VEGETARIAN ARCHITECTURE

to Momi and Milla
and
in memory of Peter Blundell Jones

jovis

VEGETARIAN ARCHITECTURE

CASE STUDIES ON BUILDING AND NATURE

andrea
bocco
guarneri

jovis

Imprint

Cover photo: Taki Yosuke

Project management publisher: Nina Kathalin Bergeest, jovis
Copy editing: Michelle Standley
Graphic design and typesetting: Susanne Rösler, jovis
Lithography: Bild1Druck, Berlin

Printed in the European Union.

Bibliographic information published by the Deutsche Nationalbibliothek.
The Deutsche Nationalbibliothek lists this publication in the Deutsche Nationalbibliografie. Detailed bibliographic data are available on the Internet at http://dnb.d-nb.de.

jovis Verlag GmbH
Kurfürstenstraße 15/16
10785 Berlin

www.jovis.de

jovis books are available worldwide in select bookstores. Please contact your nearest bookseller or visit www.jovis.de for information concerning your local distribution.

ISBN 978-3-86859-569-7

On the reference system
Cross-references between square brackets and printed in brown colour direct the reader to other parts of this book and to the bibliography. For instance, [→§5] directs to chapter 5; [→■9,10,11] to pictures 9 to 11 within the same chapter as the reference (the illustrations' numbering starts anew for each chapter); while [→B339:216] directs to page 216 of the source no. 339, as listed in the references directory at pp. 231–236.

Contents

Vegetarian architecture: a theoretical proposal

Andrea Bocco Guarneri

"The true source and analogue of our economic life is the economy of plants."
Wendell Berry [→B31:200]

"Now that technology has allowed us to reach important goals, the next advancement consists in obtaining the same results with less technology."
Reinhold Messner [→B199]

Two technologies?

I agree with Reinhold Messner, but not with his definition of technology as if it meant 'technically advanced equipment'. There is as much technology in knowing how to do simple things with simple means as there is in producing and managing complicated stuff. Perhaps, as Lewis Mumford suggested, there are really two technologies that have always coexisted in human history, one next to the other: "one authoritarian, the other democratic; the first system-centered, immensely powerful, but intrinsically unstable, the latter man-centered, relatively weak, but ingenuous and durable." [→B210:52; see also B236] Christopher Williams spoke of "machine technology" as opposed to "organic technology". The first "manipulates with overforce, it is graceless and inefficient, complicated in its manifestations but simplistic in its concepts, subject to failure and collapse. Its energies are hostile, vulgar and overextended; it reproduces itself with tiresome repetition and inspires a dull, unimaginative human life." [→B337:4] The second includes the technology he and his wife were still able to witness, practised by those he dubbed the "craftsmen of necessity"—a technology refined over generations and controlled and mastered by human hands and minds to meet their everyday needs with limited, local resources. Not only did they demand self-discipline: they also established an inherent and ineluctable relationship between human beings and the rest of nature.

Ivan Illich [→B138,140] and Ernst Friedrich Schumacher have expressed similar opinions, which have lost none of their validity in the intervening decades. As Schumacher saw it,

> the technology of mass production is inherently violent, ecologically damaging, self-defeating in terms of non-renewable resources, and stultifying for the human person. The technology of production by the masses, making use of the best of modern knowledge and experience, is conducive to decentralisation, compatible with the laws of ecology, gentle in its use of scarce resources, and designed to serve the human person instead of making him the servant of machines. [→B279:127]

Since the first industrial revolution, the history of technology is probably the history of the progressive introduction of "labor-saving devices that worked to devalue or replace the skills of those who used them". [→B31:109]

It is less important to define and distinguish between the two technologies than to assert the primacy of people over technology; and that the latter must be at their service and under their control. Mumford advocated what he dubbed a "biotechnic"—something one might now recognise as the description of an ecologically compatible civilisation. In Mumford's words,

> a sound and viable technology, firmly related to human needs, cannot be one that has a maximum productivity as its supreme goal: it must, rather, seek as in an organic system, to provide the right quantity of the right quality at the right time and the right place in the right order for the right purpose. ... A biotechnic economy would foster modes of production, transportation, and human settlement that would deliberately reduce the amount of non-organic energy required to the lowest possible level. ... An economy of plenitude would prudently seek only the optimum amount for daily use, and store surplus power for special uses or emergencies. [→B211:table 3]

Similarly, Yona Friedman coined the phrase "ecotechnic" and argued that

> nature is habitable provided that we know how to live and are able to behave according to her needs. To change ourselves and adapt to the environment is a biological law. On the contrary, to transform things to adapt them to us, and stay as much as possible as we are is the basic law of every technology. The wise dosage of these two approaches should be the subject of an ecotechnic. ... We need techniques which would imply adjustments of human behaviour instead of accumulation of a panoply of sophisticated tools. [→B96:135,91]

Such pronouncements are now a few decades old, but the tendency to put faith in the capacity of technology—maybe a 'smart technology'—to solve the problems it generated is still widespread. Unfortunately, the 'smart' way to sustainability is still far too slow and damaging to the environment. [→B33] It is therefore urgent—both for the sake of humanism and for the conservation of nature as we know it—to affirm an alternative paradigm, one based on a different understanding of the balance of access rights to resources among all living beings and on an 'appropriate technology' where humans are concerned. [→B129]

Technology is chosen

"Appropriate technology reminds us that before we choose our tools and techniques we must choose our dreams and values" [→B22]: according to Wendell Berry, then, the coming of a new tool is not just a cultural or technological event; "it is also an historical crossroads—a point at which people must choose between two possibilities". The choice about how we should use technology and what we should use it for "depends absolutely on our willingness to limit our desires as well as the scale and kind of technology we use to satisfy them. Without that willingness, there is no choice; we must simply abandon ourselves to whatever the technologists may discover to be possible". [→B30:109–112] And before Berry, Arne Næss had already formulated the principle that technology is chosen and that every new technique should be evaluated in terms of health, meaningfulness, cooperation, support network, raw materials, energy, waste, pollution, capital, vulnerability, management, and equality. In order to make such a choice, people need to have access to a whole range of information which both they and the proponents of any innovation normally lack. [→B212]

This lack of information about their possible ramifications is perhaps one of the reasons why Berry is so wary of innovations. He fears that they may reduce human freedom and wealth and introduce well-disguised, irresponsible inefficiencies:

> The farther-fetched the solution, the less it should be trusted. ... A good solution will satisfy a whole range of criteria; it will be good in all respects. ... A good solution always answers the question, How much is enough? A good solution should be cheap, and it should not enrich one person by the distress or impoverishment of another. ... [A]ny solution that calls for an expenditure to a manufacturer should be held in suspicion. ... Good solutions exist only in proof, and are not

> to be expected from absentee owners or absentee experts. Problems must be solved in work and in place, with particular knowledge, fidelity, and care, by people who will suffer the consequences of their mistakes. [→B30:140–143]

As always, Illich was crystal-clear when he observed, "high quanta of energy degrade social relations with the same ineluctability with which they destroy the physical environment". [→B139] Technological determinism is predicated on the belief that social benefit is entirely dependent on innovation, and the consequences of such dependency are very seldom questioned. [→B293]

In acquiring more than we need, we have dehumanised ourselves—while adding little if anything at all to our happiness—, have bought insecurity and have become strangers to our neighbours and to all other living beings. [→B279:20, see also B237] Neither the wealth nor the military might possessed by the entire industrialised world will be able to forestall population growth and the exhaustion of resources. The impact of our lifestyle, so far paid mostly by others, will eventually be borne by us too. [→B284]

Survival through thrift

True freedom requires learning to live without comfort and safety objectives. Free persons know how to live simply. They understand that only frugal pleasures can be sustainably and democratically enjoyed by everyone. A plentiful, healthy, affordable satisfaction of human needs can only be pursued by adopting a socially fair and economically thrifty lifestyle. [→B56,100]

In accord with Eugene Odum's theory of ecology [→B225] and with Herman Daly's theory of economy, [→B70] Edward Goldsmith affirmed that the achievement of stability or homeostasis, rather than an increase in productivity, is the purpose of ecological succession. [→B109:133] Similarly, peasants adopt a 'subsistence ethic' that aims to reduce vulnerability rather than maximise yields. [→B109:148] As Berry noted, "in a healthy culture, of course, frugality would not be difficult"; it would not even be perceived as discipline. [→B30:52]

Now, however, "the economy of extravagance has overthrown the economies of thrift" [→B30:75] on a global scale. Such powerfully attractive abundance is based on the assumption that we have a right to use as much fossil fuel as we can. Obviously, such fuel does not belong to one generation more than any other, but we have been able to ignore the claims of others by virtue of the fact that they are not here now. The 'miracle' of industrial progress is thus

> a theft of energy from (among others) our children. That is the real foundation of our progress and our affluence. The reason that we are a rich nation is not that we have earned so much wealth—you cannot, by any honest means, earn or deserve so much. The reason is simply that we have learned, and become willing, to market and use up in our own time the birthright and livelihood of posterity. [→B30:127]

Wholeness

In some ways, *Vegetarian Architecture* is the same book as David Pearson's *Earth to Spirit*, [→B239] only less anecdotal and more systematic. It is not content merely to present images that might inspire the reader—despite the difficulties in gathering sufficient data for each case study, it seeks to verify quantitatively its claims, and, what is more important, it systematically investigates their technical and constructional characteristics. In many books about 'ecological' initiatives, authors often present their findings as acts of faith that are justified by their commitment—enthusiasm is seldom coupled with technical competence. But unless we insist on scientifically verifying the quality of our research and claims, we risk discrediting the entire ecological movement. In this book I only present and analyse in detail examples on the basis of verified and verifiable information. The reputation of the *Osterie d'Italia* guidebook, [→B234] for example, may be based on the respect accorded to the Slow Food movement, but the reputation of the movement itself is based, among other things, on its ability to select taverns that offer quality traditional food at affordable prices. [→B243,241]

This book is about architecture. It nevertheless proposes a broad reorientation aimed at redefining architecture as a 'nature-steering' activity again, and advocates for expanding its boundaries to encompass agriculture and food. After all, as Friedman said, basic survival requires only two things: food and roof. [→B96]

[→■1]

A tendency to enlarge the field of a number of disciplines is emerging. Although some distinctions are blurring, words should not lose their meaning—this tendency simply seems the result of a more holistic understanding of the subject of each discipline. The 'new gastronomy', for example, is concerned with more than merely food preparation and flavour; it considers all of the processes involved in the production and transformation of food as well as agriculture's social and environmental impact.

In a similar fashion, the constitutive bonds connecting buildings and infrastructure with cultivated land should be reaffirmed. A settlement is not a juxtaposition of houses and roads; it is the way a human community transforms the environment to obtain durable sustenance. It is easy to forget this when virtually all we eat seems to pop up as if from out of nowhere on supermarket shelves. But this miracle will not last much longer, and we need to root our activities and patterns of production and consumption as close as possible to where we live.

This book consistently refers to ecologically oriented agriculture and nutrition as these appear more rooted in reality than architecture; moreover, their theory and practice have developed dramatically over the last few decades. I am referring, to name a few, to permaculture, synergistic gardening, biodynamic agriculture, modern vegetarianism, veganism, 'wholistic' nutrition, the 'new gastronomy', and the rediscovery of traditional *satoyama* ecology. Not only can architecture learn from such stances; someday it might even converge with them, thus laying the foundation for a wider, more unified understanding of the human relationship with the environment and of the human agency on it. [→B16]

My discussion uses food as a reference and metaphor because it is one of the few last things that some people still prepare themselves. [→B10] Most people find it normal to buy their clothes and not to make them. By contrast, some people still prepare their own food. Their reasons for doing so vary. For some, it may be because of the intimate relationship that exists between food and body. For others, it may be that food preparation is a form of taking care of loved ones and guests.

The Pagan (as well as the Shinto) view of nature was of an entity "alive and infused with purpose" and "aglow with seductively sensuous qualities". [→B264] [→■1] Goethe saw nature "at work and alive, manifesting herself in her wholeness in every single part of her being". [→B109:222] Building on primeval religions as well as Goethe's notion and on Odum's concept of ecological succession, which progressively converts the Earth's inorganic environment into a more organic one, James Lovelock established his theory of the planet (Gaia) as a super-living being. [→B183]
In accord with a 'deep ecology' approach [→B63,64,179], this book argues for a radical wholeness. The focus may be on architecture and building, but I want to promote the idea that we should strive to consistently respect life in all aspects of our lifestyle, from food (its production and consumption) to health (diet and behaviour) to material and spiritual issues. I do not intend to offer one-size-fits-all 'solutions': the world is made up of niches, it is the sum total of local places and phenomena. [→B285] It is not a blemish that low-technology cannot provide universal solutions: it is in fact the anti-generalist approach par excellence. [→B368] Low-tech is generated in the niches; it is suitable for residual spaces. Not only do niches have the right to continue to exist, but it is in them, as ecology reveals, that innovations emerge, it is from them that (bio)diversity is generated. Indeed, we might consider whether universal solutions even exist—it could be discovered that, even in market terms, the spaces considered marginal are much larger than believed. Instead of investigating or offering low-tech, adapted solutions to particular problems, the solutions, i.e. the products, proposed are the same and arise from the same logic. Yet, such generalist approaches—often portrayed as the only model—are only a fraction of the variety of possible approaches.

The push towards compartmentalisation remains very strong, despite frequent calls to take the larger picture and context into account. Mainstream medicine, for example, has difficulty in recognising our body as a holistic organism through which life flows, preferring to divide it into many separate compartments. Likewise, although most farmers consider their crops living beings, they view the soil in which they grow as inert. The same call for wholeness also applies when we consider the consequences of our choices. For example, I do not have the right to use a cosmetic that has formidable effects on my skin, if its manufacture requires extracting some ingredient from rare animals; indeed, if it requires taking the life of any animal. The maximisation of performance cannot be affirmed as a value in itself nor defined as a goal: Besides being harmful, it is futile to desire very high performances just because it is technically possible to obtain them. [→B334]

[→■2]

[→■3]

[→■4]

[→■5]

[→■6]

[→■5, 6] Wood dried at low (left) and high (right) temperatures
With high-temperature (about 100°C) kiln drying, timber quickly reaches the recommended moisture content, but its fragrance, stickiness, gloss are lost; and also the hygroscopy is weakened. This is because in the drying process, essential oils, aromatic and anti-moth substances, as well as lignin boil and erupt from the ends and can look as if it had exploded. Also, the fragrant smell of wood changes to smell of charcoal. Sap and resin become black and solidify. Timber dried at high temperatures does not crack on the surface; however, the fibres in the inside of the section become flaky and radial cracks may appear; this negatively affects mechanical strength. Moreover, carbon dioxide, which had been bound in the tree, is released in the process.
At Kitokuras sawmill 山一木材㈱ (Ayauta-cho 綾歌郡, Kagawa prefecture 香川県), timber is either air-dried or dried at a low temperature (45°C) in a solar greenhouse (in winter, the solar heat is supplemented by a stove that burns splinters directly from the sawmill). Before drying, a radial cut is sawn to the heartwood. The cracks that occur while drying thus concentrate around this cut, and only minor cracks are created elsewhere. Of course, timber dried at low temperatures also retains its scent and colour.
The final properties of timber obviously depend much on the quality of the raw material; compare the different thicknesses of the annual growth rings in photos 6.

The radical quest for 'good food' has produced a wealth of insights that might be applied to an equally radical quest for a 'good house'. [→B332] One can perceive what 'good' food is with one's senses, provided that they have not been distorted by social conditioning and bad habits. But in order to judge, a much more holistic understanding is necessary, one that requires information, a critical sense, and an ecological vision. [→B252] Good food nourishes, indeed protects your health and even heals you; [→B62] it does not poison you or the environment; it puts you in meaningful relation with natural cycles, with the land and those who cultivate it; and it also, yes, tastes good—indeed, it satisfies your senses thoroughly. Similar assertions can also be made for building materials of vegetal origin. [→B209]

This point calls into question the issue of despising direct experience to the advantage of abstract and complex scientific formulas. According to Giannozzo Pucci, "Two classes have thus been formed: on the one hand those who are officially entitled to certify reality, on the other hand the 'clandestine of knowledge' ... without a title to explain the universe and therefore unable to give importance to their relationship with what comes from the senses". [→B251:52] The "practical conscience" of nonprofessional individuals and groups should be as acknowledged as the "discursive conscience" of experts. [→B16] This is the reason why there is an ethical, environmental, and scientific value in developing a sensitivity to good food or to the healthiness of a space. [→B6,7] [→▪2,3] Christopher Alexander argues that an individual's sensations are the foundation for judging the validity of a space. According to Aldo Leopold, what is 'good' is simply what is conducive to life. [→B175:224,225]

What are things made of, and how?

Since it emerged in the 1980s, the idea at the basis of the Slow Food movement has continuously redefined itself in more precise terms. What started as a stated, personal preference for local, affordable, and wholesome food later developed into a movement that advocated for "good, clean and fair" food according to simple and unyielding criteria. [→B242] Similar criteria should be available to find one's way in the disorienting, noisy mass of self-proclaimed 'eco-', 'bio-', 'green-' properties nowadays stuck to whatever (see e.g. Werner Boote's film, *The Green Lie*), [→B48] building products and buildings included. I argue that we can apply Slow Food's approach to the production and consumption of food—and maybe add vegetarian, vegan, and medical principles to such approach—to how we design and inhabit buildings.

A general principle should be that of transparency and honesty. Often we are compelled to make choices and take actions based on erroneous, if not deceitful, information: We eat disorderly and too much, and we want to continue doing so; therefore we are happy to treat our stomach ache caused by such disorderly eating with some chemical medication. It would be better to examine our behaviours and assumptions. This includes taking into account the "truthfulness" of materials, as for instance defined by Loos. [→B181] [→▪4,5,6] Applied to food, this means learning to discern its quality. In so doing, one may discover that most food is grown under conditions that compromise is nutritional value, the environment, and society. The consumer is, however, largely oblivious to how it is cultivated and processed. Were consumers aware of the origins of their food, they might very well choose to produce as much food as possible by themselves. Many have argued that a vegetable garden is the handiest concrete act of opposition to consumerism and to the prevailing system of dependence. [→B30,219]

Governments have never required labels to inform consumers about chemicals used in agriculture or about residues in foodstuff. Obviously, this means that choices are less informed and often made on the basis of habit and above all price; and produce obtained from agriculture-as-it-should-be has become the exception, a market niche. [→B155]

Even fewer laws "require manufacturers to declare the full constituents of their [building] products, how much energy has been used in their manufacture and whether there are any pollution burdens". [→B338:184] Powerful multinational producers of building materials

> rely heavily on the ignorance of specifiers and customers who are unable to discriminate between the genuine and the slick marketing of environmental claims. ... Resisting this and

[→■7]

[→■8]

choosing less well known and harder to source materials requires extra effort and a commitment to environmental principles on the part of the designers and their clients. [→B339:216]

Natural materials

Using renewable construction materials is a way to reduce carbon dioxide emissions; natural-origin materials also ensure construction that is not hazardous to users, provided they are free of added toxic chemicals. [→B339:xii,3] Acquiring the skill to design a building that will make use of simple technologies, based on good craftsmanship and the careful choice of local and natural material, requires a great deal of effort, as does obtaining the permit to build it. [→■7,8] Often, such materials are not covered by environmental assessment methods and software. Even when they are, their characteristics are underestimated or just partially acknowledged: this assertion is confirmed by our calculations. [→§13] This is a crucial point, because, as Tom Woolley stated, "it does not matter if a technique is 'ecological' or low-impact: if it does not come with an assessment, it may result difficult to include it in the working project". [→B338]
According to David Eisenberg, the reason why modern codes and standards do not include "most of the traditional building materials and systems" is that they "were being abandoned at the time codes and standards were developed. And they don't have a big industry like cement or steel to support the research and testing and development needed to bring them into codes". [→B82:54] What is more, test protocols have often been modelled after standardised industrial products. "The industrial paradigm frames the whole field, demanding a high level of uniformity and predictability" in building components, [→B82:26] that evidently those made of natural material cannot offer. But assessments usually take into account only a few parameters (for which 'high-tech' counterparts show higher performances) and not the whole picture.

At the same time, it must be acknowledged that little is known about natural materials and the building techniques based on them. [→B304,305,306] A detailed and scientific understanding of their properties and characteristics should be developed, that includes both traditional and experimental buildings.

[→■9,10,11]

[→■12]

[→■12] A furniture shop in Nagoya 名古屋 initiated a project dubbed Kodama, to reconnect the mountains densely forested with *sugi* and *hinoki* trees with the city, having in mind that in spite of the high amount of tree plantations, in Japan most furniture sold in stores is made with imported timber. The first product of this project is a children's desk. All the actors in the production chain have been involved in the project. To ensure a desk, buyers must join a two-day trip to Higashishirakawa village 東白川村 where they visit both forest and factory. The desk is made up of three parts, and it is assembled so that it can respond to the growth and changing needs of the owner. Other products and services are being developed to better exploit local resources of Higashishirakawa area. Design: Murasawa Kazuteru.

[→■13]

[→■13] Ipanema table produced by the Andrea Zanini's joinery (Alba, CN) on a project by Studio Ellisse. The wood is of local origin (Boves, CN) where it is also sawn and dried to obtain boards. These are then squared in the joinery workshop; the joints include the mortise and tenon and the most modern dominoes or lamellas; in addition, vinyl glue is used for the legs. The table is then sanded and oiled with natural oils.

[→B346,347,348] Some progress has been made on this front, including the research work directed by Pete Walker at the University of Bath and that presented at the NOCMAT conferences. [→B105,222,328] Scientists and engineers are trying to find ways to 'improve' natural materials so that they can perform as predictably as industrial ones. Almost no one advocates for leaving natural materials as they are, and for deepening our understanding so that we make the best possible use of them. [→B125] [→■9,10,11]
Many designers are reluctant to rely on natural materials as this would require accepting a degree of imprecision. Outside the artificially conditioned environment of the industrial plant, there is no standardised procedure for baking, or for preparing a plaster: the exact amount of ingredients will vary as deemed appropriate by an experienced craftsperson. Such a skilled craftsperson is able to adjust the recipe and process according to the environmental conditions and the specific properties of the raw materials, which of course are not as homogeneous as artificial materials. Embracing natural materials also requires accepting change over time: thus, not only should buildings be designed so as to allow modifications and evolutions in accordance with the changing needs of their users, but the buildings' detailing should accommodate the change of the materials' performance, and their decay. Anna Heringer has observed that it is not "the missing technologies that prevent us from building sustainably. Nor is it the lack of awareness. It is actually the fear … of vulnerability and transience". [→B244:6]

Sim Van der Ryn affirmed that "people are drawn to natural materials because they stand in opposition to the industrial appetite of disassembling the organic, for destroying the soul and spirit inherent in living materials". [→B83:xv] As Christopher Day put it, "natural materials are life-compatible". [→B72:187] In his opinion, natural materials have a similar effect as contact with the natural environment. They "connect us with life", thereby invigorating and strengthening our natural immunity. Another point he makes is very subtle. It cannot, he suggests, be good for the soul to be surrounded by deception, such as 'fake' materials that pretend to look like something else. [→B72:80] [→■12,13]

[→■14]

Natural agriculture

Luigi Veronelli, the famous wine critic and quality food activist, was adamant on this score:

> It's not organic? It's not agriculture. It's the rape of the earth with the horrific products of science. … Most of today's farmers are not really—they have no respect for the land, they continue to pour tons of poison into fields, orchards, vegetable gardens. … An ancient profession has been destroyed and can now only survive with subsidies. [→B322:109]

It is not, however, sufficient for a foodstuff to be labelled 'organic', because organic agriculture regulations still permit the use of some chemicals, and because social issues are not considered relevant for the attribution of the 'organic product' label.

The kind of agriculture to which I will refer is not, therefore, strictly speaking, organic agriculture. It is something defined, based on a more radical position; one that takes a broader view. It requires the exclusion of many foods from one's diet (as at Club 99 [→§5]) [→B260] and the adoption of strictly natural farming methods, such as those proposed by Fukuoka Masanobu 福岡正信, Kawaguchi Yoshikazu 川口由一, Bill Mollison, Sepp Holzer, Emilia Hazelip, to name a few. [→B98,151,205,206,133,128] [→■14] I advocate for labour-intensive methods that are adapted to small-scale farming and are aimed at production for the grower's own family, and for direct sale of the surplus crops on local markets. [→B251:218] Such an approach to food production is more similar to tradi-

[→■15]

[→■15] Ōmishima 大三島 is a small island in the Japanese inland sea, to which Itō Toyō 伊東 豊雄 has decided to devote his energies. Initiatives are underway concerning the recovery of local buildings and production areas, the planting of vineyards, the recovery of fantastic traditional citrus groves, the construction of a community centre without any claim to leave the mark of the star architect.

tional peasant economies than to large-scale agribusiness production, however organic they may be. [→B158] Unfortunately, after World War II many decision-makers shared the notion that 'agriculture as a way of life' was inefficient and outdated. The massive subsidisation of agriculture allowed to industrialise the farming process on the one hand, and to drop the price of food on the other, to let people spend their money on other goods and services. [→B247] Alongside the economic marginalisation of farming has come the socio-cultural devaluation of farmers, against which Gino Girolomoni, the father of Italian organic agriculture, fought an almost lonely battle. [→B107]

Other than being backward and inefficient, traditional farming methods, as Miguel Altieri maintains, "reflect the priorities of the farmer, produce a varied diet, a diversity of sources of income, use locally available resources, minimise the risk of harvest losses, protect against the spread of pests and diseases, and make efficient use of the local labour force". [→B9:19] In Berry's opinion, "good agriculture is virtually synonymous with small-scale agriculture. … [S]mallness tends to be a prerequisite of diversity, and diversity, in turn, a prerequisite of thrift and care in the use of the world". [→B30:xi] He proposes that "subsistence farming is the very definition of good farming" and affirms that "how we eat determines, to a considerable extent, how the world is used". [→B31:324] Moreover, real farming establishes a "necessary and meaningful" relation to the place, [→B31:21] while "large and centralized economic entities … are not interested in the health—economic, natural or human—of any place on this earth". [→B30:155] The most obvious way to start building a decentralised system of local economies, argues Berry, "is to develop a local food economy". [→B31:8,141] [→■15]

The parallels between the production and consumption of food and the construction and use of buildings are numerous. Also the way we build implies a range of impacts on the environment both at the small and large scales. Were the construction of new buildings undertaken with an awareness of such consequences (Villa Strohbunt [→§5]), and the result of hard work (Cheia [→§2]), there would be fewer buildings, and with far less of an impact on the environment. Moreover, the rich cultural diversity of agriculture and gastronomy is echoed in the immense diversity of vernacular architecture. [→B229,230,266,267]

Principles of vegetarian architecture

Vegetarianism can be traced back to ancient religious and philosophical texts such as the *Tirukkuṛaḷ*, [→B303:251–266] and Ovid's *Metamorphoses*. [→B235] The choice to be vegetarian can be based on a variety of factors: nutritional, religious, and ethical, to name but a few. Ethical objections are usually based either on a rejection of cruel breeding practices, such as factory farming, or on the slaughter of animals. Recently, as it has become clear that a diet including meat has a much greater impact on the environment than a vegetarian one, many have chosen vegetarianism based on environmental concerns.

The phrase 'vegetarian architecture' is obviously metaphoric. [→■16] I will nonetheless try to address agriculture and nutrition in the least vague way possible. If defining a vegetarian diet is relatively straightforward, then so too should be defining a 'vegetarian'

[→■16]

building. I would then like to propose a tentative list of principles learnt from agriculture and nutrition that are ecologically oriented:

- Work together with nature, rather than against it; recognise that nature is complex, undetermined, diverse, multifunctional. Generally speaking, this also means doing as little as possible. Every human intervention alters nature. But it is indeed possible to recognise degrees—usually linked to the amount of power employed and to the attitude with which we approach nature—ranging from respectful acceptance to complete contempt, viewing it merely as something to 'improve' or exploit.
- Acquire knowledge about and make full use of available materials, even in their least transformed state. The nutritional value of foods is best preserved when they are consumed whole. In the past, many artisans have laboured under conditions defined by extreme limitations and have nonetheless been able to achieve remarkable results. [→B363] As Leon Battista Alberti observed: "Better than knowing which should be the highest-performing materials for his job, a good builder knows how to make the best use of those he has at hand." [→B4:96] Timber is 'built' by nature according to the axiom of uniform stress, realised as an average over time. Claus Mattheck pointed out that trees, for instance, lack weak places and superfluous material. "A true ecodesign," he observed, "would mean not only optimisation of the external shape but also of the internal fibre distribution." [→B193:131] This means that grain and load flow coincide. In manufacturing and construction, this remains an unexploited principle: it is usually requested and expected that natural materials be as isotropous and as standardised as possible.
- Make use of locally produced material, except for exotic imported 'spices'. Elena Barthel of Rural Studio expresses this principle as follows: "Good food is like good architecture: they both rely on the best local ingredients." Can you grow bananas here? No? [→■17] Then do not eat bananas, except on occasion, as an exception to the rule. When it comes to diet, there are many

[→■17]

reasons why ingredients of animal origin should be minimised, except for those that can be sustainably produced or hunted at the individual or basic social nucleus' scale. Only a few traditional societies were vegetarian, but their overall meat consumption was usually minimal and confined to special celebrations; and of course,

[→■18]

they ate whole foods. [→■18] Translated into building, this principle might be applied by relying on locally sourced materials and by minimising the import of exotic, high-tech components. A house has a long service life and is much more complex than a meal. Even in a vegan person's lifetime, there will be occasions when resorting to animal origin foods cannot be avoided. Likewise, in the construction industry, a certain amount of metal and synthetic materials are today unavoidable, at least in building services.

- The same goes for energy input in the production process: regardless of the possibly 'renewable' source of energy employed, growing plants in highly artificial environments has nothing to do with real agriculture and obtains standardised foodstuffs whose quality is dubious. Can you grow tomatoes all the year through in the place where you live? No? Then when you cannot have fresh tomatoes, do not eat them, or eat them as sauce, or dried. Likewise, in the building trade the use of energy-intensive materials should be minimised as much as possible.
- Employ material that can be easily absorbed by the environment, which means without any substance of chemical or synthetic origin, either during production or in subsequent processing and conservation. [→B161] [→■19] This ensures the health and stability of the ecosystem over time; [→B80] and higher nutritional quality. [→B340] The food we eat today "is grown by unnatural processes that make use of a host of chemical substances ... of which the residues are to be found in nearly all the food commercially available today. Our food is then processed in vast factories with the result that its molecular structure is often totally different from that of the food we have been adapted to eat during the course of our evolution. It is further contaminated with other chemicals ... designed to impart to it those qualities required to increase shelf-life and otherwise improve its commercial rather than nutritional viability." [→B109:302] [→■22] As Colin Campbell recommends, people should eat real food, "not industrial food transformations ... simple foods, without additives, improvers, preservatives, colorants, sweeteners, emulsifiers, stabilisers". [→B18:286, see also B375]

[→■19]

[→■20]

[→■21]

[→■22]

[→■22] Industrially grown produce is very different from naturally grown produce. On one hand, residues of chemicals used are possibly, yet likely present in industrially grown fruits and vegetables, which are by definition absent in organically grown counterparts. On the other hand, endogenous production of secondary metabolites is inhibited by the administration of exogenous substances. If a certain phenomenon (e.g. the presence of a certain parasite) is managed from outside, the plant does not metabolise the substances it would produce to cope with it. A natural fruit has more taste also because of the presence of these secondary metabolites, not only because it is not swollen with water like industrially produced ones. (In fact, the higher yield of industrial crops is partly due to the higher water content; the amount of real nourishment is quite different). This is more true for annual plants (strawberries, vegetables) than for multi-annual plants (tree fruit), whose lack of taste is rather due to the use of chemical fertilisers. In industrially grown strawberries for example, there is a massive use of external inputs (heat, light, NPK among others), so that they are virtually available independently of the season: always the same in size, hue (homogeneous on all the fruit's surface as if it was painted), tastelessness. Moreover, industrially grown fruit is usually harvested before the ripening process is completed to meet the requests of large retailers, which makes it very different from fruit ripened on the plant.

Preservatives and other chemicals in building materials encourage residents to behave irresponsibly and architects to make bad design choices. For instance, the durability of vegetal origin materials can be substantially increased by adding toxic preservatives; and this produces special waste that cannot be dumped or burnt at the end of the material's service life. On the contrary, careful selection and handling of raw materials, coupled with competent design and maintenance, and the frequent substitution of parts can obtain remarkably durable buildings, even though made of natural materials. [→■20]

- Refuse to resort to materials and processes monopolised by corporations and resolve to reduce use of industrial products more generally. Such a position is grounded on the basis of both ethical (preservation of small businesses and local economies) and health-related considerations (rejection of industrial food). It can be more easily applied, although not without effort, to nutrition. [→B238] In construction, this is more difficult and a number of modern materials and products cannot be avoided. This is also because, for instance, today's buildings attain high performance thanks in large part to technologically advanced windows. Peter Harper's "low-carbon materials + industrial vitamins" [→B124] concept perfectly epitomises a realistic, balanced position in this field. [→§13] Even the most modern projects can be built primarily with natural materials, whose environmental impact is very limited, plus a few highly-manufactured products that make some high performances possible. A few architects attain remarkable design quality without conforming to mainstream models nor surrendering to norms, certifications, and software: some examples are discussed in this book [→§§6,7,8,10,11]. Moreover, domestic preparation of food from primary materials and products should be given preference over readymade industrial products, which translates into preference for building technologies that can be easily handled at the local level. This would help preserve local skills and jobs, and minimise dependence from remote entities (see for instance [→§§5,6,10]).
- Opt for limited means of production that do not require motors. Give preference instead to manual and animal labour. This means choosing labour-intensive, small-scale production. [→■8,21]

- Do things by yourself and, when this is not feasible, rely on face-to-face, direct relationships, based on trust. In the case of food production, a direct relationship with the farmer makes it possible to dispense with certifications. Certifications encourage anonymous, indirect relationships and serve the interests of the industry, since products with the same certification are potentially interchangeable, while small-scale products are unique. Just as the best food production is individual and small-scale, when it comes to housing, use value should come before market value, **[→B315]** and locally sourced materials should not have to be certified.
- Maintain affordable prices on naturally grown, healthy produce. Labour-intensive processes do tend to be costly, and basic goods should be paid what they are actually worth: this may require a shift in spending priorities. Nonetheless, good food ought to be accessible to all and should not belong to a luxury market niche. The *Guida al vino quotidiano*, **[→B102]** for instance, shows that it is possible to offer bona fide wine at affordable prices.
- Recognise that moving towards self-reliance requires hard work, contentedness, and an acceptance of taking responsibility for one's own actions (*Verantwortung*). **[→B143]** Low-tech solutions help maintain a sense of individual awareness with respect to one's own choices and behaviours and acknowledge the true (environmental and otherwise) costs hidden in them. What is not paid here and now will be paid somewhere or some other time by someone else. There is, however, an obvious risk that autonomy is inherently antisocial. **[→B258; see also B318]** Stewart Brand declared that the idea of self-sufficiency "is flawed at the root, and works badly in practice", and that although it is important to be able to do without remote, anonymous institutions, local, systemic inter-dependency is the way nature works. **[→B18:5]** Moreover, individual choices are insufficient and new, widely shared paradigms and severe political decisions are needed if we as a society aim to build a truly sustainable future. **[→B75]**
- Re-evaluate what constitutes a satisfactory sensory experience and appreciate frugal pleasures. As Berrino explains,

  > it is reasonable to assume that the protective effect of the Mediterranean diet or other diets relatively rich in plant foods and poor in animal foods … depends on consuming fewer calories. … For over 100 years now we have been knowing that if we give animals little to eat—20–30% less than they would if they had unlimited availability of food—they live longer and get sick less. **[→B29:94]**

  In fact, "eating less activates cellular mechanisms that save energy and inhibit very energy-intensive cellular activities, such as [cancer] proliferation". **[→B29:188,189]** The main road to sustainability is to reduce the level of consumption, for example, by living in smaller houses and conditioning them at temperatures closer to the outdoor environment. **[→■23]**

The principles listed above describe the way in which the whole of humanity has been living until recently, but such principles would be difficult to maintain today. Therefore, they should be seen as ideals or goals for which to strive, not as strict requirements that can be immediately adopted.

If together with Berry, Jean Giono, Pucci, and Vandana Shiva **[→B31,106,251,288]** we define authentic agriculture as subsistence agriculture (though one that is open to the possibility of exchanging surpluses), then authentic architecture (if the name is still suitable, since it should perhaps be reserved—as throughout most of human history—to the buildings of the powerful) is vernacular architecture (*minka* 民家). **[→■24,25]**

The case studies selected in this book show different approaches to what I refer to as 'vegetarian architecture', and do not embrace all of the principles I have been enumerating. They provide examples of contemporary structures that are, at least in some way, comparable to vernacular construction. They share traits in terms of rootedness (in place and in the ecological cycles); use of materials; low impact and unobtrusiveness; care of a certain place and harmony with it; awareness of local competence; harmony and interconnectedness with the local; a

[→■24]

[→■23]

[→■25]

degree of autonomy; and an awareness of ecological constraints. [→B60,274]

When I speak of 'vegetarian' architecture, I am not advocating for the biomimicry [→B24] of plants, even though studying them can provide inspiration for more eco-oriented design. [→B119,120,186,187] Plants are living beings, buildings are not. Plants will grow, develop, or even reduce their size: no external agent is needed. Buildings will never be able to possess such adaptability of their own accord. We are very far from being able to erect a building that would possess even the mere mechanical properties of a tree.

Origin of this book

I coined the phrase 'vegetarian architecture' while observing Hungarian peasant houses, where it was evident that both food and homes emerged from the soil on which they grow; they are made of and by it. The rural Hungarian home is constructed with nothing else other than raw earth and vegetal materials, produced by the same agricultural activity that required the peasant home to exist in the first place, and often are its waste. [→B170] The same could be said of Japanese or Romanian houses, except that in these a few stones are used. [→▪27]

The vernacular buildings in open-air museums are made of wood, earth, and straw. [→B57,84,87,248,249] Wood is used for most of the load-bearing structures, for stairs, window frames, horizontal partitions, sometimes for boarding and cladding, and latticework (exposed or covered with earth in a wattle and daub work) as well as for shingle roofing, gutters, and furniture. Straw and reeds are used for roofing, as fillers for joints, and shredded for reinforcing the earth in plasters and floors. Earth for unfired brick walls, renders and plasters, floors and ovens. These were really 'vegetarian', or even 'vegan', buildings, which from a holistic point of view appear more respectful of environmental balance than most contemporary architecture, however 'low' or 'zero' they may claim to be. But the question remains: To what extent can we adapt principles from these rural buildings to contemporary, urban circumstances? And to what extent can such buildings be adapted to suit contemporary comfort and lifestyle? [→B94,108,148,228] A few examples are discussed in this book [→§§3,4].

This work was born out of a discussion I had about ten years ago with Peter Blundell Jones while working on a Marie Curie project that was not funded. My research project was aimed at investigating some case studies [→B41] of pioneering ecological architecture that emerged in Europe after the energy crisis in the 1970s. That low-tech, pragmatic, and experimental architecture differed greatly from its institutionalised counterpart, 'sustainable building', that later became common practise. Today, 'sustainability' often takes the form of regulations and directives and such things as energy certificates—an approach that is often more bureaucratic than heartfelt. On the other hand, though admirable, 1970s ecological architecture was sometimes naive and its experiments a failure. But some of those architectural pioneers have continued to work passionately and competently, and managed to achieve impressive results that I wanted to document. (Examples can be found below.) [→§§4,6,8,10,11]

Over time, I have been adding other topics to that central theme which have enriched the picture. These topics grew out of two main strands: a fellowship from the Japan Society for the Promotion of Science (JSPS) that I received in 2015, and the work I conducted on local development in marginal areas (on the field at the San Salvario Local Development Agency and performing research for *Flessibile come di pietra* and *Capacities*). [→B45] [→▪26,28,29] The case studies contained in the third section [→§§9–12] belong to this wider group of topics.

Fortunately, 'sustainability' has entered the mainstream with a whole series of 'compliant solutions', specialised products, calculation and certification systems. Hundreds of books exist that present examples of 'sustainable' architecture, [→B103,227,317] most of which are rather mainstream. In this volume, I present a selection of radical and sometimes extreme cases. Some of them are well known (the WISE building [→§11], for instance), some had not yet been published so far. Some of their authors and key persons not only strive for a low impact on the environment but try and work cooperatively towards a regeneration of the ecosystem and of the socio-economic system of which they are a part. The selection of case studies was partially inciden-

[→■26] Tamera, in Alentejo, is a typical example of colonisation: a group of people arrived from abroad, and found there a good place to establish an eco-village. It maintains good relations with the local community and the surrounding villages; however, a different way of life has come to settle in a context that has not generated it. The area was almost deserted, but thanks to the advice of Sepp Holzer, artificial lakes were created and the microclimate changed. The area has resumed agricultural productivity able to support the community of about 200 inhabitants, who are strictly vegans. In Tamera technical-scientific research is also being carried out: for example, they are experimenting with ways to increase the effectiveness of passive solar collectors.

[→■28] To my knowledge, EVA Lanxmeer in Culemborg (province of Gelderland) is the most convincing example of ecological settlement in an urban context. It was not entirely born out of a communitarian lifestyle choice, but - besides high-quality architecture and systems - it is also based on the common acceptance of working rules (e.g. about management of water cycle and traffic) that involve a high level of responsibility. The project was initiated by a group led by Marleen Kaptein according to the master plan designed by Joachim Eble.

[→■29] The Kumagais くまがい have added a permanent exhibition on the qualities of wood, an educational space for meetings with a small library, a shop, a cafeteria and a children's play area to their family sawmill, now in its third generation. All this to promote the culture of natural wood to the public, in self-designed and self-built buildings made of local timber. The project is called Kitokuras キトクラス, lit. 'living with trees'.

[→■26]

[→■27]

[→■28]

[→■29]

tal but also based on available documentation. (Most drawings have been thoroughly re-made to present them here in a unified way and, what is more important, to inventorise the materials and investigate the processes involved in their construction.) I attempted to cover different European geographical areas and to include examples from my Japanese experience: I have observed buildings (and the cultural problems behind them) in mature economy countries and have privileged quality over quantity. I tended to give preference to not-so-recent examples and to somewhat ordinary constructions that do not require a host of specialised designers and technicians.

The case studies

The core of the book is arranged into three main sections, and it is complemented by a concluding discussion.

The first section is dedicated to four case studies of traditional buildings. Two are substantially unaltered: an Edo-period peasant house now relocated in an open-air museum (Hirose House **[→§1]**) and a late-nineteenth century Romanian peasant house relocated to a place close to where it used to stand, which is currently lived-in (Paraschiva House in Cheia **[→§2]**); and two larger and more affluent ones, which were recently refurbished: a nineteenth-century peasant house in the Swiss mountains (Casa Steila Mar **[→§3]**, and an eighteenth-century half-timbered building in a German town (Sandberghof **[→§4]**).

I open the book with a consideration of traditional buildings, because of their conceptual primacy and because they come first chronologically. The notion of sustainability led to a new way of looking at traditional architecture: "traditional cultures and indigenous architecture [have been] reprioritized to be considered as important repositories of knowledge about the environment". **[→B293:173]** They provide examples of how to exist harmoniously with life-supporting systems. **[→B21,88,231]** In addition, there is much more to learn from vernacular architecture, both didactically and theoretically, than from modern architecture. If nothing else because, unlike the latter, vernacular architecture is technically comprehensible upon viewing it. In fact, they provide what Stewart Brand called "an economic grammar of construction". **[→B53:134]**

Open-air museums preserve, on the one hand, precious and sometimes unique archaeological and ethnographical heritage, which includes not only the traditional buildings but also the know-how embedded within them. **[→B256]** They also provide, on the other, societies that are in danger of impoverishment and of losing meaningful ecological connections with their environs, with possible strategies for survival, **[→B96]** and a catalogue of practical examples. Yet, focussing on the buildings themselves is insufficient. What is needed instead is a thorough comprehension of a life and production system, which would include looking at the relationships between the buildings and their environmental, social, and economic context. The most forward-thinking museums, such as Ballenberg in Switzerland, **[→B280,281,282]** but also smaller historical sites, such as Haithabu in Schleswig and Düppel in Berlin, **[→▪18,31]** are embracing this approach.

Both plants and vernacular buildings show that attaining the maximum performances is neither necessary nor sustainable. Franz Volhard has argued that "today's high-strength building materials are … in many cases stronger than they actually need to be". **[→B326:10]** Already in the 1970s, Giorgio Ceragioli discussed the notion of 'excess performance'. **[→B69]** Mattheck has observed that increased expectations with regard to individual safety leads to increasing the dimensions of load-bearing structures and therefore to "a more rapid destruction of the environment and thus the destruction of the species as a whole". **[→B193:221]** Reducing expectations makes it possible to keep costs low. This, in turn, frees up funds for situations in which more costly, technologically advanced solutions are truly necessary.

The principles found in vernacular architecture do not belong only to the past. They can also be applied critically today, to steer 'sustainable' choices. **[→B149,194,270,296]** I chose to include Casa Steila Mar **[→§3]** and Sandberghof **[→§4]** because they represent examples, out of hundreds of possible alternatives, of the competent and judicious rehabilitation of traditional buildings to meet current living standards, while using natural materials. As Olivier Sidler remarks, in addition to preserving the environment, retrofitting extant buildings entails significant socio-economic benefits. Recovery should be aimed at respectful, functional improvement of existing

[→■30] Olivier Sidler has been working for decades in the field of low-consumption buildings and passive houses. He has been a consultant to the French government in the field of energy policies and the implementation of technical solutions to lower the energy consumption of French buildings.
In the 1980s, he bought an old rural stone building in Félines-sur-Rimandoule (Drôme) that he partially rebuilt and extended. The total area is about 500 m^2 and included both the home of his family of four and his energy consultancy company, Enertech, which employed up to twenty-two people. The company contributed enormously to the economy of the small village.
To the south façade of the house, Sidler added a two-storey high, unheated greenhouse that contributes to the passive performance of the building. Its proper functioning requires careful management of the openings. In January, a temperature higher than 19°C is recorded there for a minimum of 4 hours a day: you can have lunch at Christmas there, and there grows a banana tree that bears fruit. The ground floor of the house is very deep and therefore there is little light in the rooms that overlook the greenhouse. As its roof is opaque, summer radiation inside the house is prevented, while sunlight penetrates it in winter.
In 2016, Enertech moved to a new building in the neighbouring village; Sidler is now retired.

[→■30]

[→■31]

[→■32]

buildings. [→B289] [→▪30] One should not let oneself be captivated by the outstanding performances that new buildings may offer. Instead of constructing new buildings, we should drastically reduce the energy requirements and environmental impact of existing ones. [→▪32] While there may be new products which allow buildings to have a low operational impact, such products are however heavily burdened in terms of embodied energy and consumption of rare materials. Its long history notwithstanding, "natural building is still at a pioneering stage", as Woolley puts it. [→B338:9] Today, both professionals and the institutions responsible for releasing building permits "consider materials, that were in use for centuries, very dangerous and are much more happy to have faith in synthetic, untested materials, that are likely to degrade in ten years." As Schumacher pointed out, industry tends to prefer artificial materials to natural ones (because they can be modelled on the basis of requirements and a perfect quality control is applicable), and machinery work to living beings' labour (because more reliable and predictable). [→B279:88] In a similar vein, Eisenberg observed that "industrial replacements have typically been developed to reduce the labor and costs of construction, not necessarily to improve the quality or safety of buildings. ... Their widespread use today is more a testament to the investment of money and effort in understanding and managing these problems than to their perfection or superiority over their non-industrial predecessors." [→B83:26] Nor are natural materials less durable: in Europe and elsewhere, there are many, centuries-old, well-preserved buildings that are made of earth, timber, and straw. [→B159,226,298] [→▪16,25,27]

The second section of the book consists of four chapters that describe buildings constructed within the past two decades with natural materials, with a more or less large complement of artificial and synthetic materials. Case studies were chosen to exemplify some of the techniques now available, without the intention to cover all of them—for instance, hemp-lime construction (which according to David Lea might even be used with no additional load-bearing frame in small buildings) is not covered. The discussed cases are the Villa Strohbunt in the Sieben Linden Ecovillage, [→§5] almost entirely free of artificial or synthetic materials (except for building services); two small office buildings—one in Switzerland, the other in Slovakia—that use straw bales as a load-bearing material; [→§6] a temporary, post-disaster, community facility built with a bamboo framework in a coastal hamlet in Japan that had been hit by a tsunami; [→§7] and a single-family house on the southern coast of Norway that uses timber not only as a load-bearing frame but also as a thermal and moisture-regulating material. [→§8]

Should one comply with norms or be ahead of them? Eisenberg thinks norms are better at preserving the status quo than encouraging sustainability. He is engaged in promoting a cultural shift so that security is understood more broadly than today, so as to include both immediate issues—such as structural strength—and deferred concerns: buildings should be "safe for their users and other inhabitants of earth, present and future." In his words:

> We think we've eliminated or greatly reduced the risks associated with buildings. What we've actually done is move those risks in space and time. We've moved them away from the building site out into all the natural systems on the planet—our life support systems[—]and from the present to our children and grandchildren and all the future generations of all the other species on whose welfare our welfare also depends. ... Yet those who are trying to design and build to minimize all these kinds of impacts, while also dealing with the risks that the codes address ... often have a much harder time getting their projects approved than those projects that contribute the most to such hazards. [→B82:26–32]

One of the few possibilities for truly sustainable, environmentally and socially conscious construction can be found in 'informal' practices and in niches—perhaps 'grey areas' overlooked by authorities because they do not clearly fit into classifications, or are in very marginal places, which are inconvenient to visit for inspection. [→▪34,26] The Italian Genuino Clandestino movement, that fights "to return to having the right to feed us with the stuff our grandmothers made" [→B250:17] and to exchange seeds, is an apt illustration of this point. So is Rural Studio's experience in Alabama where most buildings could be erected without a permit. [→B93] [→▪33] Some

[→■33]

[→■34]

[→■35]

[→■33] Rural Studio, a part of Auburn University in Alabama, is arguably the most famous Design and Build programme in architecture worldwide. It is located in the village of Newbern in Hale, one of the poorest counties in the USA. The Studio educates architectural students through creating new resources for the local community **[→B93:12]**. Since 1993, it has designed and built over 150 projects. The overall coherence of the project and the orientation towards sustainability led to the inclusion of food as well. "The place is a [fresh] food desert, which threatens the health and well-being of people." **[→B93:21]** This prompted the Studio to initiate in 2010 the Rural Studio Farm (RSF), a demonstration project for small-scale local agriculture whose most direct purpose is to provide staff and students with healthy food that does not harm the environment, and which would ultimately redesign the Campus as well as its occupants' lifestyle and promote food culture in the local community.
The organically farmed vegetable garden extends on an area of 1,700 m^2 with an annual yield of 3,000 kg, which are enough to meet 70% of the 4,300 annual meals goal. One-tenth of the surface is occupied by a greenhouse, which "serves as a manifesto of the whole RSF project", says Elena Barthel. It works with no external inputs and includes a hoop house and a seed house. A thermally massive wall, formed by several rows of water-filled barrels, encloses the north side of the construction; a slope of earth abuts to it to protect the greenhouse from winter winds. Rainwater is collected in four underground tanks totalling 20 m^3. From here it is pumped during the day (thanks to the electrical energy produced by PV collectors) into a cylinder from where, at night, it is released by gravity to the drip irrigation system.
During the two academic quarters, the RSF produces onions, garlic, vegetables to be consumed fresh (salads, chicory, carrots, roots, rocket, tomatoes), as well as vegetables to be cooked (collard greens, kale, spinach, Swiss chard, potatoes, sweet potatoes, red beets). In the summer months, on the other hand, produce to be preserved for the winter is grown, such as peas, beans, cucumbers, tomatoes for sauce, banana peppers, black-eyed peas, aubergines.
As in a sailing school, everyone has to take turns in taking care of the garden, as well as washing dishes, for a total of 12 hours per semester.

[→■34] In Tateyama 館山市 (Chiba Prefecture 千葉県) a group of students of Professor Okabe Akiko 岡部明子 has restored a building with a straw roof, starting by recommencing the cultivation of *kaya*, because it is obvious that if there is no grass for thatching, you can not make a grass-thatched roof. The building is intended for the village community and has a social function.

[→■36,37] The Swedish architect Bengt Oscar Warne theorised [→B92,329,330,331] that (rain)water, waste, soil, and plants would be included in the design of the houses. Ordinary log houses would be placed at the core of larger, enclosing greenhouses. A space for activity and cultivation would therefore be created between the greenhouse and the core house. A favourable microclimate for growing flowers, fruit, and vegetables would be created, and this arrangement would help reduce the amount of energy required to heat the building.

The Sikhall *Naturhus* (Brålanda, in the Vänersborg municipality, on the western shore of Lake Vänern) was built from 2001 to 2004. While the concept is to be ascribed to Warne, the final project was developed by self-builder Anders Solvarm for his family of five. The 145-m^2 single-storey core loghouse is enclosed by a 315-m^2 prefabricated, steel greenhouse.

The greenhouse effectively reduces the need for space heating from March to May and from September to October; in other words, it shortens the heating season but cannot completely eliminate the need for space heating in winter. [→B316]

Fresh air is supplied through a well: it then flows through two long, underground pipes, and it is released in the buffer space. This system allows continuous operation, naturally and with no energy input. The greenhouse vents are operated automatically by two weather stations.

Water is fed into the system from a private well at no energy expenditure, except for pumps operation. On average, 300 litres of water are needed per day, summing up all uses. Black and grey water and kitchen waste flow into tanks in the basement, where it is anaerobically purified and sorted in floating and sinking substances. 300 litres of nutritious liquid solution are pumped every day to the *jordbädd* (plant beds) in the buffer space and on the flat roof of the core house. [→B110] Water exiting from the system is periodically checked and found to be swimming quality. Overflow is released into a small artificial pond near the house, where red carps live.

Chemical-free cultivation takes place in three areas.

In winter, cultivation is limited to lettuce and rocket that grow in pots in the back half of the living room, thanks to natural light from the skylight and extra LED lighting.

On the flat roof the temperature is considerably higher than at ground level and this allows to grow plants such as lemon, paprika, chili pepper, squash, and figs. Tomatoes, pumpkins, aubergines and courgettes have also been introduced, as well as flowers such as geraniums and cyclamens, which attract butterflies and small insects. Even small birds can enter the greenhouse. At ground level, strawberries, kiwi, lettuce, tomatoes, and cucumbers are planted along with apricot, lemon, and fig trees. In addition, herbs are grown such as mint, sage, laurel, parsley, rosemary, and basil. Vines show to have found an unexpectedly suitable habitat.

Root vegetables such as potato, carrot, beetroot, parsnip, as well as herbs are grown in sixteen beds outdoor.

This house is worthy of note for the non-negligible amount of vegetables it allows to grow, in spite of the high latitude (the total annual yield is 500 to 1,000 kg of fruit, vegetables and herbs, which means around 20% self-sufficiency on average) and much more so because it makes the consequences of the actions of the inhabitants evident, and obliges them to willingfully take responsibility. Solvarm explains that the water treatment system would not accept a person to take heavy drugs, like those for cancer treatment, as this would kill the plants. It is also to be remarked that to function, a *Naturhus* requires that you live there, as the whole water cycle is designed on the basis of the inhabitants' water consumption.

[→■36]

[→■37]

buildings in this book have somehow managed to slip through the cracks of local building regulations.
While certificates and standards may protect the public good, they also promote the interests of aggressive companies and restrain innovation. Consider, for example, the rules that are meant to protect public health. These same rules also drastically reduce diversity and eliminate micro food production activities, the only ones that still follow traditional and low-impact methods. Another problem with such regulations is that they discourage the use of non-conventional materials and processes. Authorities require that they pass time-consuming and costly assessment and certification procedures, simply because they do not fit into the expectations created by industrial standards. [→B156]
All five examples in this second section show attempts to do well substantially, while not respecting conventions in structural matters, energy, etc., and making minimal use of industrial products (e.g., by avoiding the installation of mechanical ventilation systems or reducing the size of the foundations). Although some have an iconic value, aesthetic authorship is never a central aspect of these projects. They are instead in tune with the "spatial agency" approach that tends to eliminate, or at least to scale down, 'authorship': a building is meaningful in as much it is a (working) tool and not the product of an individual's creation. [→B16]
Ugo Sasso used to tell the story of a South Tyrolean family that thanks to their 'Klimahaus'-certified home spent so little money on heating that they could afford a holiday in the Caribbean every winter. Similarly, it would make just as little sense to live in a brand-new *Passivhaus* in an 'unspoilt' place, such as in the mountains, and then commute one hundred kilometres every day in a car. What matters is the total environmental impact—the sum total of diet, transportation, and the building's operational energy.
The above considerations tend to shift the discourse onto a field that architects disregard, deeming it outside of their jurisdiction: collective and individual behaviour. Yet an heretic architect, Bernard Rudofsky, had already noted eighty years ago that "We don't need a new way of building, we need a new way of living". [→B265]
In many instances, ecological impact can be reduced at zero cost by changing habits instead of buying and running newer and more advanced appliances. It is crucial to take responsibility for our choices, to be aware of their consequences, and to acknowledge ecological constraints. This is what Lucien Kroll has in mind when he refers to "techniques versus humanism". [→B167; see also B165,166] [→■35] A sailboat and a motorboat are different in terms of engineering and operation; so are the skill and awareness needed to steer them. [→B90] The same can be said in regards to the design and management of a passive house [→B195,341] as opposed to one whose operation would rely largely on (active) services: one needs skill and bravery to actually obtain—not just intend to obtain—excellent performances, minimising the use of services. [→B26] [→■36,37] The buildings in the second section prove that this is possible.

This book uses the term 'vegetarian' metaphorically. It also understands the term 'architecture' in a very broad sense—as Rudofsky [→B268,269] and Friedman [→B96] did—to include all human activity that modifies the environment spatially.

[→■38]

There are a number of places where intelligent actions to create an ecologically sustainable future and to develop sociality are being put into practice; catalogues of such actions are available to draw inspiration. [→B190,345; see also B189] Although there are great design opportunities in the field of sustainable, local development, originality should not be the main priority. Designers should be bold enough to carry out or accept small, often invisible, unspectacular things that may require a great deal of time and dedication before they produce any results. [→■20,29,35,38,39]

[→■39]

The four experiences of rural revitalisation that make up the third and final section [→§§9–12] present an utterly not reassuring, not conservative character. [→B184] To begin with, they have depended heavily on attracting new residents, an illustration of which is the 'highlanders by choice' theory. [→B61] In the case of the towns of Wangelin and Kamiyama, locals may have initiated, at least in part, certain processes that were crucial to the success of the project; but since the population was shrinking, attracting new residents was a major goal against which to measure their success. And indeed in most other cases, some of which I discuss, newcomers were responsible for launching the needed regeneration processes.

In many such places, the first question is the demographic survival of human communities, and of their ability to make persistent, ecologically competent use of the territory. In addition to the human settlement and to the vitality of traditional and new material cultural practices, the agricultural and dietary elements are always present and often key to the project's success. [→B12,307] The easiest and most effective measure is to begin by establishing some type of local economic base for agricultural production, also because today many other products could not be produced differently than by the industry. Obviously, "the economy of a healthy community based in agriculture or forestry ... cannot be the present colonial economy in which only 'raw materials' are exported and all necessities and pleasures are imported": [→B31:203] a local, 'circular economy' has to be reintroduced. Veronelli suggested that each community should discover and claim its own particular, inalienable assets and self-manage a production of wealth based on such assets. [→B321,322] Architecture can and should contribute, but it is only one tessera in a much larger mosaic. [→B130,313]

It would have been simplistic and rigid to include in this book only examples that fall within the definition of 'vegetarian architecture' I have tried to give above, without taking into account the socio-economic, cultural and environmental context. Especially in this third section, I preferred to discuss examples that, despite only partially corresponding to the characters I listed above as typical of an ideal 'vegetarian architecture', show to have been the result of a comprehensive vision of the socio-cultural and ecological environment in which they are immersed.

Captive vernacular: Hirose House at Nihon Minka-en

Andrea Bocco Guarneri

Nihon Minkaen 日本民家園, the Japan Open-Air Folk House Museum, **[→B374]** was founded in Kawasaki City in 1967, with the aim of preserving examples of the rapidly vanishing *minka* (folk houses) from the Edo period (1615–1868). It extends across a 3-hectare (ha) park and is similar in arrangement and principles to many other open-air museums established in Europe since the late nineteenth century. The museum's founder, Ōoka Minoru 大岡實, was to have two such museums in Japan, one located in the east the other in the west. Each would feature roughly forty-five buildings, two per prefecture. The acquisition and reassembly process took place over the course of the late 1960s and early 1970s, ceased for a decade and then resumed much more slowly later on. The last addition to the collection dates from 1994. Today, the Minkaen includes twenty-five buildings, most of which come from Kantō, Chubu, and Tohoku regions. The museum's policy has been to rebuild the relocated buildings as close to their original form as possible, disregarding alterations that took place while they were still in use. The museum published reports on the dismantling, relocation, and repair of every house. **[→B99,232] [→■2]**

The Hirose House is a farmhouse whose original location was a hamlet called Kamihagiwara 上萩原, in the Enzan district 塩山 of Kōshū City 甲州市 (Yamanashi prefecture 山梨県). The place lies at an altitude of 770 m above sea level (m a.m.s.l.), and is subject to the strong winds that blow from the Japanese Alps. The winds tend to erode the light, volcanic ash soil and make local agriculture a hard job. Yet, agriculture persisted as the main activity in this area. In addition to subsistence agriculture, the crops cultivated for monetary exchange have remained largely the same over time: a local variety called Hagiwara tobacco, which is famous for its spicy taste; silkworm breeding; and later fruit.

Interviews with those who once lived in the Hirose House **[→B221]** revealed that on the fields above the house, they alternately grew maize and wheat. In other places, they cultivated barley and wheat. In early summer they sowed corn along their edges that they later hung around the house to dry. Other crops included konjac 蒟蒻, millet, azuki 小豆, and

[→■2]

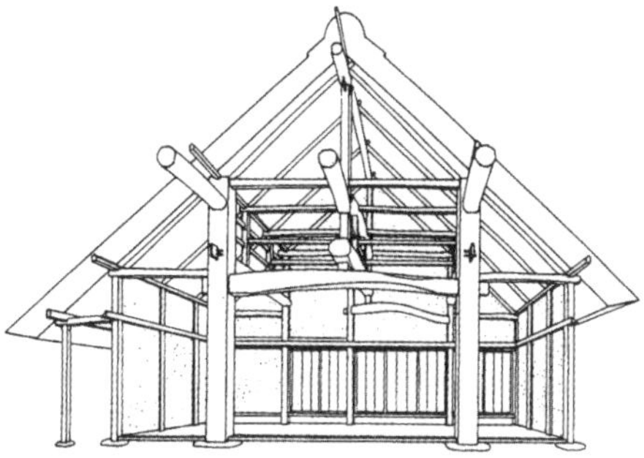

[→■1]

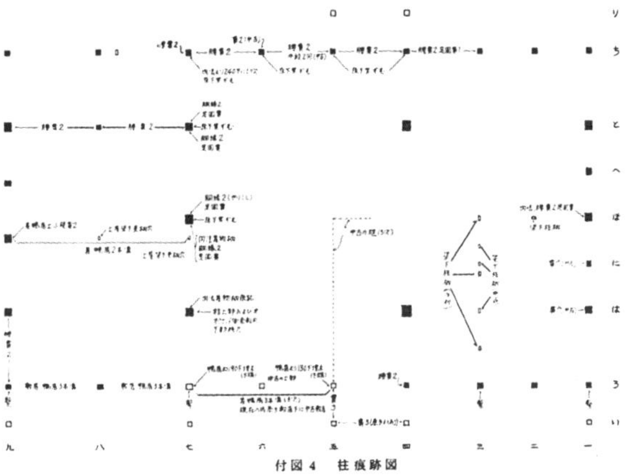

[→■3]

[→■4]

other types of beans. Because water was scarce and the ground steep, farmers arranged just a few rice fields on labour-intensive, stone-walled terraces near the river. The Hiroses owned the small land they cultivated, but they were not rich. They did not even produce enough rice to feed the entire family. They must have nonetheless occupied a somewhat privileged position. This is indicated by the fact that, in contrast to the foundations that were typical for the region—posts stuck directly into the ground—, at their home the foundations were *ishiba-date* 石場建て, that is posts that are placed at the top of foundation stones. **[→■7]** Moreover, the house contained a reception room (*zashiki* 座敷) and a horse stable (*umaya* 厩), supposedly reserved for upper-class visitors, who might have wanted to rest overnight and get a fresh horse. On typological grounds, the house was ascribed to the late seventeenth century, as it is thought that the early houses of the Kōfu 甲府 basin are characterised by four posts (*yotsudate* 四つ建, literally 'stand of four') constituting the core of the load-bearing frame. **[→■1,3]** From the second half of the following century on, subsistence agriculture was complemented by silkworm breeding. This was a fairly good source of income and impacted the form of the local buildings. They added, for instance,

[→■5]

[→■6]

[→■7]

[→■9]

[→■8]

[→■10]

[→■11]

lofts to create an elevated section of the roof over the central part of the upper floor (*tsukiagenikai* 突き上げ二階). [→■4] This aided in obtaining better lighting and improved ventilation. Though such lofts were a typical feature of the Kōfu basin *minka*, reflecting the history of its economy, the museum chose not to rebuild the one still existing in the Hirose House. [→B233:62]
The reconstruction of the Hirose House, which lasted a mere few months, took place at the Minkaen in 1969 after having been acknowledged as an "Important cultural property" and having been surveyed by the Yokohama National University. [→233:4] The museum then published a report on its dismantling, relocation, and reconstruction. [→B283]

Among the many buildings conserved at the Minkaen, I chose to report on the Hirose House because of its archaic simplicity and possibly because when I first saw it, it was "richly endowed with the beauty that comes from gradual ripening over many years", [→B233:6] as the curators of the museum put it. [→■5] Moreover, moss had grown on large areas of the thatched roof, somehow making it a perfect visual epitome of 'vegetarian architecture'. [→■6] (An aside: it's worth noting that in an occupied building, moss would not, of course, grow that way. In real life, it would indicate a bad state of repair or an abandoned building.) Recently, the roof has just been rethatched. The structure is composed of a *jōya* 上屋 (nave or 'upper house') plus *geya* 下屋 (aisles or 'lower house') and a *matageya* 又下屋 (another more external aisle, only on the main facade, which was originally exposed to the east). [→■1,2] The gross internal area is 114 m²; in its original location, the house sat on a property of slightly less than 1,000 m².

First, villagers set a bed of stones at the bottom of a hole dug in the ground, forming a sort of pad foundation much larger than the emerging foundation stone itself. They then beat these stones into the ground vigorously, filling the space between them with gravel. Next, they placed large foundation stones that they then tamped to ensure stability; finally, they infilled sand all around the emerging stones, which they again beat down into the ground. [→B233:18,19] Villagers performed this hard, labour-intensive work: it was one of the *fushin* 普請 works, that is, a social reciprocal duty fulfilled by the community. "Any house was actually built by the entire village." [→B233:16] The *ishiba-date* was chosen in view of the frequent earthquakes, as this loose, pin-joint-like connection between foundation stone and timber framework "is doubtlessly very appropriate", to borrow Heino Engel's judgement. [→B85:81]
Engel also noted that "the sole function of the foundation is to keep the wood posts clear from the usually damp ground". [→B85:79] In the cold season, however, the temperature of the foundation stone drops and dew condensation occurs, so some moisture penetrates the column from the end touching the foundation stone, and decay eventually occurs. [→B217] The foot of many columns was in fact substituted when the house was rebuilt at the museum, connecting a timber section with the same dimensions to the bottom of the undamaged part of the original column. For the same reason, the ground floor of traditional buildings was always raised, except in the *doma* 土間, the space where the main productive activities were carried out, and around which the entire house was organised. [→■7,8,10]
The next step was the fabrication and erection of the frame. The carpenters assembled on the site the elements they had made beforehand. [→B233:20] [→■9] They never assembled the frame horizontally and then tilted it up, as was the case in Europe: they assembled every member individually, in its final position, fixing them together almost entirely with timber joints, and with scarcely any nails. This form of setting up the framework is very fast: only three months were needed to complete the rebuilding at the museum's site.
According to Nakao Nanae 中尾七重 and Futani Tomoo 布谷知夫, [→B217] in the Hirose House chestnut was originally used for columns and lintels (*kamoi* 鴨居), pine for rafters, and *keyaki* 欅 (*Zelkova serrata*) for girders. The members which had become unusable at the time of reconstruction were replaced following the original. The total amount of timber used in the house is 9,600 kg.
Mariya Stoycheva, who has studied the Hirose House in detail, explains that columns are mostly prismatic and made from squared heartwood, but some columns and all beams are round and slightly curved,

[→■12]

and close to the natural state, although sapwood is removed. In farm houses, round posts made from the trunk of a single young tree were often used since straight, quality timber was reserved for the upper class and the temples. Only at the joints did they square the round beams in order to obtain precise and elaborate connections. Joints are Japanese interlocking connections. They are not, however, the sort of ready-made solutions found in handbooks, which rather stem from a later abstracting and typifying tendency. [→B55] The carpenters who built the Hirose House were quite free and creative in how they approached construction; they did not repeat the same joint even for similar intersections, and adapted their solutions to the timbers at hand. [→B295] [→■11]
The surface of the poles—as well as that of the floor and wall boards—was regularised with a hand adze (*chōna*, 手斧): the house was built before the plane became popular. [→■12]
In keeping with the typical Japanese way of building framed structures, the house's frame is a simple post-and-beam construction without braces or struts; [→B85:72] [→■1] both the *jikugumi* 軸組 (lower frame, corresponding to the height of the walls) and the *koyagumi* 小屋組 (roof frame) are capable of resisting vertical pressure only. Yet, thanks to the stiffness of its joints and the elasticity of its members, the house has survived without any damage the many earthquakes that have taken place over the course of the fifty years since its relocation, even the earthquake in 2011. The Hirose House is one of the museum's *minka* that are considered completely safe, despite their obvious lack of conformity with current seismic regulations. A survey showed that ten other *minka* are not so earthquake-proof, and two have since been reinforced. [→B122]
The gabled roof (*kirizuma* 切妻) is supported by *munamochi* 棟持 posts, that are posts which rise to the full height of the structure to directly support the ridgepole (*munagi* 棟木) and are set in the gable walls. [→■2,9,13] The roof truss system is nevertheless an *odachi-gumi* 真束組: such full-height posts are not present in the core of the house, where the king post (*shinzuka* 真束) sits on the *jōyabari* 上屋梁 beam: a larger column-free area is therefore created in the *doma*. [→B233:14]
The roof is thatched: almost the entire work process was traditionally undertaken by the village people as a co-operative unit. [→B233:22] [→■13]
Horizontal bamboo rods called *yanaka-dake* 屋中竹 are laid on the roof rafters at intervals of about 500 mm; a further layer of bamboo rods is laid running along the slope (*taruki* 垂木) at about 230 mm intervals. All such rods are tied in place with straw rope. On the *taruki* are attached split bamboos at intervals of 150 mm. All around the eaves and the gable verges (*keraba* 螻蛄羽), a continuous bamboo perimeter element called *kayaoi-dake* 茅負竹 is attached to

[→■13]

secure the edges of the thatch. [→■14] In the Hirose House, the *kaya* 茅 (thatch) is *Miscanthus sinensis* (*susuki* 芒); leaves are removed from the stalks and the length of the sheaves is made even. The *kaya* sheaves are laid starting from the eaves and gable verges and then working up along the slope until the ridge is reached; they are set lengthwise along the eaves, transversely up the verges, and radiating at the corners. At given intervals, each layer is secured with bamboo rods called *oshihoko-dake* 押鉾竹 which in their turn are tied to the bamboo grid structure beneath the *kaya* with straw rope passing through the thatch. There are three layers of thatch about 150 mm thick each, which make up a total of approximately 400 mm once compressed. A smooth, even surface is created by beating the *kaya* with a special tool called *ganki* 雁木. The *kaya* is bent over the ridge; in the Hirose House, there is a grass ridge (*shibamune* 芝棟) constructed by applying layers of *kaya* on top of each other, then wrapping them in three waterproofing layers of cedar bark, and covering them with more bundles of *kaya*. Turf is spread over and planted with *Selaginella tamariscina* (*iwakiba* 巻柏) because the soil weights down the ridge, but will eventually dry and will be washed away by rain. The plants' roots, however, reinforce the soil and prevent it from drying and eroding. The final stage is trimming the entire roof starting from the ridge and working downwards using special shears; the horizontal stakes that had been tied onto the slope and used as ladders by the workers are then removed. [→B233:22,23]

All the materials employed—such as *kaya*, bamboo, and straw rope—were close at hand in an agricultural economy: nothing had to be bought. The total amount of *kaya* used in the roof of the Hirose House is 26,000 kg. In total, thirty-eight rope rolls of 150 m were used for the roof's entire construction, including thatch binding and also the scaffolding.

Since its reconstruction at the Minkaen, the roofing replacement work took place two times: the first time in 1993, the second during the winter 2018/19. The last re-thatching work cost 48,300,000 yen (387,860 €), including the remaking of a French drain, scaffolding, and taxes—an extremely expensive intervention, the sort of which only a museum could afford. This shows how remote traditional building practices have become from contemporary ones, which tend to be based on formal tenders and specialised services that only a handful of contractors offer. Traditional construction, by contrast, relied on unpaid cooperative work in the village.

After the roof, came the walls; bamboo wattle and daub walls commonly used in *minka* because the materials were readily available. **[→B233:24]** The first stage was to prepare the wattle, which was then daubed in the *arakabe* (粗壁, 'rough wall finish') fashion, exactly as described by Emily Reynolds. **[→B257]** **[→■15,16,17]** As Engel observed, the Japanese climate "is always wet and there is no difference in temperature and humidity between inside and outside, there is no movement of the wood and therefore there is no need for beads": **[→B85:98]** the durability and the precision required for a contemporary, conditioned house would be completely different. In the reconstruction at the museum, the earth walls were rebuilt with new material.

Some parts of the perimeter walls and most of the internal walls are made of timber boards. Posts and beams are not grooved; the 13-mm-thick boards are butted against each other and pegged to the noggins (*nuki* 貫).

The *ōdo* (大戸, main door) slides and is made of boards (*itado* 板戸). The only room with substantial openings to the outside is the *zashiki*, which has two *shōji* 障子 screens, while elsewhere the windows are actually small ventilation openings where the *shinkabe* latticework has not been daubed with *arakabe*. **[→■18]**

Entering the house through the *ōdo*, you encounter a large space. **[→■19]** The part with an earth floor is known as the *doji* (or *doma*) and was used for cooking, agricultural work, and the storage of foodstuffs; the horse stable (*umaya*) is on the corner on the right-hand side. In farmhouses, the *doma* was often called *uchiniwa* 内庭 (internal yard). In both the internal and external yard 外庭 (*sotoniwa*), works such as threshing, hulling, winnowing, and polishing of harvested grain, as well as the making straw rope, were undertaken according to the weather. The internal *niwa* was also used for making pickles, *miso* 味噌 (bean paste), and *shōyu* 醤油 (soy sauce), and here these

[→■14]

[→■15]

[→■16]

[→■17]

foodstuffs were kept in pots; because its function as a place for food preparation was essential to survival, it had a semi-sacred character. Moreover, this was the place where the farmer's family spun cotton and silk, weaved, made clothes, and dyed yarns and fabrics.

To the left of the doorway, there extends a living area called *idoko* 居所, which was the place for many everyday activities, including consuming meals; it has two sunken hearths (*irori* 囲炉裏) dug into the ground. [→■20] Beyond it, at the far end of the house, are three rooms—the *zashiki*, *nakanando* 中納戸, and *okunando* 奥納—arranged in a line, one behind the other. The *zashiki* was a formal guest reception room (that could also accommodate overnight guests), and in the more recent past was also used as a children's

bedroom; the *nakanando* was the young couple's sleeping room, while the *okunando* at the farthest corner was the elderly couple's sleeping room and a storage space for the family's valuables. At the time of its dismantling, the farmhouse was inhabited by four different generations; it had stayed within the same family since its erection. **[→B221]** *Okunando* and *zashiki* have sliding doors that make them directly accessible from the *idoko*. **[→■20]** The *nakanando*, by contrast, is only accessible from the *zashiki*.
Even today, in Japanese houses there prevails a hierarchy of rooms, according to the levels and the kind of flooring. The *doji* (*doma*) has a tamped earth floor. The *idoko* has a *doza* (土座) floor, a floor made of straw bundles spread over tamped earth and covered with thin rice straw matting (*mushiro* 筵). **[→B233:62]** **[→■21]** This was once very common among the common people: in *minka*, rooms with *tatami* floors were still a luxury in the eighteenth century. **[→B233:7]** The *doza* floor is contained in wooden sills resting on the ground; the difference in level—about 100 mm—between *idoko* and *doji* is due to the thickness of the floor layers. The three rooms have a wooden board flooring, elevated about 320 mm above ground level. There is no ceiling, not even above the three rooms: from inside the house, one sees, if light allows, the lower surface of the roof; however, there is a floor for storing hay on top of the *umaya* that partly extends over the *doji*.

Before relocation, there was a *kamado* 竈 (cooking stove) in the *doji*. **[→■22]** Once transferred to Minkaen, the building was restored to its supposedly original state; the *kamado* was therefore not rebuilt because there was no evidence about its original position. This decision left the building incomplete, because without the *kamado* a house would not have been able to function properly.
The *irori* was the focal point of the household and its fire was never allowed to go out, also because it was necessary to preserve the *minka*, since its heat and smoke not only kept insects away but also protected the timber structure, the earthen walls and, more crucially, the thatched roof from damp and consequent decay. **[→B233:39]** However, this fire was not effective at heating the house: the Japanese custom was to warm up the people—for instance having a

[→■18]

hot bath—, not the rooms. **[→B73]** Firewood and the skin of white birch collected from mountain trees were burnt in the *irori*. At the site where the building was originally located, in winter there was a very strong and cold dry wind. The temperature was low, but it did not snow very much.
There was no sink or other washing equipment (*nagashi* 流し) inside the Hirose House. Water was collected in big pots from a stream early in the morning, when it was still clean. For washing they used the water of an irrigation channel running behind the house. On the premises there was a diminutive Shinto shrine with a spring whose water was very clear so that it could be used for drinking. An outside toilet adjoined the house.

For breakfast, the last people who lived in the house ate *morokoshidango* 唐黍団子 (a ball of corn flour) and *oneri* 御練り (*satoimo* 里芋, daikon and pumpkin mixed with corn flour). It was eaten boiled or grilled and seasoned with *miso*. Sometimes they ate the leftover food from the night before. For lunch, they had *han-meshi* 半飯 (half rice, half barley). They ate mainly cereals other than rice. For dinner they had *obōtō* お餺飥: a long, *udon*-like pasta made from wheat flour that is eaten in soup with many vegetables; the *dashi* 出汁 (broth) was prepared with *katsuobushi* 鰹節 (bonito).
At parties, they had *nimono* 煮物 of *daikon* and *satoimo*, seasoned sweeter than usual, or *kinpiragobō* 金平牛蒡: a popular dish with roots (*gobō*, i.e.

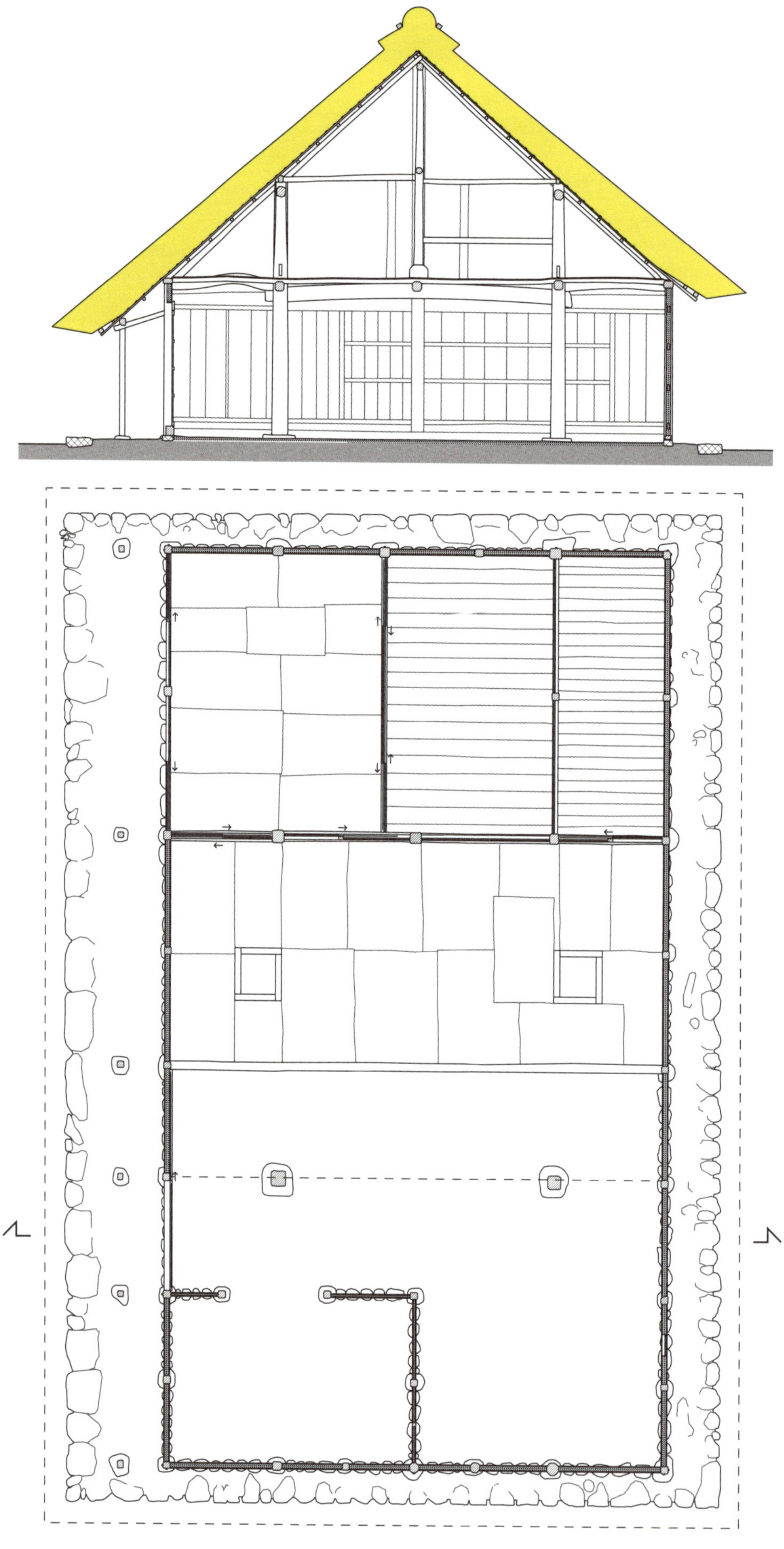

[→■19]
Section and plan, scale 1:100

[→■20]

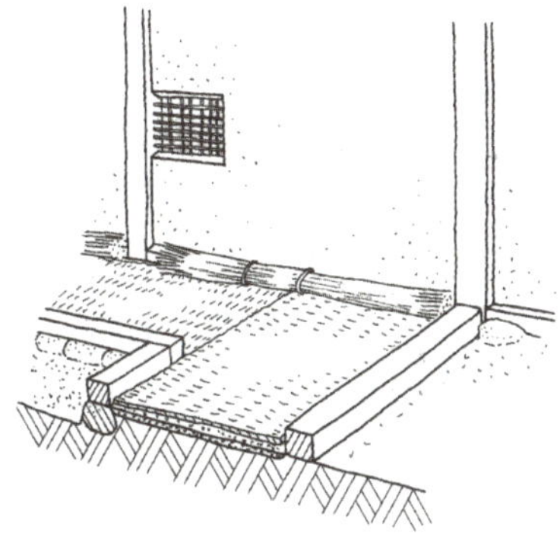

[→■21]

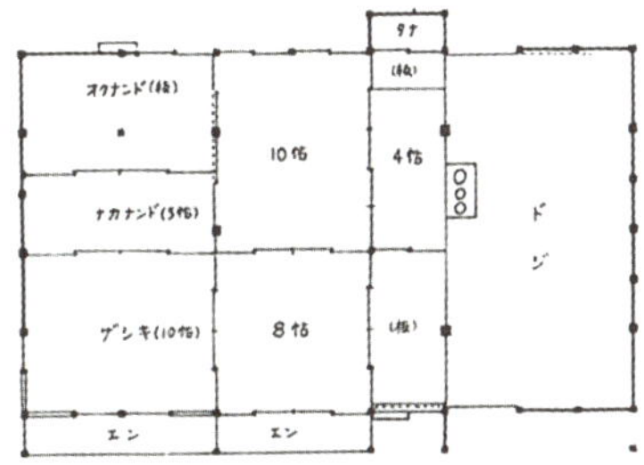

付図 2　移建前平面図

[→■22]

scorzonera or bardana, and carrot) chopped and sautéed with soy sauce, sugar, sake, and sesame oil. For Obon and other special celebrations they also ate *okowa* 御強, a steamed glutinous rice for *mochi* 餅.

They had two horses used for working the fields and for transport. Horses ate grass in summer and dried corn leaves, straw, *sasa* 笹 (bamboo leaves) in winter. They were sold after the head of the family was summoned for war. After that, they kept two pigs, some cocks, and hens.

No one lives in the Hirose House today. Extracted from its original setting, the house no longer has the same spatial relationship to the territory and landscape that surround it, even its orientation is different. What is more, all the relations between the building and its socio-economic context have been lost. Because the museum chose not to reconstruct any elements related to daily life and production, as they sometimes do at other open-air museums, it lacks any meaningful connection to daily life. Its maintenance is no longer an act of daily care performed by its occupants, but by specialists who do not live there. The only act of continuous care is performed by the volunteers of the Robata no kai 炉端の会 group, who keep the domestic hearths lit during the day both to witness a semblance of the life that was once inside of them and to help preserve, with their smoke, the thatch roofing. [→B233:5] Similar to Paraschiva House [→§2] and most vernacular buildings, the Hirose House was conceived to be easily and continuously maintained and renovated.

Today it would not be permitted to use such foundations, to fix joints this way, or to have this type of roofing. Nor would it therefore be possible to create a thoroughly 'authentic Japanese' house with techniques and materials consistent with tradition, but modern in the use of space, in the exploitation of natural light, and in comfort. Yet, one of the Minkaen's most relevant roles is to preserve at least the material embodiment of "principles of thrift and care that are indispensable to the survival of human beings". [→B30:75]

Wild vernacular: Cheia

Andrea Bocco Guarneri
with Daniliuc Sorin

The great vastness of forests in Romania stimulated the development of a wooden architecture with single-material walls, where the load-bearing structure was one with the envelope. In many regions, timber was the most widely used material in architecture until the beginning of the twentieth century. **[→B57,58,59,294]**

The wood used depended on the resources offered by the forests; fir, spruce, beech, ash, and oak were of common use. A skilled craftsman had to be able to analyse the qualities of the wood and identify the most appropriate for the construction's requirements. For sizing the structural timber, the carpenter based his judgement mainly on experience and tradition; this meant that the structures were often oversized. Likewise, knowledge gained through experience also directed the craftsman's evaluation of the wood to be used in relation to the place where the tree had stood; for ordinary dwellings, they preferred trees that had grown quickly in swamps or sunny slopes—despite their quicker decay—because they were easier to work. They acquired, on the other hand, stronger wood from trees that grew slowly in dense forests. For even harder wood, they chose trees that had grown very slowly on the crests of hills or mountains. **[→B17:55]**
The timber was prepared long before the construction work began. The most regular trunks were chosen, taking into account the age and size of the trees in order to maximise the amount of timber that could be obtained. The felling was carried out in winter when the vegetative activity was minimal, bringing work in the fields to a standstill. The trunk was cleared of branches, which were used as firewood or abandoned. Logs were dragged on the ground or rolled down along slopes, until they could be loaded on carts drawn by horses or oxen. At the construction site, they were debarked to facilitate drying and stacked in open air. There they were sheltered from precipitation and sunshine and stored for at least twelve months.

In wooden Romanian vernacular architecture there are three main construction techniques: a framed structure with wattle and daub infill, which is the oldest (*din furci* with *nuiele şi lut* infill); followed by

the framed structure with sill beams (*talpă* or *tălpic*); and finally the *Blockbau* (log house), which was the most widespread technique.
In the latter, the logs were worked to obtain angular joints (*cheotoare dreaptă* joints), either protruding or flush (in this category is the dovetail joint); [→■11,20] the latter required more time and tools than protruding joints. The logs were positioned and only afterwards were the joints worked. In general, constructional concepts and building details are evident, so that there is no question of how elements stay together or what their function is. [→B337:69]

Cheia is a hamlet in the Râmeț Commune in Alba county, located in a lane-shaped depression of the same name in the now-wild landscape of the Trascău Mountains, a part of the Apuseni mountain range. [→■1] It lies at less than 600 m a.m.s.l., a position more sheltered from the wind compared to neighbouring Bradeşti, which is on a ridge at slightly less than 1000 m a.m.s.l. along the county road coming from Aiud; however, like all settlements located at the bottom of a valley, the cold and humid air tends to stagnate there. Cheia is surrounded by limestone mountains whose peaks reach around 1200 m a.m.s.l. The village was possibly settled in the sixteenth century by a group of people who were trying to escape the taxation and religious oppression of the Habsburg Empire by forming a secluded settlement. From Bradeşti, Cheia is about an hour's walk along a winding path through the forest and along a stream that, a century ago, turned the wheels of twelve mills; another option for reaching Cheia is to walk up the same stream through the flooded gorges of Râmeț. Until 1940, between fifty and sixty families, or roughly 300 inhabitants, lived there. It was a village with a pastoral character and scattered houses. Local communities, including Bradeşti, relied heavily on Cheia's water mills, which made up a relevant part of the livelihood of its households. Because the community rejected electrification, which the communist state would have introduced, the village remained largely untouched by modernisation. It thus eventually lost its economic base and was ultimately almost completely abandoned.
The recent, massive depopulation of villages in the Apuseni Mountains has led to the almost irreversible loss of many of the region's traditional practices and crafts, and to the degradation of many of its historical constructions. [→■2] It is said that a house resists as long as it is inhabited; e.g., a thatched roof begins to rot soon after it is left unattended.
Journalist Valentin Şchiopu, who reported about the region, explains that the residents that remain, though now old, never complain about the harshness of the winter. Nor do they complain about loneliness, even as they confess that they miss their children and grandchildren, who rarely come back to visit them in the 'middle of the wilderness'. When they are no longer able to sustain their lives in the village and have to leave the places where they were born, they leave everything in order: a cup and a blanket on the table, work clothes hanging on the hook, as if they were to come back shortly. For them, the city is like a cage; in most cases, it is the place where they will close their eyes. Their abandoned homes stand one after another, along paths upon which only tourists venture. [→B277]
Places have changed over the past few decades. Fifty years ago, the peasants in Cheia cut the hay from behind their house to the top of the mountain. The area was only sparsely forested. Now trees have come back, covering the former pastures and much of the remains of the former human settlement, whose erosion has accelerated in part because of the compostable character of their construction. At present, only the duct channels and the stone foundations of the old mills can still be seen.
Only six people remain in Cheia today, including a nun from the Valea community. Cheia has nevertheless potential as a tourist destination, as it lies at the confluence of several mountain tracks and next to the nature reserve of Cheile Râmețului. Gabriel Suliman explains: "The Apuseni do not have the heights of Fagaras, but there are some trails that bring you to the end of your tether. Here people who like to hang out in the mountains, gather in the evening around a fire, with some mulled wine and a guitar, discovering a refreshing silence." [→B277]

The Suliman family make up two thirds of Cheia's population. Cristina, from Bucharest, and Gabriel, from Constanța, both psychology graduates, had been living in the capital for many years. She taught

[→■1]

[→■2]

[→■3]

in a Waldorf school, he worked as a graphic artist in a multinational firm. They have two children, David and Alice, and thought that Bucharest was not the most suitable environment for raising them; they felt the need to spend more time with them than it would be possible in a typical, big-city lifestyle. While still living in Bucharest, they spent years searching for a different sort of place and in the meantime began to accustom themselves to a thriftier lifestyle, doing without a refrigerator, for instance.
At first, Gabriel thought of commissioning a cottage in the Făgăraş Mountains, restoring it and offering it to tourists, but when in 2012 he discovered Cheia (he installed his tent exactly where his house now stands), he immediately understood this was the place he had been searching for. 'Grandma' Laura Praja was the first person that Gabriel met when he got there, and through her he was able to buy some land for about 3,500 €. Within a few months the Sulimans sold their apartment and in 2013 they moved to Cheia, with the project of restoring traditional homes and providing accommodation to friends and tourists. [→B297]
They have established supportive relationships, but these are extremely loose compared to the types of relationships that used to be sustained in Cheia. Some of this lack is compensated by modern technology: Gabriel's 'neighbour', who lives in the adjacent valley, calls him on his mobile phone to warn him that his mares are there. In addition, the Sulimans arrived just in time to meet the last inhabitants who still maintained the traditional lifestyle, and have been able to draw on their knowledge and experience. Open-air museums collect houses but do not always have specific knowledge about the habits and customs adopted in their places of origin. The Sulimans, by contrast, are gathering practical and experience-based knowledge of traditional techniques, almost from scratch. Gabriel learned to ride and do things he had not even imagined before. [→B36]

The land they bought was a meadow where the villagers, after the long mass, danced in a circle and drank *palinca*, and where the men fought. They bought two old houses and moved them to this plot of land. During the reconstruction of their new home, which took almost three years, they stayed in the former village school across the creek, directly opposite their future home.
In addition to the farmhouse, within a Rumanian *gospodărie* (roughly corresponding to 'farm') enclosure there were toilets, a stable for animals, the outbuildings necessary to carry out agricultural, breeding, and handicrafts activities, and warehouses to store the various tools, and sometimes a well. [→B290:11] [→▪3] The Sulimans have enclosed a part of their land with a fence and created something like a traditional *gospodărie*, including the cottage where they sleep, another house which is rented to tourists, an outdoor kitchen, and an outdoor dining table they use all year round, a cellar mostly excavated in the slope for storing perishable foodstuffs, a shelter for stacked firewood, an outdoor fireplace, a vegetable garden, a chicken coop, a hutch, a washing machine; the outdoor shower, dry toilet, and goat enclosure are right beyond the fence. [→▪4]
This is in keeping with traditional practices when houses contained no cooking implements nor—obviously—a toilet. This was in part because both things were considered sacrilegious. The family's daily activities are not contained within the cottage, calling into question the notion of the boundaries of a home. Cristina explains, "in an apartment, the intimate space is the bed. It took years to harmonise with this new situation, but now I feel that the entire *gospodărie* is the home and the cottage is the intimate space. ... it is even bigger than the bed in the apartment." Like traditional peasants, they live a lot outdoors, in all seasons and even in bad weather. Regarding the cooking outside, Cristina comments, "In an hour an atmosphere is created, it's not cold." Being substantially alone in the middle of nothing means also that "here, if you have a fight, you must have settled down before nightfall".
The homestead is provided with spring water taken from a cave 70 m uphill and brought down in plastic pipes laid by Gabriel. A sink leans against the north wall of their cottage. They use lye to wash clothes and hair. So far, the kids and Cristina wash with water boiled on the stove, while even in winter Gabriel washes in the river. They have not had a TV since they left Bucharest, but they have access to the Internet and can watch a Netflix series or BBC documentaries. The laptop is charged with a solar panel.

[→■4]

Paraschiva house
outdoor kitchen
outdoor dining table
dry toilet
cellar
goat enclosure
gate
firewood shelter
outdoor shower
gate
washing machine
PV collector
Casa Gavrilă
vegetable garden
gate
fireplace
chicken coop

[→■5]

[→■6]

The outdoor kitchen has a cooking range fuelled with cylinder gas and two earthen ovens. [→■5]
They are vegetarians; they keep some lard made by a neighbour and slowly smoked with leaves, just to offer it to guests. During my stay I was fed, among other things an onion omelette with a pinch of mustard, a delicious vegetable *ciorbă* (soup) made with the water in which the *brânză* (fresh cheese) is preserved, and pan-fried *turta* filled with goat milk *brânză dulce* (sweet fresh cheese) and cumin seeds. I also ate the best apples I have possibly ever tasted; [→■6] next to the abandoned houses, many trees were loaded with apples that no one collects anymore.

The Sulimans do not own a car anymore. They either walk or go on horseback. Alice is eight years old, David twelve. When they settled in Cheia, Alice was two: her earliest memories will be linked to this place. She has developed a skill for identifying and collecting wild herbs; at ten, David already knew how to build an earthen stove. Matt Ross's *Captain Fantastic* comes to mind. [→B263] Every third week, the two children go to Râmeț school (I-VIII class), where there are nine pupils in all, and spend five days in the boarding school. The six bedrooms, with about twenty beds, are for them alone. Cristina stays there too, since there is no night caretaker anymore to look after the children. During the rest of the time, they do homeschooling. Cristina follows the teacher's sheets, but the method is adapted to the Waldorf system. Children and parents are together all the time, sharing both play and work, as was the case with peasants. In accord with Rudolf Steiner, the Sulimans believe "this is essential at least in the first seven years, if not until the age of fourteen to fifteen, when the child naturally feels the need to move away". Gabriel says he expects them to attend high school in Sibiu, Alba Iulia or Cluj, and that he does not know whether or not they will return to Cheia after they graduate.
Although they work hard—maintain a household routine; carry out seasonal work such as the cutting and carrying of hay; transport foodstuff and materials—they also take time to live. They have goats, dogs, and cats, plus chickens and guinea fowls, one rabbit and two mares. On a small plot of land they grow onions, garlic, and herbs, which they also collect in the wild. [→■7] In a nearby house, which until a few years ago was still inhabited, Gabriel distils *palinca* from hundreds of kilograms of apples picked in the area, and he sells it for 25 lei (about 5 €) per litre.
"From the historical time we have slipped into a profound and restructuring ritual time [which] aligned us in the course of life," says Gabriel. [→B255] At night, darkness and silence are almost absolute. [→■8] The dormice sing. When you wake up, from the sound of the stream you know if it has been raining—the thatched roof is an excellent acoustic insulator.

Both houses of the Sulimans' *gospodărie* were dismantled in 2014 at their original locations; reconstruction work was finished in 2017. No building permit was required, since they have no foundations. Their original orientation was not respected, as it was never considered relevant; to the peasants, the important thing was for the houses to face the inside of the courtyard. [→■9]

The simple cottage where the Sulimans live is a typical construction from the end of the nineteenth century. [→■10] They refer to it as Casa Gavrilă as it belonged to Gavrilă and Nastasiea Petruț. It is a small building (3.6 x 3.4 m), similar to those used only seasonally. The cottage is a Blockbau made of finger-jointed, rectangular-section heavy beech logs, notched and pinned with wooden nails. [→■11] The logs are visible on the outside, while the inside has been plastered using yellow clay mixed with straw applied over sapling branches that have been split

[→■7]

[→■8]

in half and then diagonally tacked onto the log wall. [→■12] In keeping with tradition, dry tree moss has been used as a filler in the interstices between the logs. The two small windows were once fitted with sheep's bowel membranes, but are now fitted with single glass sheets instead. The ground floor rests directly on the flat ground and is made of massive fir joists, covered by two layers of 80–100-mm-thick fir planks; for thermal insulation, the cavity between the two layers is filled with straw and with a clay binder and ash—the latter is to prevent mice and dormice from digging their burrows into it. The upper floor is built similarly to the ground floor; the beams are left exposed from below and the planks overlap. The straw-thatched, hipped roof is very steep in order to allow rain and snow to move down as quickly as possible.

The plan features a porch (*prispă*, which in Transylvania is called *târnaț*) [→B141:27–39] and a single room, which is entered from the porch. The room functions as a place for sleeping, a reception area for winter guests, and occasionally also as a dining room and kitchen. [→■13] It contains a stove made of stones mortared with clay, [→■14] a small table with a few stools by the south window, a bench (*lavița*) against the west wall on which the parents sleep, and a bed in front of the door where the children sleep. Various objects hang from the ceiling; toys and other stuff are stored beneath the bed. The cottage has a double circuit 12V DC/230V AC; the AGM deep-cycle lithium ion battery lies on the floor in a corner. Electric wires run in exposed pipes inside and outside the house. The yearly firewood consumption is about 3 m^3 for the whole *gospodărie*, that is, including the guesthouse.

[→■9]

[→■10]

[→■11]

[→■12]

[→■13]

[→■14]

[→■15]

As in the Hirose House [→§1], the act of living in the house preserves it. The smoke comes up in the attic in a pipe that ends up under a basket covered inside and out with clay, sand, and horse dung. [→■15] It is used to spread the smoke gently and drop the soot to the floor. The smoke forms a glossy, protective tar layer on the straw roof and cements it—when you want to dismantle an old roof you need to work hard with the peak or the axe. As time goes by, the smoke cannot escape from the ridge anymore but progressively lower from the sides—you easily spot the level of the sealing tar layer from the outside because the straw changes its colour.

The other house—called Paraschiva House because it belonged to Ion and Paraschiva Buta—is used as a guesthouse for tourists. [→■16,17] It cost 500 € and its disassembled parts were ox-carted and shouldered from a neighbouring village, După Deal (Ponor commune), 4 km away. The transportation alone took a whole summer. The house has been certified in the agricultural register since 1900, but it is likely somewhat older because there is evidence that it had already been disassembled and moved once, before being brought to Cheia.

Originally, the house had a stone basement; now it stands on short, reinforced concrete columns infilled with cordwood on the front façade, creating a storage space in the slope. [→■18,19] Walls are made of 150–200-mm-thick, squared beech and aspen logs; [→■20,21] there are twelve logs per side. At least two logs were salvaged from an older building. The total timber employed is 19.6 m^3. Wooden pegs were used to connect the superimposed logs; their heads protrude beyond the wall. As in Casa Gavrilă, the outer face of the log walls is left exposed, while the inner face is plastered over diagonal laths; the base layer is a mix of earth and chaff, while the finish coat is earth, sand, and lime. Both floors were remade with new timbers, and the height of the rooms was increased. There is a white-painted band at the perimeter of the ceiling of both rooms, both on the planks and the beams. Here cracks form easily and must be filled with clay and then covered with a coat of limewash. The four windows were enlarged, and new frames were installed; the windows do not rotate on hinges; to allow in air from outside, the entire frame has to be removed. The two doors—one for the entrance and one inside between the rooms—are connected to the log walls by *țâțâni* (wooden hinges).

Thatched roofs are the thickest (about 800 mm) and most durable (roughly eighty years) way of roofing found in the Romanian building tradition. [→B20] The original ones were made of long-stem rye straw. Unfortunately, straw is no longer what it used to be: straw from cereals cultivated with fertilisers in the flatlands grows too quickly and is therefore weak and rots easily. Moreover, Gabriel reports that rethatching the two houses with the machine-harvested wheat straw that comes in round bales was difficult because it is too short. This meant that they could not apply traditional techniques without modification. To have something long to start with (straw is laid loose, starting from the eaves which are supported by curved maple elements), they had to add ferns to the straw. The first layer of thatch was then placed on a bracket consisting of a twisted rope braided and fixed on wooden pegs at about 300-mm intervals. In the thickness of the thatch, approximately every metre, there is a horizontal birch pole to keep everything in place and compress the straw a bit. To rebuild the Paraschiva house's roof, over 6,000 kg of straw were used.

The layout is archetypal—two rooms plus a *târnaț*. One accesses the house via a flight of steps, via the *târnaț*, which has four-edged columns joined by a wooden parapet that was painted with exhausted machine oil for protection. From the porch one enters the *tindă* (small room or mudroom), which had multiple purposes in the traditional home: entrance, place for food preparation, and handwork. [→■22] In front of the door there is a stove for cooking (locally called *ploaptan*), made of clay and stone, without a metal hob. The stove extends underneath the *camnița*, i.e., grandma's sleeping place, built from loam and large rubblestones (*de codru*). This system was traditional in the Apuseni region where winters are long and cold. The second room (*odaie*) is a sleeping room, also equipped with a bed stove; it was also the good room, i.e., where guests were received and special events took place. Both rooms are now mostly used as bedrooms for paying guests. The interior has a modest but pleasant appearance; Gabriel chose to keep things simple, if not a little austere, for visitors

[→■16]

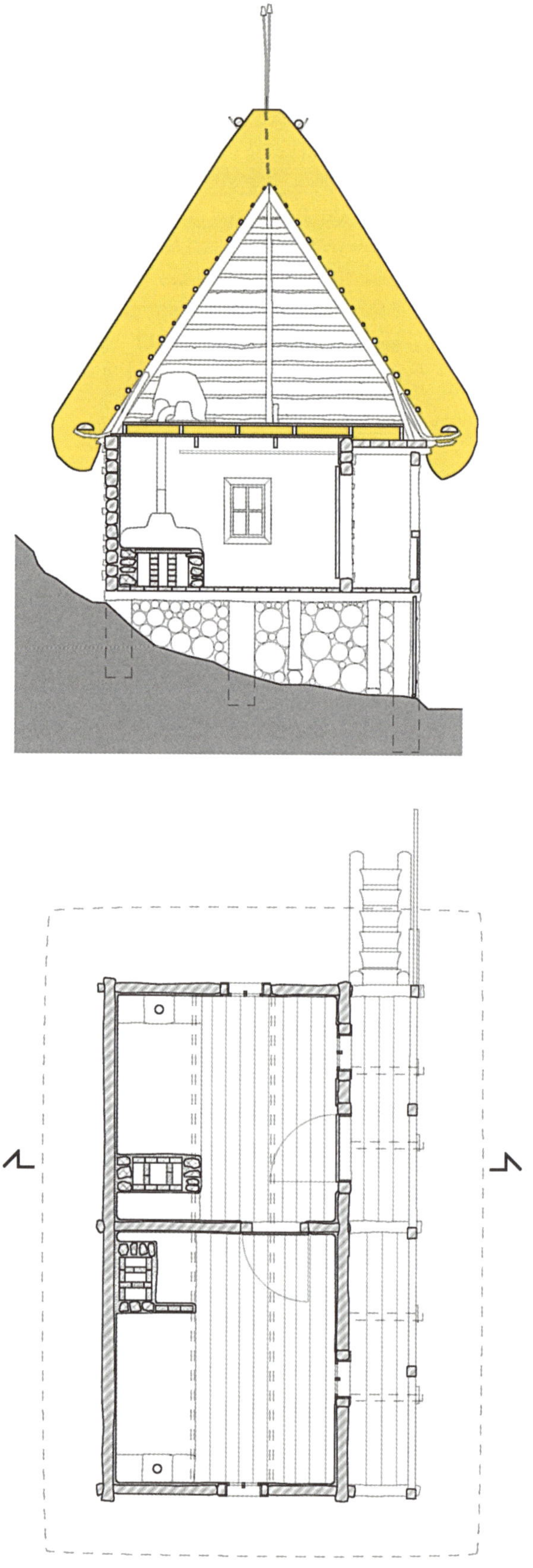

[→■17]
Section and plan,
scale 1:100

[→■18]

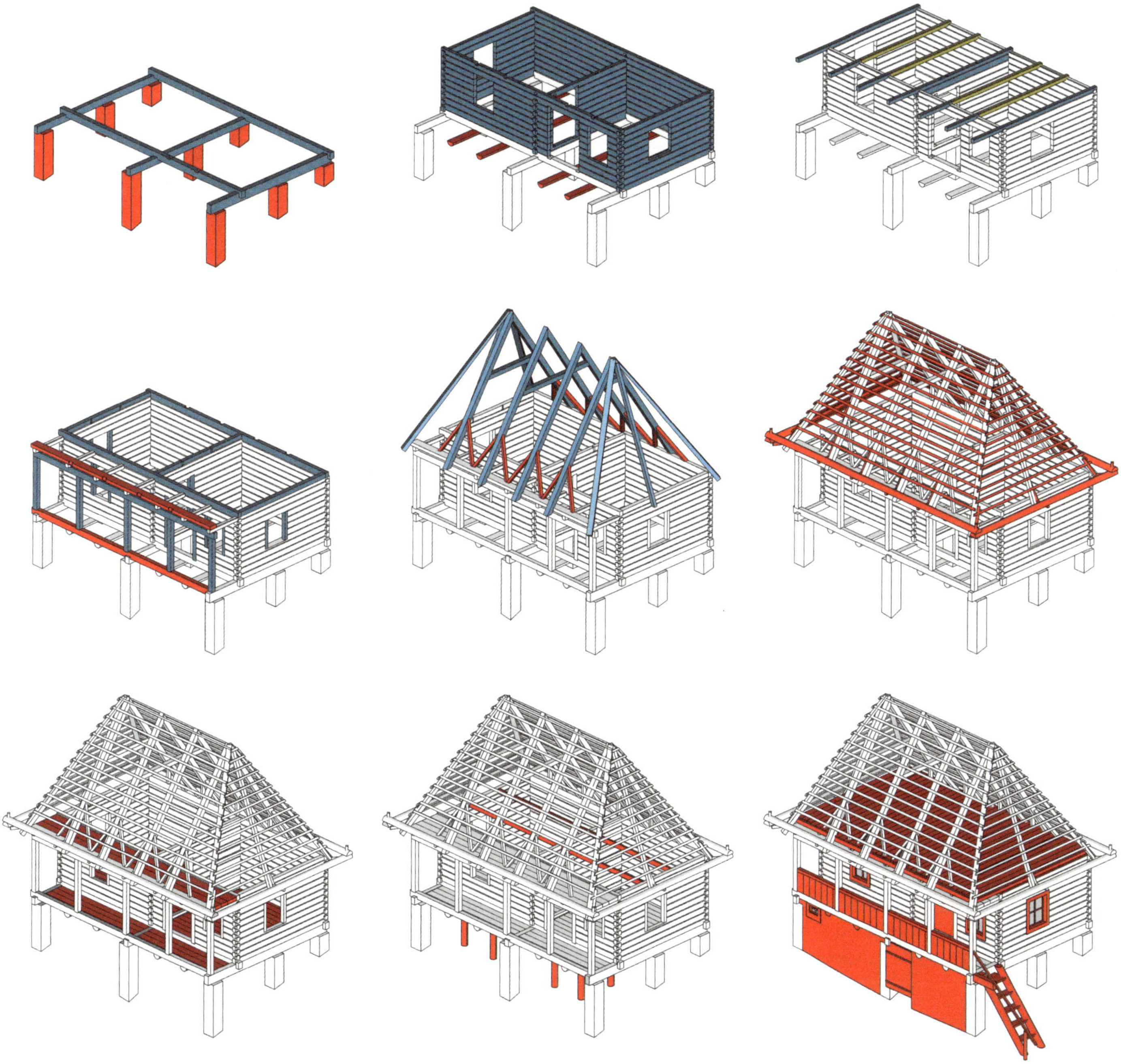

[→■19] Construction phases

[→■20]

[→■21]

from the cities who might have different notions of comfort. In spite of the enlarged windows, inside it is dark; rooms are illuminated with kerosene lamps that emit a strong odour. Yet the house offers simple delights such as the mattresses stuffed with hay and aromatic herbs, which are changed once a year.

Both houses, and especially the Paraschiva House, look a bit like those of open-air museums, in that there are traditional handcrafted items put on display: hemp, cotton and wool cloths, earthenware, wooden chests, furniture (dowry box, table, table with chairs). [→■13,22] A fabric hung in the room where I slept was given to them by an ethnographic museum; it is a very valuable piece with traditional geometric designs. There are black clay pottery pieces from Maramureş and Bucovina, continuing the tradition of Cucuteni culture, hand-moulded and engraved, made smooth and water-repellent by polishing the surface with a stone; their curvatures recall the shape of the female body. There are also wooden objects perfectly adapted to their function, simple and executed with the right wood, made based on traditional models especially for Cristina by an elderly master; a ladle with a very long handle, decorated with wolf teeth and other motifs; a wooden bowl for storing flour; another small one for kneading bread: it is rounded in plan and section, so that all the dough can be picked up by one hand, with one easy gesture. Cristina is deeply familiar with and passionate about Romanian folk culture.

This year, Gabriel plans to take an old water mill from a neighbouring village, which he will then rebuild with the help of a group of volunteers on the creek's riverbed next to his house. Gabriel hopes the mill will become an additional tourist attraction and will give visitors a chance to learn about peasant techniques and crafts in their natural environment. At present, there are very few operating water mills in Romania, even for demonstration purposes. [→B356] Construction costs will be covered through an online fund-raising campaign. The mill will produce electricity and grind corn for the animals. Additional projects include the construction of a shelter for the goats, a hut for computer work, as well as a newly built third house to expand available accommodations for tourists.

[→■22]

Straw-based retrofit: Casa Steila Mar

Andrea Bocco Guarneri

Niches, like the ones found in some Alpine valleys, allow for experimentation without creating too much fuss. Matter-of-factedness can be established. Like in nurseries, innovations and even heresies can be cultivated until they are strong enough to be brought to the fore. I think I am not a victim of suggestion if I say that, in the case of Sepp Holzer **[→B133,134,135]** or Werner Schmidt, the very remoteness of the places in which they have worked presented the opportunity to develop original ways in agriculture and architecture.
Based in Graubünden, architect Werner Schmidt specialises in ecological building, usually with straw bales. **[→B44]** He combines modern products and designs with low-energy, minimally processed natural materials: his work shows that a natural approach to architecture does not necessarily produce 'hairy' buildings. It also shows that concern for ecological balance need not come at the price of attractive architectural design.

For decades now, there has been a debate about whether it is better to retrofit or replace old, inefficient buildings. Nils Larsson recommends performing a *triage* on existing buildings, one interpretation of which might be that those located in less densely-populated areas that cannot be easily retrofitted should simply be abandoned. **[→B43]** Robert and Brenda Vale have maintained that "when it comes to reducing environmental impact, the critical issue is not so much new build versus the refurbishment of existing houses as longevity". **[→B319:184]**
A cost-benefits analysis of energy—not of money—would likely reveal that in most cases, refurbishing or retrofitting a building is more energy effective than new construction. Future research should focus on retrofitting existing structures, not on developing excellently performing new buildings.

Most of Schmidt's works are new buildings, but over the course of the past decade he has been experimenting with using straw bales in retrofits. His largest project was the Complemedis headquarters (in Trimbach/SO, 2014) whose envelope was thermally insulated with prefabricated timber elements filled with 500-mm-thick straw bales and clad with bamboo culms. He also undertook the thermal

[→■1]

retrofitting of House Ervin Jacomet, a building from 1883 in Sumvitg/GR. The 650-mm-thick perimeter stone walls were wrapped with straw bales stacked between OSB boards that had been fixed to the walls at 500-mm centres, using L-shaped metal brackets and wall plugs. This was somewhat tricky, because it is not always easy to drill stones and obtain a good grip. Retrofit work took four months in 2011 and involved all family members: Schmidt came out of this experience persuaded that such a technique was too time-consuming, and only feasible in a DIY process. He thought that a cheaper option would have been to detail prefabricated elements just to fit openings or other special places where precision is needed, and that the perimeter wall could be insulated by erecting a straw bale wall against it: a technique he experimented with in Susch a little later.

Sur Punt is the old part of Susch, a village in Engiadina Bassa, and lies on the right bank of the Inn River at about 1300 m a.m.s.l. Just across the bridge, a former medieval monastery cum brewery has recently been converted into a contemporary art museum, Grażyna Kulczyk's Muzeum Susch, which opened to the public in January 2019 after a long restoration and extension process designed by architects Schmidlin and Voellmy. At the other end of the village, Casa Steila Mar ('Starfish House') is a typical Engiadina traditional, stone-masonry house built in several stages starting around 1850, the oldest being the north end facing the street. [→■1] The property, covering 5,000 m^2 in total, was bought eight years ago by Maitreyi (Dorothee) Piontek and her former partner. "It would be worth moving to Susch even just for the quality of the water," she claims. She is a well-known Swiss author and seminar leader whose work focuses on a "holistic, transforming path of development that should free women from old personal, social and collective bondage and constraints". [→B373] Her books, especially *Weibliches Manifest* ("Female Manifesto"), describe a new spiritual feminism. [→B246] Her first book, *Das Tao der Frau*, dates from 1995 [→B245] and remains her most successful and most widely translated work. [→B382]

In 2013, she hired Werner Schmidt to transform the house into a healthy, low-energy environment: the building was to have a new, ecological, and well-insulated envelope. The whole project was to be centred on natural materials, both inside and out. Schmidt's plans included Piontek's two-storey apartment/studio in the old stable area, a space for seminars, and three apartments to be rented for short periods in what used to be the residential area. [→■2,6] Piontek lives alone in roughly 570 m^2 of the house, but envisions it as an 'open house' that can accommodate up to fifteen people. The opening of the Muzeum will bring more tourists to Susch; still, Piontek plans to open her home to a mixture of visitors, including some tourists, and to participants in her seminars, which are typically ten to twelve people who stay for about five days.

Apart from the thermal retrofit, Schmidt's project comprised 'tidying up' Piontek's house: the position and size of the openings were regularised, closing some of the existing ones and opening a few new ones, especially at the northern corner; [→■3] a small building abutted against the northeast façade was demolished and replaced by a balcony; [→■4] two of the large openings of the former barn at the southern end of the building were replaced by windows, whereas the third one was closed; [→■5] the small

[→■2]

[→■3]

[→■4]

[→■5]

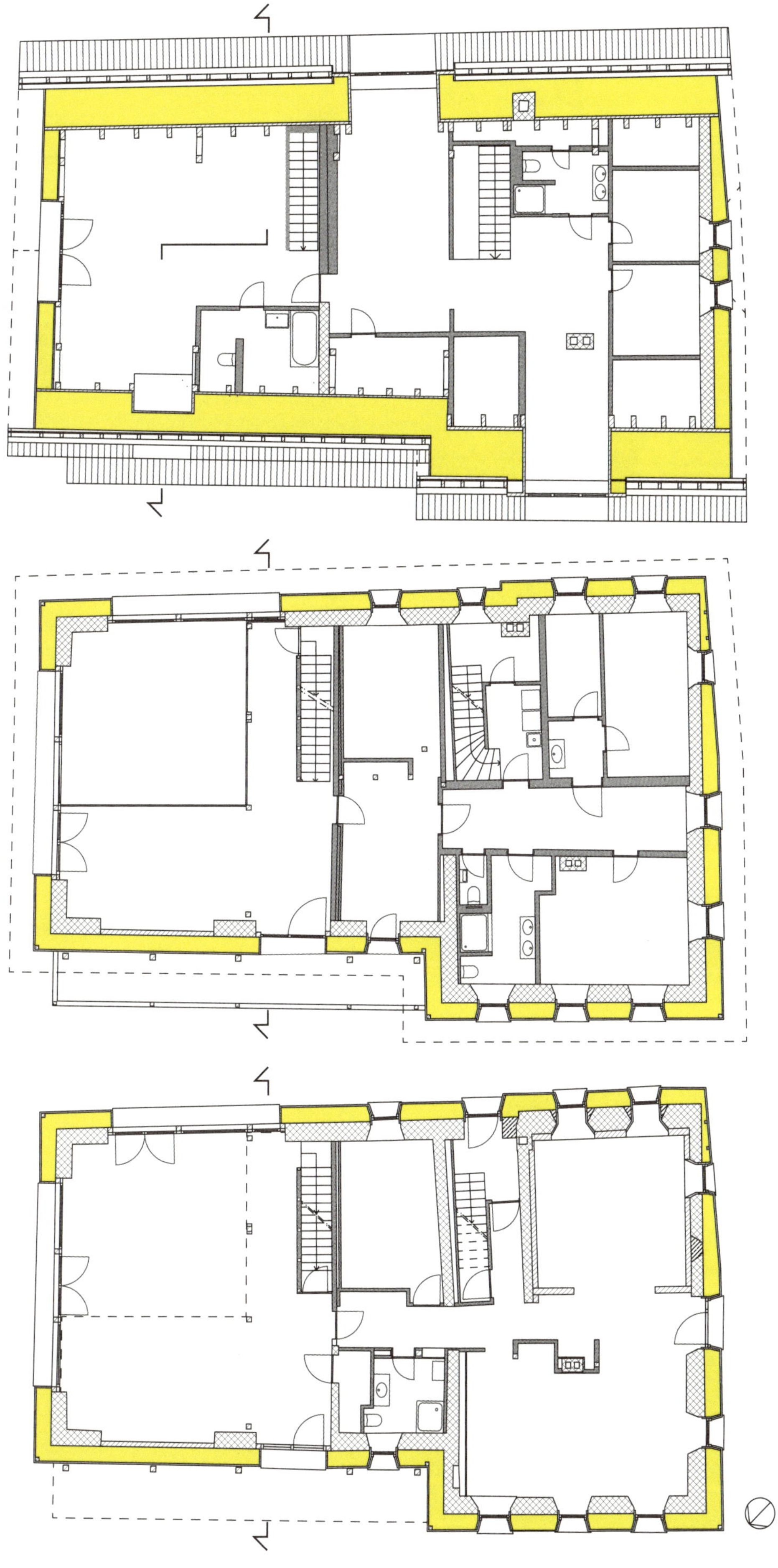

[→■6]
Second, first and ground floor plans, scale 1:200

[→■7

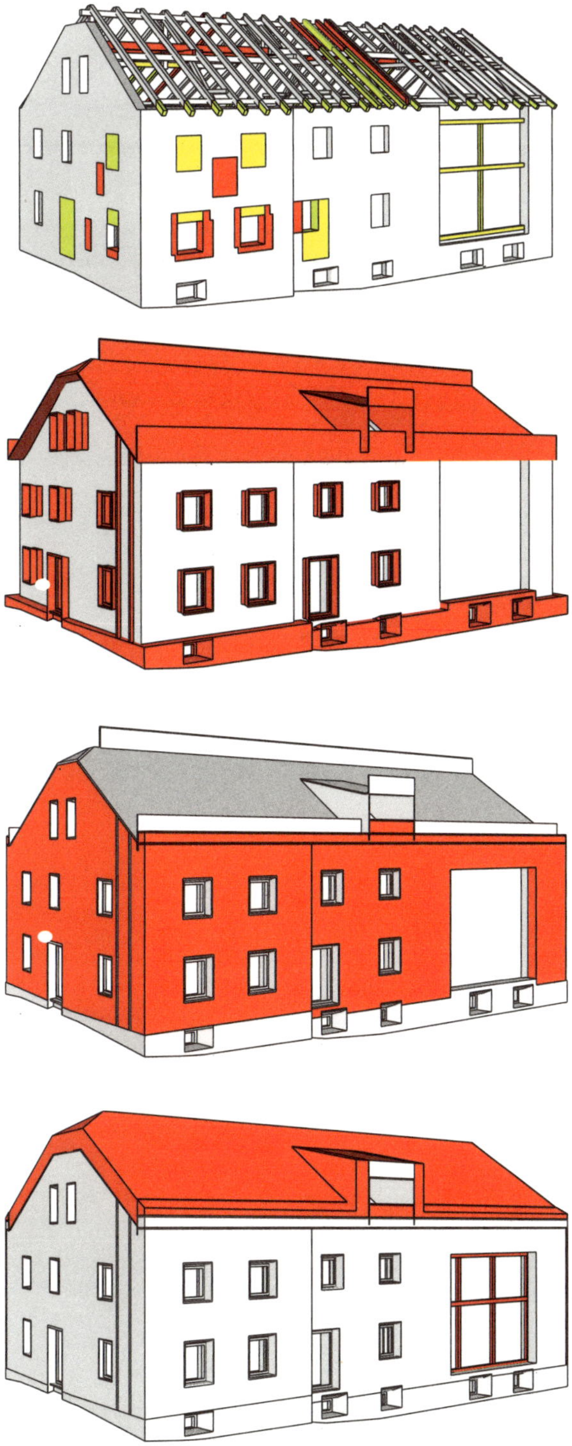

[→■8]
Construction phases

and numerous dormer windows in the roof were replaced by three much larger ones; even the position of the floors in the former barn was modified to adjust the internal heights. [→■8]

The final appearance of Casa Steila Mar is unique: the mass and proportions as well as the *Krüppelwalmdach* shape of the roof are obviously those of a traditional masonry building, and even the surfaces and edges are slightly wavy with a pleasant chiaroscuro effect. [→■7] However, the whiteness of the render, the absence of decorative elements, the precision of the window frames, the large glazing of the former barn, and the roofing material impart a clean, modern appearance. [→■9] Schmidt explains that the gently irregular edges are not so much an aesthetic choice, as they are the consequence of working without excess precision; an obsession with precision in places where it is not necessary generates complex and expensive solutions.

The window frames were dismantled and prefabricated OSB wooden boxes were built to measure for each opening. [→■10] These boxes are splayed in order to capture as much light as possible through a wall, which was already quite thick (550 mm) and was almost doubled. In addition, the splayed reveals allowed the boxes to match the dimensions of whole bales or exact fractions (½, ⅓, ¼ …). This means that no window box has the same dimensions and angles, as was the case in traditional Engiadina houses. This feature was the result of Schmidt's novel technical solution. In general, he prefers simplicity and practicality in his projects: in many straw bale houses, the edges of the openings are rounded to show that the wall is made of straw; [→B144,157] Schmidt prefers to leave the straight and clean finishes of the wooden frames visible—a rounded corner would require more rendering work.
As in House Ervin Jacomet, Schmidt detailed an insulating straw bale layer (1,000x500x350 mm) to abut against the stone perimeter walls, but here the bales lie flat. In a few places, horizontal OSB panels were placed to prevent the bales from tipping over, which were left to freely move vertically to follow the settlement of the bales under their own weight. Otherwise, the straw bales were held by the splayed window reveals. [→■3,11] Piontek laments the fact that the new system of laying the bales led to a few cracks in the render and for some of the straw bale leaf to buckle. She thinks Schmidt should have used ties or straps to hold the bales. Placing boards and

[→■9]

[→■10]

[→■11]

[→■12]

bales horizontally allowed Schmidt to increase the thickness of the insulation layer and, more importantly, to save considerable labour. The bales rest on a foamglass curb that separates them from the ground. The whole façade was then lime-rendered; as with all of Schmidt's projects, the base coat was sprayed onto chicken wire.

The roof height was increased to accommodate 700-mm-thick 'jumbo' bales. [→■12] To support this additional load, the roof structure had to be reinforced by doubling the longitudinal main beams. Over the existing joists, the pre-existing tongue and groove boarding was maintained, and a vapour membrane was added; the straw bales were laid (vertical panels were used only at the eaves, at the verges, and at the ridge); finally, a deck was placed over the straw bales together with a waterproof membrane and fibre-cement roofing.

The detail of the spot where the top of the wall meets the roof eave is worth examining, as this is where the settling of the bales might have created a thermal bridge. [→■13] To avoid this, Schmidt placed them under compression with an additional horizontal board that is also free to move down as the bales settle. The detail, besides being clean, requires only single (planar) cuts in the eave bale and in the bale at the top of the wall. The total amount of straw bales employed was about 1,100 small and 100 'jumbo' bales.

Piontek coordinated with the different contractors. Richard Fliri—the owner and builder of arguably the most remarkable of all buildings Schmidt designed—was hired to build the straw wall and to render it. The total cost of the renovations designed by Schmidt, which were largely complete by March 2015, was 1M CHF (895,000 €, roughly 1,300 €/m^2).

Piontek also had a new horse stable built, with an additional small apartment upstairs. (Schmidt was not involved in this project.) She adopts dogs and ponies who have been abused and rents 3 ha of pasture to graze her horses.

In November 2017, interior work in the northern half of the house began according to Piontek's own project. Most partition walls and part of the floors were dismantled; an internal staircase was added; and the inhabitable area of the attic floor was reduced by 30%. With the help of a meticulous 27-year-old South Tyrolean carpenter, ancient timbers were salvaged and used as 'rustic' cladding, deciding day by day which use to make of them. New timber was imported from South Tyrol. Wood surfaces were brushed and treated with white soap. Plasters were made of lime produced locally, according to traditional methods; and surfaces were painted with limewash and natural paints. [→■14,15,16]

The use of natural surface materials contributes to the multisensorial and spiritual experience of living there: the place, indoor and outdoor, conveys a sense of well-being and quiet. Though not perceivable, even the straw coat conveys a sensation of a natural, healthy atmosphere. The gypsum fibreboard in the apartment above the stable, by contrast, suggests something manufactured and artificial.

Work on the site is not yet complete: a terrace with an emergency staircase, which were already present in Schmidt's project, will be attached to the southeast façade. [→■17] The main access on the southwest façade that leads to the new staircase still has to be detailed. The courtyard to the east of the house will be closed by a gated fence; Piontek will make two or three raised beds for herbs there. An asphalt embankment will be built at the base of the northeast façade to drain water away from the cellar.

Casa Steila Mar is equipped with a firewood and central pellet boiler, plus two stoves; a third one can be used for emergency cooking. Heating pipes run underfloor. Because of the mixed nature of the fuel—even old timbers from the house itself are burnt, and it all comes in a single bunch of various sizes—it is difficult to measure the energy consumed at Casa Steila Mar. Piontek is nonetheless certain that "it is little": in the winter of 2017/18, the northern part of the house was not heated at all, but remained sufficiently warm. Calculations performed with the ENTECH 380/1 software have shown an energy requirement for heating of 22 kWh/m^{2}a: a remarkably low value given the high altitude and the very long heating season. Of course, considering the large size of the house, this does not automatically translate into low-energy consumption all together.

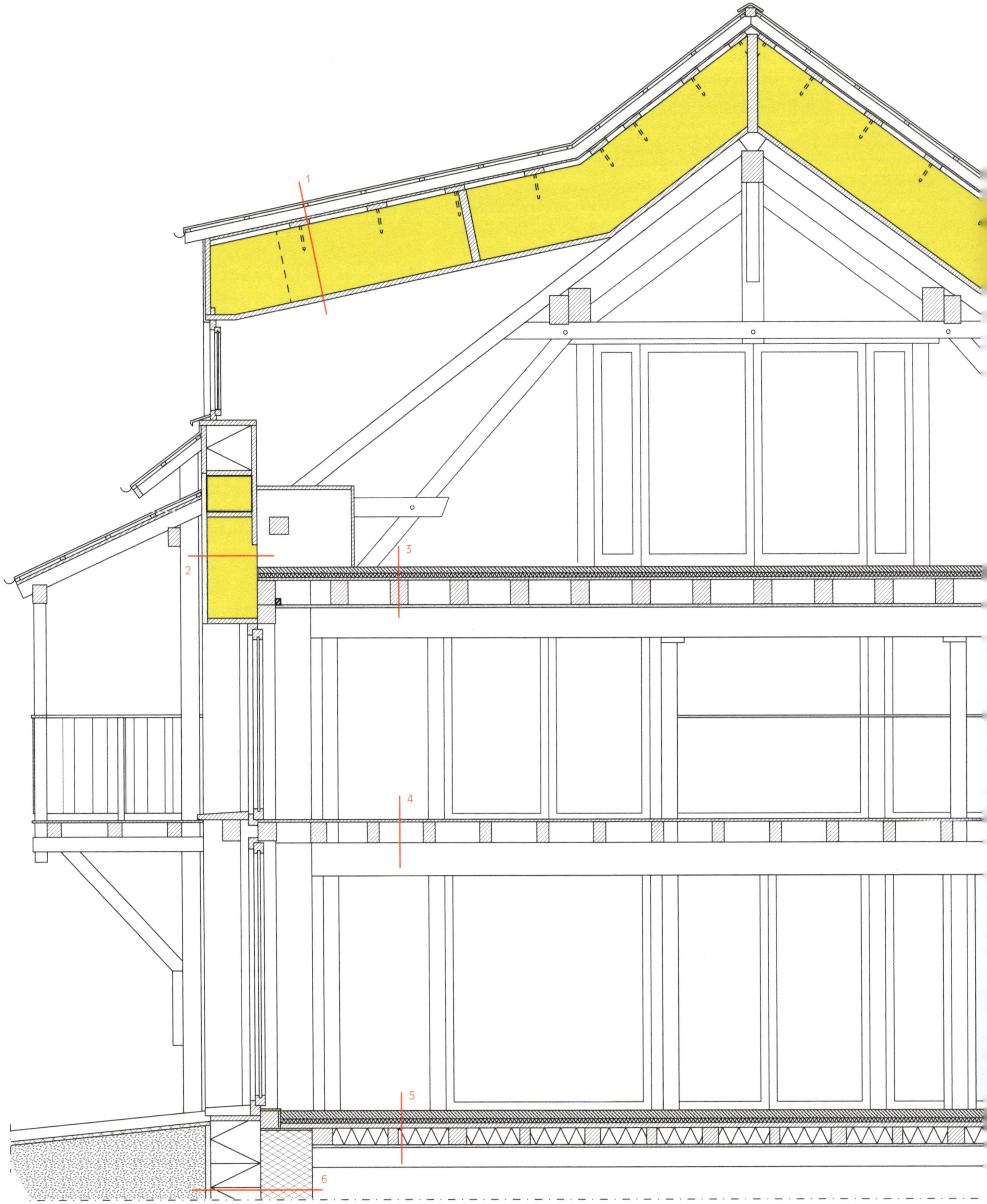
1
2
3
4
5
6

[→■14] [→■15]

[→■16]

[→■13] left page
Section, scale 1:50

1 double-layer fibrocement roofing; 30/50 mm battens; 100/80 mm counterbattens; vapour-permeable under-roof film; 18 mm HDF board; 45/250 mm scaffolding boards; 700 mm straw; trickle protection fleece; 45 mm double-grooved timber boards

2 50 mm lime render; plastering mesh; 500 mm straw; (42 mm 3-ply panel for window box, 750 mm deep, placed 200 mm from outside edge of wall)

3 60 mm cement screed; 40 mm stonewool; 40 mm wooden planks; 240/180mm joists @ 600 mm centres; 18 mm plasterboard

4 25 mm wooden decking; 200/120 mm joists @ 550 mm centres

5 80 mm cement screed; 40 mm impact sound insulation wood fibreboards; 160/180 existing beams + 160/100 reinforcing beams + 160 mm stonewool; 18 mm plasterboard

6 gravel filling; 50 mm cement render; geotextile; 500 mm compacted cellular glass in metal gabions; 600 mm pre-existing quarry stone masonry

[→■17]

Earth-based retrofit: Sandberghof

Martina Bocci and Andrea Bocco Guarneri

Throughout Central Europe numerous examples of Neolithic buildings with wooden skeletons and reed frames, presumably clad in earth, have been unearthed over the years. Apart from a brief respite in the seventeenth century, when there was a temporary shortage of lumber, *Fachwerk* (half-timbered construction) remained the predominant method of construction ever since. **[→B104]** Not until the onset of industrialisation in the mid-nineteenth century did it go out of fashion. **[→B326,349]**

A brief interest in earth-based traditional construction methods occurred after World War II, with some self-construction taking place in rural areas. In anticipation of the shortage of housing at the end of the war, a draft ordinance had already been drawn up, which then became official in 1951 (DIN 18951), but was withdrawn twenty years later, as it was considered outdated. The 1973 energy crisis reignited interest in earth-based building, but initiatives were hampered by the lack of qualified artisans and builders and by the absence of products on the market.

Franz Volhard is a pioneer of earth building and has contributed to the revival of traditional construction techniques in Germany, also reinterpreting them with manufactured products. He is a partner of the Schauer + Volhard associate studio in Darmstadt. **[→B380]** Since 1980 he has been carrying on the first pioneering attempts to resume lightweight earthen construction methods. The renovation and extension of the Houses L and S (Darmstadt)—probably the first modern straw-earth buildings in Germany, date back to this period. **[→▪1,2]** Since then he has designed and constructed numerous 'light earth' buildings, and his research has given rise to new methods of applying straw-earth mixes.

In 1983, Volhard published *Leichtlehmbau. Alter Baustoff—neue Technik*, **[→B324]** in which he systematically examined 'light earth' construction techniques with the goal of promoting their implementation and standardisation. This was the first modern treatise on earth building in Germany. **[→B136]** His choice was clear: notwithstanding the opposition against light earth shown by other authors, **[→B201:53]** in Volhard's opinion other traditional earth construction techniques like cob or rammed earth are not suitable for contemporary buildings, at least in perimeter walls. (Also, he is rightly quite puzzled and worried by a

[→■1]

[→■2]

[→■4]

[→■3]

certain aestheticising and technically inappropriate tendency in today's fad for 'earth architecture', whatever one might mean with this).

In the 1990s, contractors began to offer earthen construction services. The number of companies specialising in this field increased, as did demand for manufactured building products. In 1992, various experts in the field, including Volhard, founded the Dachverband Lehm e.V. (DVL), [→B355] a non-profit organisation that promoted the merging of know-how based on old standards with contemporary practice. The *Lehmbau-Regeln* ('regulations on the use of earth in construction'), based on the DVL's work, were published in 1998, and incorporated into the building codes of almost all German federal states. [→B327] They refer to unstabilised earth only, as stabilised mixes cannot be fully considered earth construction and are not reversible. Volhard was the project manager and principal author of the regulations, together with Ulrich Röhlen. Departing from the previously adopted system based on building techniques, the *Lehmbau-Regeln* consist of definitions, building materials, and structural components (*Begriffe, Baustoffe, Bauteile*). They therefore avoid confusing the properties of materials with those of components. As Volhard explains, "We stopped thinking about construction methods in earth and started thinking about earth as a building material." [→B325:7] To reflect the new classification, Volhard changed the title of his book to Bauen mit *Leichtlehm. Handbuch für das Bauen mit Holz und Lehm.* [→B326]

The book contains an exhaustive overview of the 'light earth' construction technique, and shows the results of research carried out over the course of almost forty years. Among other things, Volhard explains that "wood and straw embedded in dry earth can be preserved intact for hundreds of years. Earth reaches its very low equilibrium moisture level quickly, making it an ideal environment for wood." [→B326:162,163] This might well explain the high durability of traditional half-timbered buildings.

Also fibre-clay plasters and renders show remarkable performances, as they are "very elastic and warm, due to [their] thermal dissipation. Even without an additional coating, [they are] resistant to water erosion, even in outdoor use. The traditional technique is to use a fibrous earth undercoat plaster with a thin hair-reinforced lime render top coat, less susceptible to thermal expansion, more elastic and therefore more tightly adhering to the wood." [→B326:174] Historical methods such as the use of horse urine instead of water for the preparation of the earth provided resistance and improved malleability (as at the Bokrijk Open-Air Museum); diluted boiled linseed oil or stand oil, with the addition of earth pigments, were useful to protect exposed timber against moisture ingress and UV light.

Volhard claims that "the thermal retention, moisture resistance, fire protection and sound insulation properties of light earth walls are better than those of straw bale walls." [→B326:202] His book is concluded with a statement that is very pertinent here: in a building "the earth is dry, and only in the vicinity, whereas medicinal applications [of clay] are wet and in direct contact with the body. [T]his said, how many other ... building materials have the same non-toxic qualities as foodstuffs?" [→B326:232]

From the work of Volhard, I have chosen to explore the restoration and transformation of a historical building. This project is part of a small housing scheme and can be considered a catalogue of techniques in straw-earth construction, a practical application of Volhard's treatise. Volhard and Schauer carried out an admirably accurate analysis of the building and also described the restoration work in a very detailed way in two unpublished reports. [→B272,273]

In 2001, three couples started their own community-life project. [→■4] Interested in creating cohousing for the elderly, in 2003 they bought a property at Sandbergstraße 4 from the City of Darmstadt. [→■3] The complex is in the centre of Bessungen, a village which was incorporated into the City of Darmstadt in 1888 and has since become a quiet residential suburb. Its narrow streets are lined with traditional half-timbered buildings that date mainly from the eighteenth century. The group chose to move from several cities in the region to Bessungen for its optimal location, with a dense infrastructure able to meet the needs of its members (for instance in terms of public transport and green areas such as the Orangerie park), and for a specific interest in the main building. In addition, the property also included a masonry building, once used as a granary, and a few minor outbuildings.

The purchase price was 191,700 €, the construction costs were 1,268,750 € plus 30,260 € for the external areas; all costs were covered by members. Work on the complex lasted from 2005 to 2007. Residents carried out some of the demolition, clearing, joinery, masonry and plastering work, allowing them to save about 10% on construction costs.

Lothar Helm, a member of the GbR Sandberghof, declared:

> There is an affinity between the conviction that older people are not a socially worthless form of existence (even though we are only just beginning to discover the possibilities of this phase of life) and the willingness to cautiously rescue an old house, which is closely linked to the history of the district, from decay and develop a form of life in it—namely 'living together in old age'—, in which we see an alternative to loneliness and isolation. [→B379]

Once they had identified additional members, the group adopted as its legal form the Gesellschaft bürgerlichen Rechts (GbR), where all members are shareholders. This association commissioned Ute Schauer and Franz Volhard to design the project, and assumed the role of contracting authority during works.

Upon completion of the renovation work, the common areas remained the property of GbR, while the individual apartments became the property of the residents. The use of apartments for speculative purposes is prohibited. In addition, GbR asserted the right of first refusal when apartments are offered for sale, thus ensuring that only people who share the group's ideas and objectives can live there.

The aim of the project was to prevent social isolation through shared living and mutual support—it was sensibly crafted around the group's intention to build itself as a small community and also to establish meaningful relationships with the neighbours. The complex was to accommodate living and working spaces, as well as leisure areas. [→■5] The group wanted a residence suitable for their current and future needs and therefore was fully involved in the planning through a democratic decision-making process; for instance, all spaces had to be barrier-free (e.g., no raised shower tray) or at least adaptable in view of possible reduced mobility (e.g., the width of staircases is such to allow the installation of a stair lift). [→■6] The project sought to respect the original characteristics of the buildings and to resume their original construction techniques. Relatively small but autonomous housing units were thus formed, which were integrated with communal and outdoor areas to provide services and spaces for conviviality. [→■7]

[→■5]

[→■6]

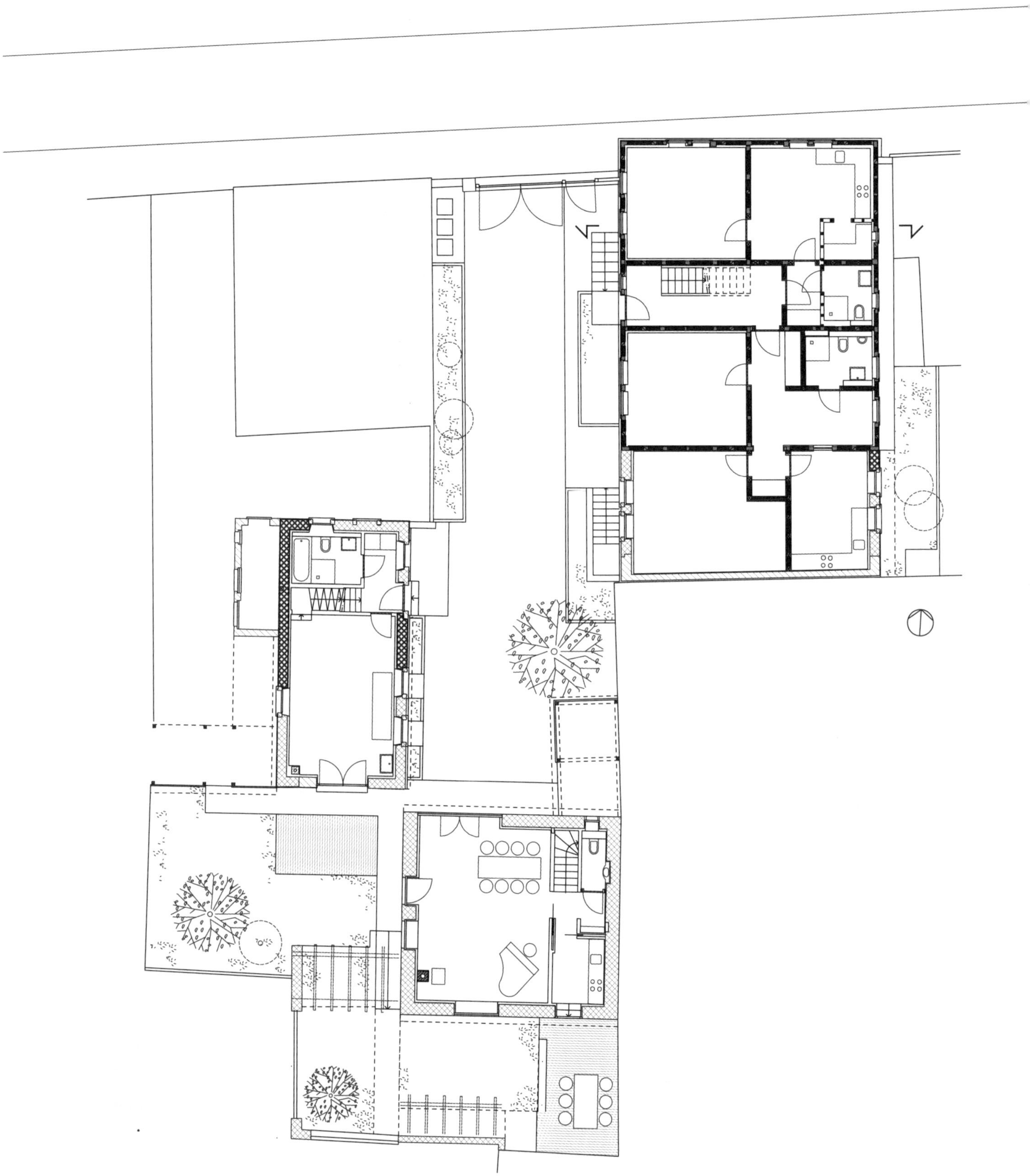

[→■7]
Plan, scale 1:200

[→■8]

[→■9]

[→■10]

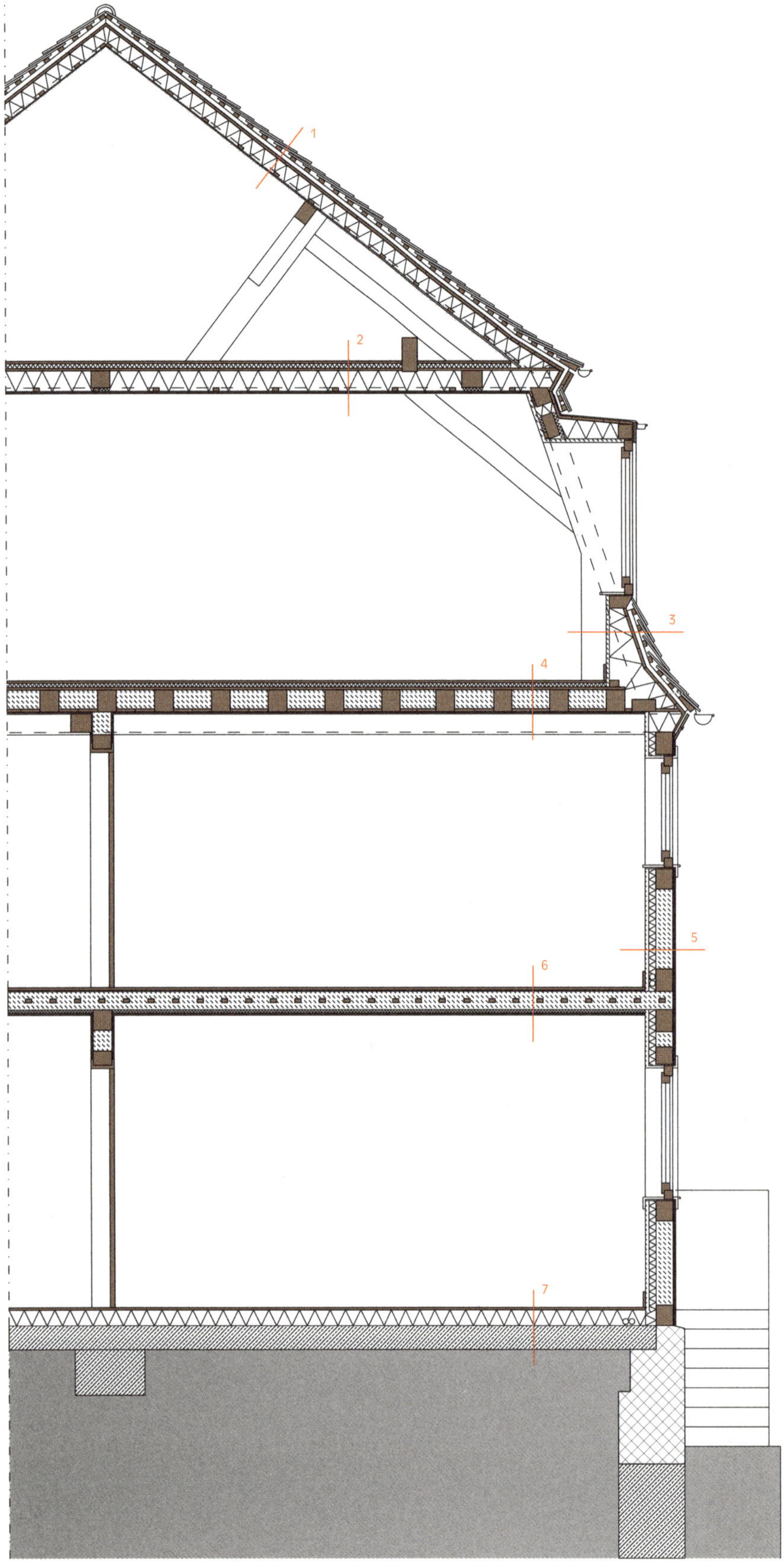

[→■11]
Section, scale 1:50

1 plain tile roofing; wind seal; 30/50 mm battens; 35/50 mm counterbattens; 25 mm boarding; 125 mm cellulose fibre; 25/50 mm wooden laths; 12 mm gypsum fibreboard

2 20 mm timberboards; 40 mm soft, wood-fibremat; 20 mm OSB; 142.5/160 mm new beams + 170 mm cellulose insulation; 28.5/50 mm wooden laths; 20 mm reed mats; lime plaster

3 reused plain tiles; 30/50 mm battens; 35/50 mm counterbattens; wind seal and convection barrier; 25 mm boarding; 180–380 mm cellulose insulation; 28 mm light earth panels; 5 mm lime plaster

4 20 mm timberboards; 40 mm soft, wood-fibre mat; 20 mm OSB; 160/180 new beams + 160 mm raw earthbricks; 20 mm shuttering; 20 mm reedmats; lime plaster; old beams

5 24 mm lime render; reed mat; half-timbered structure with remixed light earth infill or new infill of light earth bricks; min. 60 mm cellulose fibre; 28 mm light earth panels; 5 mm lime plaster

6 22 mm floating floor boards; 10 mm soft, wood-fibre mat; joists + light earth rolls; 20 mm reed mats; lime plaster

7 20 mm timber floor boards; 130 mm cellulose fibre; 200 mm reinforced concrete floor slab; sand filling

[→■12]

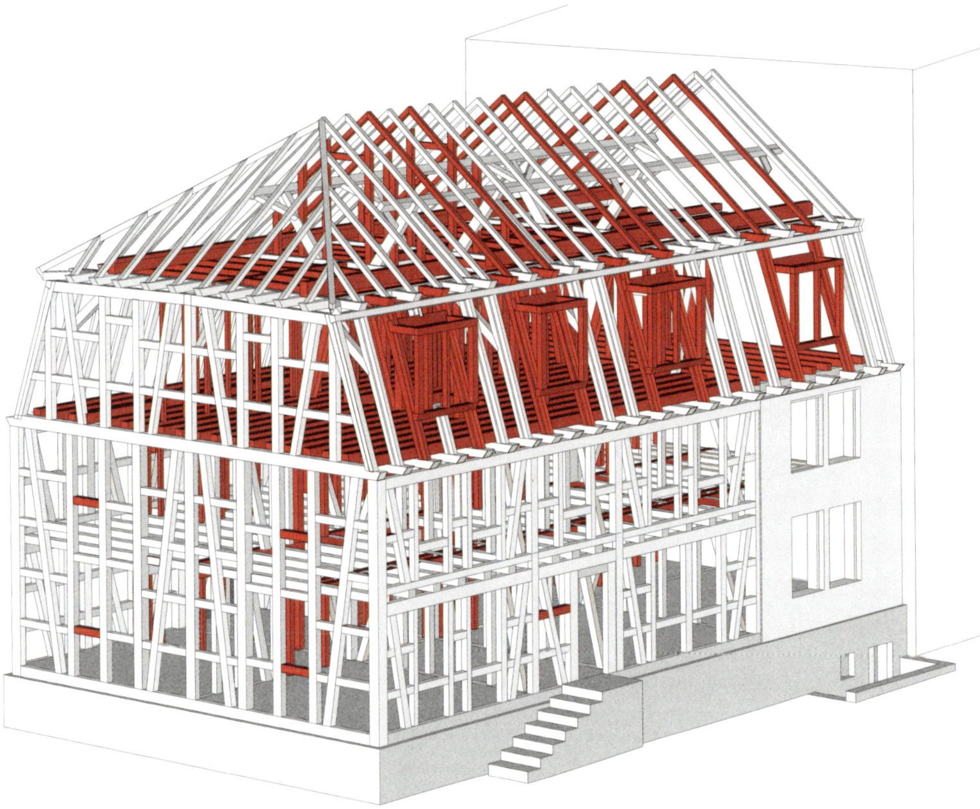

[→■13]
Axonometric projection of the load-bearing structure. New timber members are in red.

[→■14]

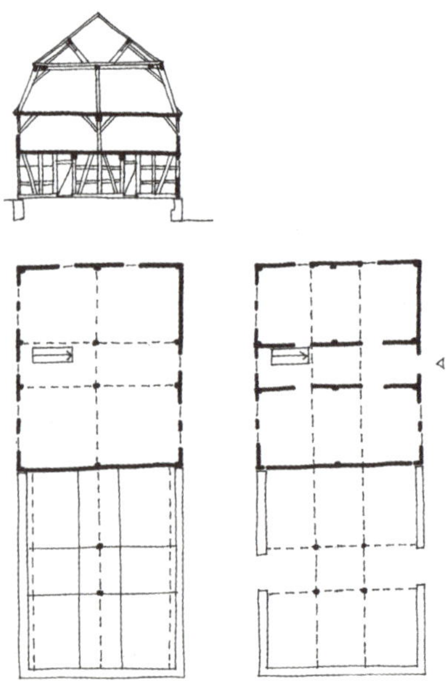

Section, first and ground floor plans of the original building, scale 1:500
[→■15]

[→■16]

[→■17]

In order to improve the quality and increase the extension of the outdoor areas, all recent additions were demolished, freeing up the main external space that the three buildings overlook. [→■8]

The shared spaces cover a total area of 108 m². The former barn is the main community space: a large and bright room, opened up towards the outdoor area, it is used as a dining room, library, and music room. The attic has been transformed into a study and guest room (for instance, visiting children) and can be easily converted into a small apartment. [→■9]

The laboratory has been maintained in its function, with French doors facing the south garden; [→■10] it also contains a laundry room and a large bathroom with a bathtub (to save space, the apartments' bathrooms just have showers); in the basement there are a sauna and a mechanical room accommodating the central boiler and the hot water tank.

These shared spaces are rich in variety and living quality, and their diverse arrangement allows both gathering and seclusion. The gardens are well-tended and host fruit trees, vegetables, herbs, and flowers. [→■18]

[→■18]

Concern with construction costs and conservation led the architects to substantially preserve the main building's structure and layout. [→■11,12] By conducting a dendrological analysis of the north gable, they were able to date the origins of the building to roughly 1758. It is very likely that the original use was as a workshop, factory or warehouse. [→B272]

The building overlooks the road to the north, while the entrance is from the courtyard; [→■3] the neighbouring building to the east is only 600 mm away, while another two-storey building abuts to the south. The total length is 16.25 m. The older, half-timbered section is 11.5 m long and the stone masonry one is 4.7 m. The latter is the remainder of a three-bays-long granary building: [→■13,14,15] at some point in the past, two bays were demolished and the remaining one was transformed into a dwelling.

The building has been subdivided into four private apartments: three of similar size (67–77 m²), one of which has two levels, plus a smaller one (44 m²). Each couple has been assigned two rooms that can be used flexibly, a dining room/kitchen with a pantry, and a bathroom. [→■17] The attic is used as a warehouse and the unheated cellar to store food and beverages.

The original foundations were very shallow: a new foundation wall was therefore built to the outside of the entire perimeter, while internally this was considered disadvantageous and non-essential, and separate portions were built instead. The new basement floor is a concrete slab, covered with sand fill, cellulose insulation, and timber flooring.

Due to the excessive load of the wall and the thrust of the sand fill, the basement, which was made of 1.5 m of rubble masonry, had begun to tilt outwards. Once the missing masonry had been integrated and the foundations restored, the framed structures were then returned to their original position by means of winches. The basement was restored leaving the masonry exposed, and the sill beams (*Schwelle*) were restored or replaced on new substructures made of cast concrete.

In the half-timbered building, there are twelve oak posts extending without interruption across the first two storeys; [→■13,16] between these the walls were arranged. Originally there were only transverse walls on the ground floor, which formed two large rooms that opened onto an intermediate corridor. The upper floor and the double-height attic, probably used as a granary, lacked partitions. [→▪12] Around the end of the eighteenth century or at the beginning of the nineteenth, in the half-timbered part of the house, the attic was adapted to become domestic spaces. In the mid-nineteenth century, the attic in the masonry one was similarly converted for habitation.

The timber skeleton creates a three-dimensional system capable of providing structural stability as long as the size of the rooms is not too large; however, some more beams and welded steel profiles had to be added to stiffen the connections between beams and uprights. Individual timber members were replaced only where strictly necessary. Over the centuries, the building has been gradually sinking into the ground, which has led to differences in height of up to 200 mm. To level the floors, entire parts of the building were thus raised or lowered.

Two oak girders run along the entire length of the building on the first floor. Over the years, the west end of the beams, anchored to the perimeter half-timbered walls, were severely damaged, causing the stone portion to sink in slightly. The joists were maintained; the span between girders and external walls was halved by introducing new glulam beams. Where possible, the light earth rolls that infilled the floors were preserved. Otherwise, they were replaced with new straw-earth rolls that were placed between the joists when they were still malleable. Then, where it was to be plastered, the lower face was smoothed and levelled by applying a clay mortar. The space above was filled with straw-earth, until level with the upper edge of the joists. [→▪19] Finally, the board flooring was laid on battens inserted into grooves that had been carved into the earth rolls.

A single central girder (*Wandrähm*) supports the upper floor, which has a height of 2.15 m. To obtain an apparent increase of such height in the half-timbered portion, the infills between the joists were removed, thus reaching a maximum height of 2.3 m. [→▪20] To stiffen the floor, new beams were bolted transversely above the existing joists. The space between the new beams was infilled with unfired bricks. [→▪22] In the masonry part of the building, the upper floor was completely remade in timber covered with a layer of loose earth.

The mansard has been partitioned, creating a new floor level with truss ties, with joists and cellulose insulation between them. This makes the 2.4-m-high rooms more comfortable and intimate. To adapt the mansard to residential purposes, five dormers covered with zinc sheet were created. The damaged timber truss elements were removed and replaced. [→▪21] A bituminous membrane that is wind and waterproof was laid on the entire surface of the roof. And finally, original tiles or vintage ones were laid on battens to allow ventilation.

New, larger staircases were built in the timber-framed part of the building, replacing the old stairs, which were not only in poor condition but also far too steep. The steps are oak. Strings, risers, and parapets were painted with an oxidised red. The stairs in the masonry part were demolished.

The infill panels of the internal and perimeter walls were earth and straw on wattle (*Flechtwerk*). [→▪14,16,23] The walls made from perforated bricks and concrete blocks were demolished, but the earth panels were maintained and repaired with materials similar to what was used originally. Light earth bricks bonded with fibre-clay mortar—held in place by triangular sectional strips on the side faces of the uprights—were used for new partition walls. [→▪24] This choice helped ensure shorter construction times, greater simplicity, and cleanliness in the laying process. It also ensured better quality control. In order to improve sound and fire resistance, a new wall on the southern side of the building—decoupled from the existing one that belongs to a neighbouring property—was also erected.

On the ground and first floors, the openings in the north wall were doubled by demolishing the infill panels at the sides of the existing windows. The openings with sandstone lintels in the west wall of the masonry part of the building were also enlarged and new sandstone blocks inserted. Doors and windows were replaced with new ones that use contemporary details but recall historical examples.

In the west and north perimeter walls, which are more exposed to the weather, the poor condition of the timber members made it impossible to keep the structure visible, as this would have been too costly

[→■19]

[→■20]

[→■21]

[→■22]

[→■23]

[→■24]

to do, and would also have resulted in lower durability and required intensive maintenance. [→■4] The solution was to clad the walls in reed mats fixed to the panels, then spray them with limewash, followed by two coats of lime render and a water-based paint. In the east façade, by contrast, the half-timbered structure was kept visible; and only the panels were rendered. [→■25]

The load-bearing frame is not visible from the inside. A reed mat was placed on the internal walls and intrados of the ceiling to provide support to successive layers. Both the light earth panels and mats were covered with lime and gypsum plaster, 5–8 mm thick. The residents then limewashed the walls.

Great care has been taken to obtain an optimal indoor climate: the result was a thermal transmittance of the envelope ($U=0.4\,W/m^2K$) that is half of the admissible value according to ENEV 2004. [→B273]

To avoid altering the proportions of the building and to maintain part of the external characteristics of a half-timbered building, the insulation layer was

placed inside. This also helps avoid excessive heat accumulation in summer, especially if combined with ventilation at night (sample measurements have shown that performance is influenced by the occupants' behaviour). The placement of insulation on the inner face of perimeter walls, together with low thermal conductivity cladding materials, allows individual rooms to be heated temporarily.
60–100 mm of cellulose were infilled in a cavity created with thin light earth panels screwed on uprights; mineral wool insulation covered with plasterboard was used in wet areas. Volhard determined that a greater thickness would have taken up too much space, and that thermal resistance would have not increased much. Interstitial condensation was avoided by using vapour-permeable, capillary insulating materials that dry naturally from the warm side.

Similar problems were to be addressed in the energy retrofit of the Kleine Freiheit *Gründerzeit* social housing in Hamburg (2007) by Daniel Scherz (ZzB) and the Corti-Rigano House in Padova (2009). **[→B261]** These examples show that it is possible to improve considerably the energy performance of heritage buildings without changing their appearance, yet installing an uninterrupted thermal insulation layer. At Kleine Freiheit, the consumption fell from 315 to 42–53 kWh/m²a and at Corti-Rigano house from 280 to 49 kWh/m²a.
The performance at Sandberghof has significantly improved; it is interesting to note that the energy requirement of 92 kWh/m²a (calculated on the basis of ENEV, with tools that often fail to embrace the wide range of facets that characterise ancient buildings) is substantially worse than the measured consumption (2007–2011), which ranges between 56–70 kWh/m²a. Klaus Schillberg's manuals propose retrofit solutions with materials and techniques similar to those used by Volhard, which confirm their reasonably good transmittance values. **[→B275,276]**
A central, gas-fuelled condensation boiler is complemented by vacuum solar collectors installed on the roof of the barn. Heat is provided by standard radiators.

With this meticulous and respectful renovation, which used an array of earth products and methods, Schauer and Volhard were able to give new life to a

[→▪25]

three-centuries old complex that would otherwise have been demolished. The results are impressive: a high-quality refurbishment, which fulfils the clients' desire to make Sandberghof an oasis of harmony and a place for sharing.
The high quality of the result is no doubt to be also ascribed to the commitment of the clients themselves, which they cultivate in their everyday lifestyle. Residents are in charge of the complex's management. They meet on a weekly basis for this, and one more weekly gathering is for eating together. Discussions are arranged to avoid internal conflicts; individuals or small groups have chores (such as garden care, cleaning of common areas, administration, small repairs); each member has to offer two days of cooperative activities per year. Art and cultural events, dinners and other activities, sometimes open to the neighbourhood, are held in the communal living room. They have a car-sharing system and encourage the use of public transportation and bicycles.
Subsequently, the building at Sandbergstrasse 6 was also restored: currently twelve people, between the ages of sixty to eighty, live on the property in five housing units. The group has been quite stable during the twelve years of their cohousing project: ten of the current residents were already there at the start.

Radical vegetarianism: Villa Strohbunt at Sieben Linden

Andrea Bocco Guarneri
with Martina Gerace

It is somewhat reductive to analyse a single building within the Sieben Linden Ecovillage, [→B381] instead of looking at the entire village as an ecosystem. [→B179] [→■1,2] However, this was the subject of a previous publication [→B46] and in the future I hope to return to examining the village as part of a larger study of human regenerative action, e.g. in terms of its role in increasing biodiversity. For this reason, in this section, I focus on Villa Strohbunt as a case study for considering the possibility of constructing a building manually, without the aid of machinery. Indeed, in light of the fact that today we have available powerful machinery and very low-priced energy, it was a challenge to show that it is possible to erect a building using only manual tools, while attaining contemporary performance standards.

The aim of Sieben Linden Ecovillage is to represent a "model of socio-ecological settlement for climate- and resource-conscious lifestyles and regional development". [→B291:5] The community's vision and goals are set out in a series of guiding principles, to which new members must adhere and which affect all aspects of life. [→B291:1] Special emphasis is placed on self-sufficiency, environmental protection, and conscious use of natural resources. In Sieben Linden live people from diverse social and cultural backgrounds, and from different age groups. Sieben Linden is an active member of the Global Ecovillage Network (GEN) and has engaged in an increasing number of cooperative activities and educational programmes.

The settlement was established in the municipality of Beetzendorf in the Altmark in Saxony-Anhalt in 1997, when the ecovillage cooperative bought a farm, which consisted of an old building and 20 ha of forest and agricultural land, close to a railway line. Sieben Linden's founders chose the site because it was affordable, already possessed its own infrastructure, and because it was accessible by public transportation.

Based on the methods and the three basic principles of permaculture—care for the earth, care for people, fair share—they then began a global planning process. [→B132] The plan prioritised making the area suitable for the production of food, and for the creation of spaces for work and recreation. In 1998,

[→■2]

[→■1]

[→■3]

[→■4]

the local municipality approved the development plan for a new rural settlement for 300 people, earmarking a buildable area on agricultural land. In addition, the community obtained permission to host a maximum of fifty-six trailers that would serve as temporary housing until work on the village was complete. The old farmhouse was then refurbished according to the principles of ecological architecture, becoming the ecovillage's community centre ('Regiohaus'). [→■3] Inside the community centre are, among other things, a communal dining area, a library, and seminar rooms. In the building's north wing ('Nordriegel') are also a bar/dance club, a few shops, and the community's administrative offices. [→■4]

Founders planned the village to be independent of any grid supply of energy that did not work regeneratively. To fill their energy needs, initially they had intended to rely on biogas plants and a gas network for cooking, and on a solar-powered, central heat storage system. But these installations were not implemented. After a few years of relying on their own water wells, they were forced to connect to water mains; they still manage an independent sewage system, however. Since 1999 they have had a basic infrastructure in place, such as paths (circulation within the ecovillage is restricted to walking and cycling), wells, electricity and telephone lines, reed beds, a pond, and an open-air amphitheatre. Most of Sieben Linden's inhabitants make their living within the village.

Land once devoted to industrial agricultural production has gradually been transformed into land farmed with horses, and into valuable, organic vegetable gardens. A portion of the village's land is managed as a communal garden that provides vegetables for the whole community, and a portion is managed as an independent enterprise, which includes a fruit tree nursery. [→■5,6,8] The Sieben Linden land has now increased to approximately 100 ha; it includes 64 ha of forest, 25 ha of arable land, 6 of gardens, and another 6 of buildable areas. The forest is a pine and fir plantation created before the community bought the land that is now being slowly renatured and converted into a mixed forest. The community uses the forest as a source of firewood and construction timber; [→■7] timber from the forest was used in the construction of some of Sieben Linden's houses. The forest is more than a source of raw materials, however. It is also preserved as a place of peace and tranquillity.

[→■5]

In 2000, the first residential buildings were built, and the village has continued to expand ever since. [→■9] About one hundred adults and forty children live in Sieben Linden. There are now thirteen houses, about fifty trailers, a community centre, a space for seminars and guest accommodations, an organic food shop, an information centre, a meditation house, a food storage space, a sauna, several outdoor kitchens and toilets, as well as a carpentry workshop, and a horse stable. Since 2010, educational activities in the ecovillage have continued to expand. Their educational programmes, workshops, and seminars attract people from all over Germany. A new building is planned opposite to the Regiohaus, with additional bedrooms for guests and spaces for seminars and workshops.

Silke Hagmaier, who was part of the ecovillage project from the beginning, wanted to establish a vegan settlement based on radical environmental, philosophical, social, dietary, anti-consumerist, collectivist principles. She envisioned the village as one that was largely self-sufficient, maintained a common economy, and practiced free love. [→B336:11] Her vision was dismissed as too radical for the whole ecovillage. At the northeast corner of the buildable area (Nordschonung), she nonetheless succeeded in establishing a sort of autonomous republic within the ecovillage, where such a social experiment could

[→■6]

[→■7]

39/1
30/6
BIRNE VON TONGERN
GELB-MÖSTLER
BOSCS FLASCHENBIRNE

[→■8]

[→■9]

take place. Her group, called Club 99, settled there in 1999 and began experimenting with an alternative lifestyle. Club members committed to a "resource diet" that was meant to ensure a sustainable lifestyle and to fully respect all living things. [→B342:38] To attain this, Hagmaier deemed smaller, gradual measures as insufficient to the task. For instance, when speaking of diet, consuming organic food was not enough—one should eat organic, vegan, regional, fair food grown without fuel, and not packaged in plastic. [→B291] An ecological goal of Club 99 was to reduce the energy and material consumption to 10% of the national average, which, according to the study *Zukunftsfähiges Deutschland* by the Wuppertal Institute, [→B182] would have to happen throughout Germany if all people on earth were to be granted the same access to globally available resources.

Group members had to refrain from using power mains and mains-powered devices. They could also only consume or use what they had either produced, and could dispose of, themselves, or what was thrown or given away by others. In other words, the group's quest was to see how does a life feel within self-imposed restrictions. Although motives had been different, the lifestyle their ideology required was no less demanding than the lifestyle that prevailed in Cheia. [→§2] Club 99 also wanted to explore the dematerialisation of prosperity, as a means of understanding which inner and outer changes are needed to experience a 'simple life' as a 'good life'. In other words, their ideal was "the maximum of well-being with the minimum of consumption". [→B31:233] Apparently, this worked for some members, at least for a time; Michael Würfel observed, "I even had the impression that the Club residents could enjoy themselves extraordinarily well." [→B342:39]

Yet, such a radical approach distanced Club 99 from the majority of Sieben Linden villagers, and the group size always remained small. Such lack of growth implied a high workload for the group members, whose number fluctuated between three and ten, most of whom, not surprisingly, were young adults without children. Hagmaier and Stengel were the only members who stayed on from the beginning. Over the years, many people came to Sieben Linden attracted by Club 99. But because they found its strict principles difficult to maintain, they ended up settling in other neighbourhoods. "The directness and perhaps also the relentlessness that the attempt at an always authentic communication (including its regular failure) entailed was exhausting. ... [Over time,] conflicts remained unresolved. The reason why the joint project was terminated differs according to the parties involved." [→B342:40–42] Würfel speculates that some might have been losing confidence that every member was contributing their fair share to the community's economy. Others might have felt confined by the rigidity of their assigned roles and by the group's high expectations. Hagmaier's pregnancy in 2010 brought the experiment to an end. The closure of such a pioneering project represented a shift from the founding principles of the ecovillage to a less radical lifestyle.

The buildings in the Nordschonung are Villa Strohbunt, two straw bale domes attached to each other (Strohballenkuppeln), and Villa Communia; in addition, there are several trailers, and a house called Einhorn that was recently completed. [→■10]

[→■10]

Villa Strohbunt is a two-storey building designed and constructed by Björn Meenen, Stengel and Hagmaier between 2001 and 2004. It was the first straw bale house with an official building permit in Germany.

They consciously chose straw bales as they are one of the most ecological building materials available, and the ecovillage wanted to become the first large straw bale construction site in the country. In order to mark out this new path, David Eisenberg and Harald Wedig were invited to lecture in Sieben Linden. Wedig, together with Martin Oehlmann, is credited to be behind the first prototype of a straw building (LebensGut Pommritz, 1995) ever constructed in Germany. (He went on to build more model houses of straw bales in 1999 at the Nordisches Folkecenter für erneuerbare Energie and in a nature reserve in Viersen.) [→B278] The building permit for Villa Strohbunt was issued as a case-by-case agreement (*Zustimmung im Einzelfall*), something that required extensive negotiations with state and federal building authorities and that was backed by expert opinions; TÜV Braunschweig (Technischer Überwachungsverein, 'Technical Inspection Association') conducted a test that showed that a clay-plastered straw bale wall could withstand fire for 90'.

The 'village architect', Henning Müller, was in charge of the site. Roughly one-third of the work was DIY, one-third commissioned to craftsmen, and one-third done by volunteers. Up to ten workers were on the site at any given time. [→B314] Hagmaier recalls: "To our erotically relaxed and natural lifestyle belonged being comfortable, namely naked. [This] might happen when driving to the carriage or during work on the roof, although legally compliant with safety shoes and helmet!" [→B291] The construction process was thoroughly experimental and based on the "resource diet" principle: in order to achieve 90% savings on the environmental footprint, members agreed to dispense with the use of machines and with machine-made building materials. [→■11]
The pine and fir timber came from the ecovillage's forest, hand-felled and hand-worked, and transported with horses to the building site; it was dried naturally and assembled using traditional tools. Straw was partly from the first organic harvest of Sieben Linden fields and partly purchased from a local organic farmer. The clay and sand were dug from the ground of Sieben Linden; the digging work constituted the occasion for creating a constructed wetland. Foundation granite stones, floor tiles, wooden ties connect-

[→■11]

ing the straw bales, windows, doors, clay bricks, gutters, pantiles, pipes, glass, and even most nails were salvaged from other buildings. [→B336] There were only three exceptions: some cement for a few unavoidable joints in the foundation and the chimney; mechanical pressing of straw bales; a few cubic metres of engineered timber panels for stairs and shelves. [→B291:39] Motor machinery was only employed to transport foundation stones, straw bales and clay to the site. They chose to reject any subsidies as they came with the condition that construction last no more than one year, something that could only have been achieved with the use of industrially manufactured building materials and machinery.

The energy-saving concept of the house was to be apparent to outsiders. They thus sought to avoid unnecessary, complicated building forms that might have had a negative impact on the house's overall energy balance. [→B314:40] As a result, the house has a very simple appearance; it is a solid geometrical block softened by a sandy colour and numerous glazed surfaces, and by its unconventional roof. [→■12]
Soil sealing was minimal. The house's foundations consist of twenty-four granite blocks that support two orthogonal layers of beams that are detached from the ground, forming a crawlspace. [→■13] It has

[→■12]

[→■13]

[→■14]

a braced *Fachwerk* of round pine logs connected by worked joints. [→■15,24] Efficient and accurate joints are not easily obtained with round wood, but with the help of Harald 'Harry' Mayer, the construction team leaders, Meenen and Stengel, were able to master the skill required to bring this about. By using a solid timber floor, made by installing beams squared on three sides across the whole room (*Dippelbaumdecke*), they were able to dispense with columns in the house's 4.5x7 m interior. The thickness of the unprotected planks and beams ensures constructional fire protection. Stored too long in the forest, unbeknownst to the builders, the logs were infested with longhorn beetles, requiring treatment with borax, boric acid, and herbal remedies. [→B314:42,279]

The straw bale envelope was erected on the outside of the load-bearing frame, just interrupted by a few beams that support the roof overhangs. Perimeter walls were clay-plastered and rendered. [→■14] The gables, however, were clad with additional vertical boards. The partition walls were made of clay bricks that were usually plastered. [→■17]

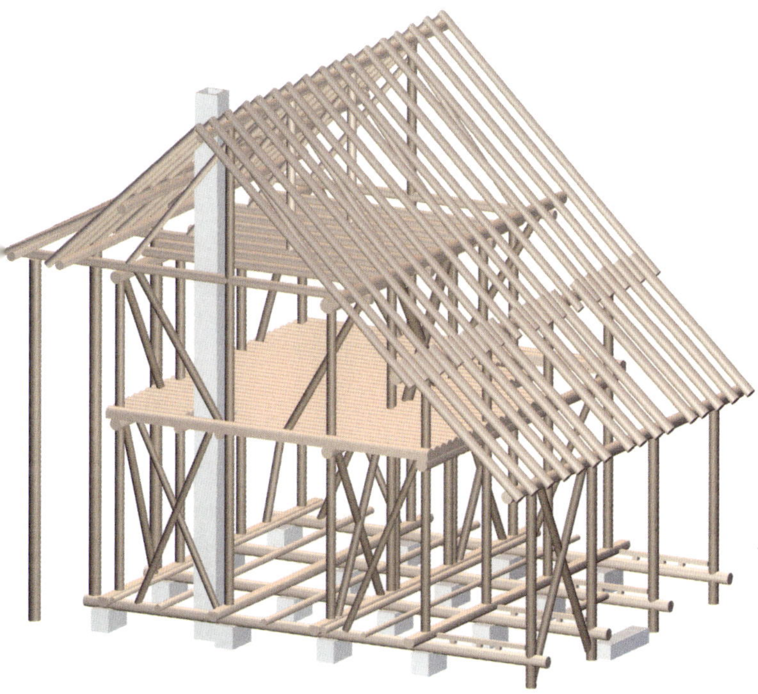

[→■15] Axonometric projection of the load-bearing structure

The roof is asymmetrical. [→■15] The ridge sits roughly at one-third of the depth of the building, determining a much shorter slope to the front (south) of the house, where both stories open up with large windows, and a much longer slope to the back (north), where it extends to cover a relatively deep entrance porch. [→■16,23] The roof structure is a secondary log frame supported by the core house underneath it, as well as by free-standing columns outside. In this way, the south overhang shelters the south façade. The roofing is pantiles; a damp-proof layer was intentionally omitted. Hagmaier recalls that "in addition to sleepless nights, [this decision] brought us comments from 'experts' that one never wanted to hear". [→B291] If the house is subject to the constant observation of the inhabitants, it can do without a waterproof layer, as it was obviously the rule in traditional buildings.

The technical services are easily accessible for maintenance. Heating, water, waste water systems are designed in such a way that they can be repaired by the inhabitants themselves. [→B314]

Villa Strohbunt, also sometimes referred to as Villa Strohbund, was built as a community house for Club 99. The name is a reference to Pippi Longstocking's Villa Kunterbunt (literally, 'many-coloured villa': the German name for Villa Villekulla). The 'villa' was created as a shared space for communal activities such as cooking, eating, and seminars. It has a single, relatively large room on each floor with two large windows facing east and west, and an even larger one towards the south. [→■17] Rounded windows reveals have broken mirror pieces embedded in the plaster, so as to increase natural light. Downstairs there was a kitchen/living room, upstairs a group room totalling 103 m^2 GIA (gross internal area) if the smaller rooms on the north side are included. [→■18] There are three such spaces on the ground floor: the buffer entrance space in the middle, which also gives access to the staircase, and two small rooms on either side; and a recess and a storage space on the first floor. [→■19] Such definitions are very loose as rooms were flexibly used. Until 2009, the office of Club 99 and the computers were located in the Nordriegel.

After the closure of Club 99 in 2010, Villa Strohbunt was converted into a dwelling for the co-parenting-

[→■16]

[→■17]

[→■18]

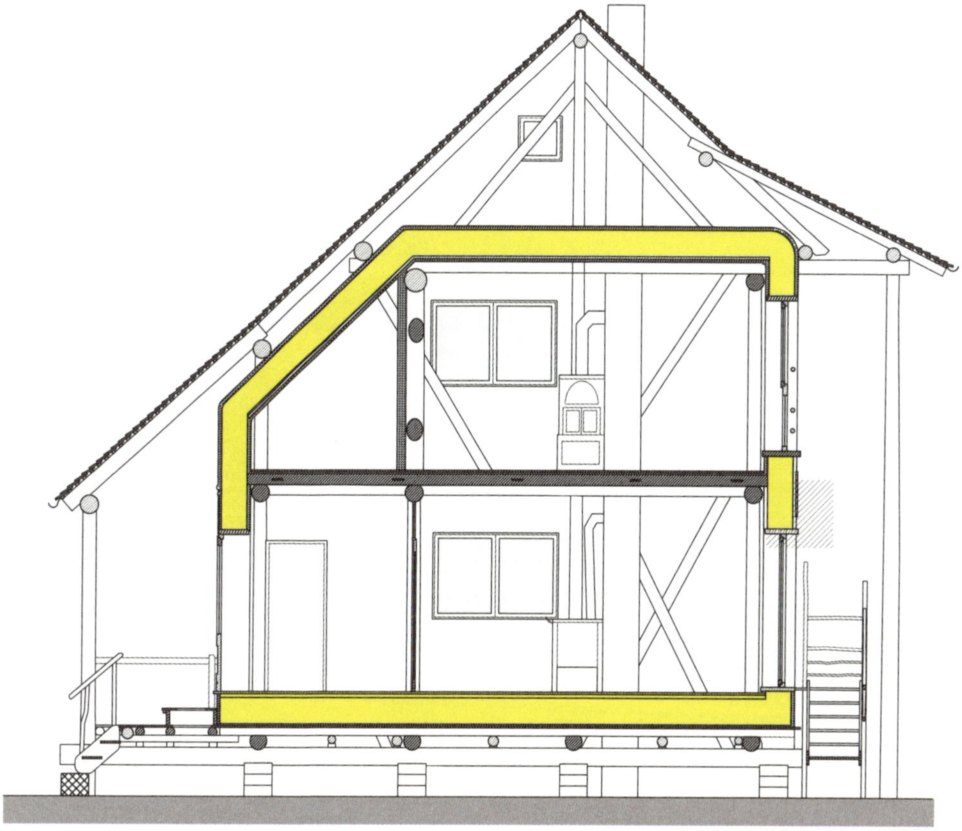

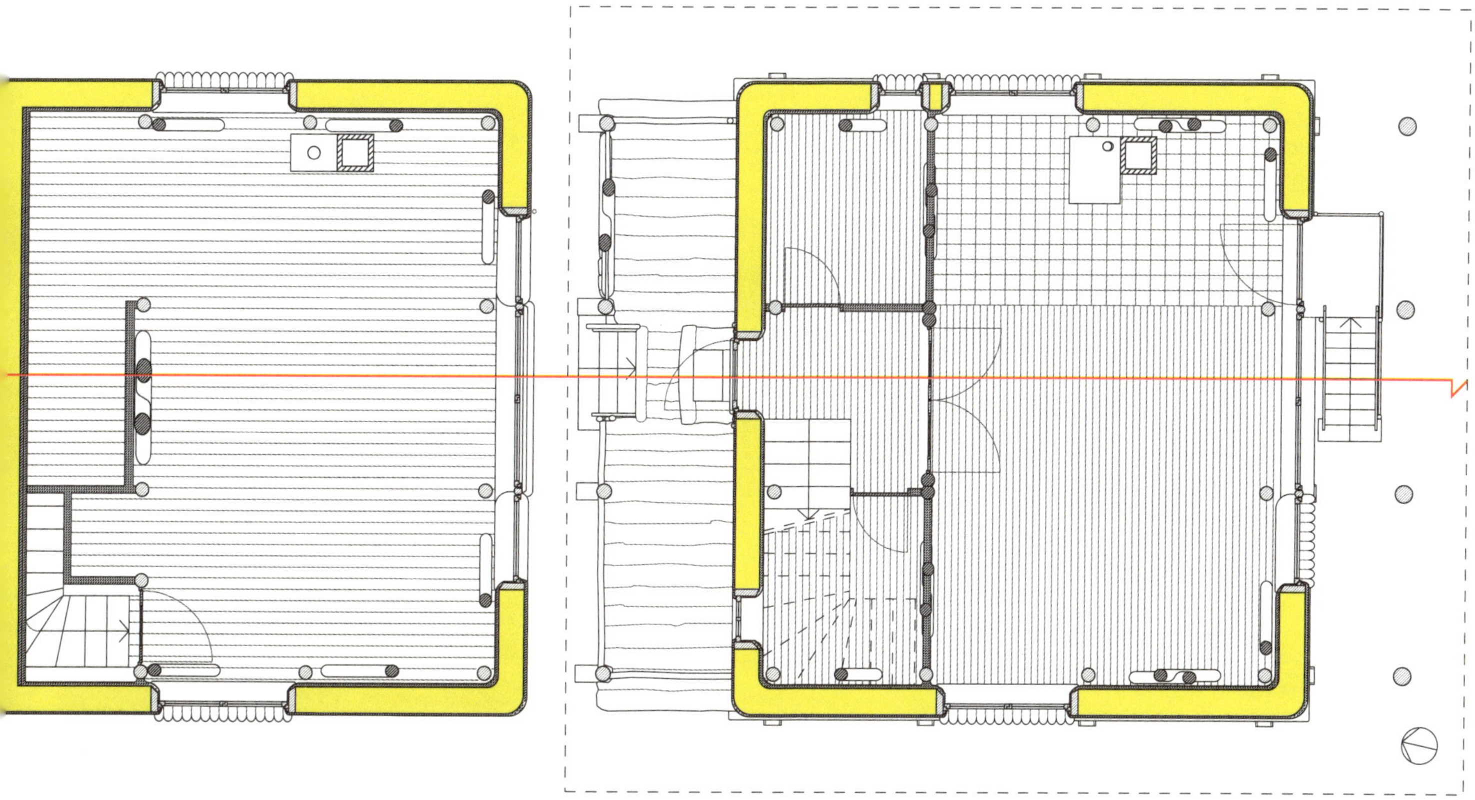

[→■19] Section, first and ground floor plans of the original building, scale 1:100

[→■20]

[→■21]

[→■22]

[→■23]

[→■24]

community, Gemely, which consists of four adults and two children. Physical changes included the connection to the central heating system of the neighbouring House Einhorn, for space as well as sanitary water heating (the house used to rely on two stoves, one at each floor; the one on the ground floor being a cookstove); and the connection to electricity mains, so to allow the use of a dishwasher and a refrigerator. They also installed solar panels and new windows for better insulation and constructed a dry partition wall (*Trockenbauwand*) to create a second room on the first floor. Today Villa Strohbunt is owned by the recently founded association Blühende Landschaften ('Flourishing Landscapes').

As with every other building in Sieben Linden, Villa Strohbunt was and still is heated with local firewood. The heat loss is reduced by the storage capacity and good thermal insulation (U_{wall}=0.15 W/m^{2}K. It is not possible, however, to calculate the exact fuel consumption, as Sieben Linden residents pay a flat fee for firewood and fuel consumption is only recorded at the village level, not by individual dwellings.

In Hagmaier's opinion, the creation of Villa Strohbunt was the biggest achievement of Club 99, as it opened the road to Sieben Linden being one of Europe's main sites for straw bale building and it also encouraged the establishment of FASBA, the German association for straw bale building (Dirk Scharmer was involved in the construction of the villa, as was Burkard Rüger [→§10]). What is perhaps more important, it showed that the "resource diet" preached by Club 99 was compatible with contemporary requirements in terms of insulation and quality of life. A study by a group of students of the TU (Technische Universität) Berlin found that its embodied footprint (on a time span of eighty years) was around 3% of that of a theoretical conventional building with twice the floor area. Our own analysis suggested that the "Villa Strohbunt model" is actually the only one that can guarantee a radical reduction of a building construction's footprint, even though another Sieben Linden house, Libelle, showed (also thanks to its expert execution) a lower energy requirement. [→B46] [→■20]

In 2003, Stengel, with the help of two guests, built two straw bale domes behind Villa Strohbunt; one is a guest room, the other a shared bathroom with two bathtubs and a wood-burning stove. [→■21] (The Villa itself has no bathroom or toilet; residents still use the communal outdoor toilets on the plot or those built later in Villa Communia). The domes were built of load-bearing straw bales, similar to igloos, and rendered with clay. A freestanding roof with a log-framed structure and tile roofing protects them from the weather.

Villa Communia was built in 2007 with some compromises with respect to the principles of Villa Strohbunt; [→■22] some machinery was used (the time and effort needed to build the Strohbunt were deemed as excessive), and a telephone line and power sockets were installed, which allowed to move the Club 99 office from its former location in the Nordriegel. The house was meant to serve as a residence for more than Club 99 members alone. By the time Villa Communia was erected, the straw bale building technique had evolved. It thus has a wooden frame infilled with straw bales, as opposed to Villa Strohbunt where the load-bearing structure is detached from the insulating envelope. Yet, the basic building materials are the same, as is their origin (timber and loam from Sieben Linden land, straw bales from the area). Both sites also avoided the use of concrete, mineral insulation materials, and new bricks. In the end, Villa Communia was judged as possibly closer to the target of reducing the embodied environmental impact by 90%, as compared to the average German house (no investigation has been seriously attempted to verify this, though). Initially, Villa Communia did not include a bathroom, because residents would use the bath dome, but later a bathroom was added for more convenience.

Massive structures: Createrra and Gartist

Andrea Bocco Guarneri with Guillermo Ráfales

This chapter focuses on two buildings, Createrra and Gartist, that are comparable in size, use, setting, and type of client. Each was designed by an architect, Gernot Minke and Werner Schmidt, respectively, who is committed to 'alternative' building methods based on natural materials, in this case, load-bearing straw bales. In an effort to reduce construction costs and environmental impact, Minke and Schmidt both sought to limit the use of wood in the roof construction. To do this, Minke introduced vaulted structures into the design of Createrra. Such a choice was in keeping with his earlier work, such as at the Indian Institute of Technology in New Delhi of 1990, where he used bricks, or at the Wangeliner Garten [→§10], where he used straw bales. [→B203] Schmidt, by contrast, turned to a false-dome structure for Gartist, a concept he has been developing for some time, such as with unrealised projects like la Donaira [→B44:144–149] or temporary ones like the tower at the Lenzburg Agricultural Fair in 2013. With Gartist, however, he was finally able to carry out his vision in a permanent structure.

Besides such differences in technology and design, the two buildings exemplify two approaches: the first relied on workshops and the help of untrained volunteers (Minke affirms that "hands-on workshops and learning by doing [are among] the most exciting and effective ways … to learn the architectural profession"), [→B198:289] the second relied on professionals, even though with the help of untrained assistants. The first approach leads to 'hairier' results, [→B77] the second to more 'clean-cut' ones. While Minke is mostly known as a workshop trainer and author of publications on alternative construction methods, also based on the pioneering research he performed at the University of Kassel's FEB (Forschungslabor für experimentelles Bauen), [→B185,200] Schmidt is famous for his professional practice, known for his commitment to detail, and for being at the forefront of high-quality straw bale building. [→B44,89] Schmidt has a transparent approach to his work and to his methods. On his website he provides a wealth of information regarding the techniques he adopts; this is consistent with the open-source character which many advocate straw bale building should retain. [→B144,350] Minke, by contrast, is more protective of his methods, preferring to transmit knowledge through books and seminars. [→B201,204,361]

Createrra

Minke has been experimenting with construction with sulphur concrete, cans and bottles, old tyres, paperboard, Hogan structures, bamboo, green roofs, superadobe, raw earth (including extruded loam strands), statically optimised domes, and in the last two decades with straw bales, which he embraces as the most robust building technology available that can meet current energy standards. He favours vaulted and domed constructions. During his travels as a student to the Balkans and Turkey, he developed a fascination with domed rooms. Already attracted to the pleasant, calming effect of such spaces, he decided to study them after spending the night in an earth-domed room in New Gourna, Egypt. He then went on to design numerous structures that made use of vaults and domes, such as with his own house and with the Vaakerstrasse students' dormitories in Kassel, a kindergarten in Sorsum, the Picada Café in Rio Grande do Sul, a house in Bad Schussenried, and housing modules in Tamera. [→■1,2]
The Createrra building lies at the northern edge of Hrubý Šur/Hegysúr (Senec district) on the Danube plain, about 20 km east of Bratislava; the building

[→■1]

[→■2]

stands just next to the private house of Bjørn Kierulf and his wife Zuzana Kierulfová.
Kierulf is a Norwegian industrial designer. He came to Slovakia to learn the language and eventually settled there in 1989. Together with his wife he established the architectural practice Createrra that specialised in the design of *Passivhäuser*. Createrra has won several national awards and has influenced the evolution of *Passivhäuser* in Slovakia since its foundation in 2007. Createrra is also where Kierulfová's not-for-profit organisation, ArTUR (trvaloudržatel'ná architectúra or sustainable architecture), is based. Founded in 2001, ArTUR promotes constructing with natural materials,

[→■3]

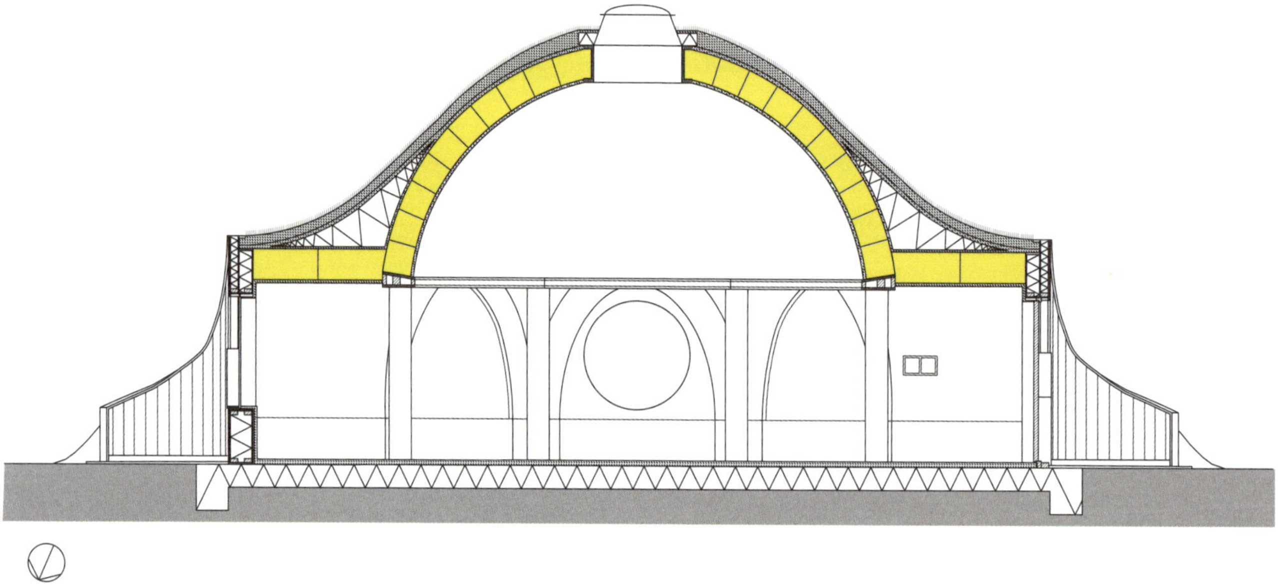

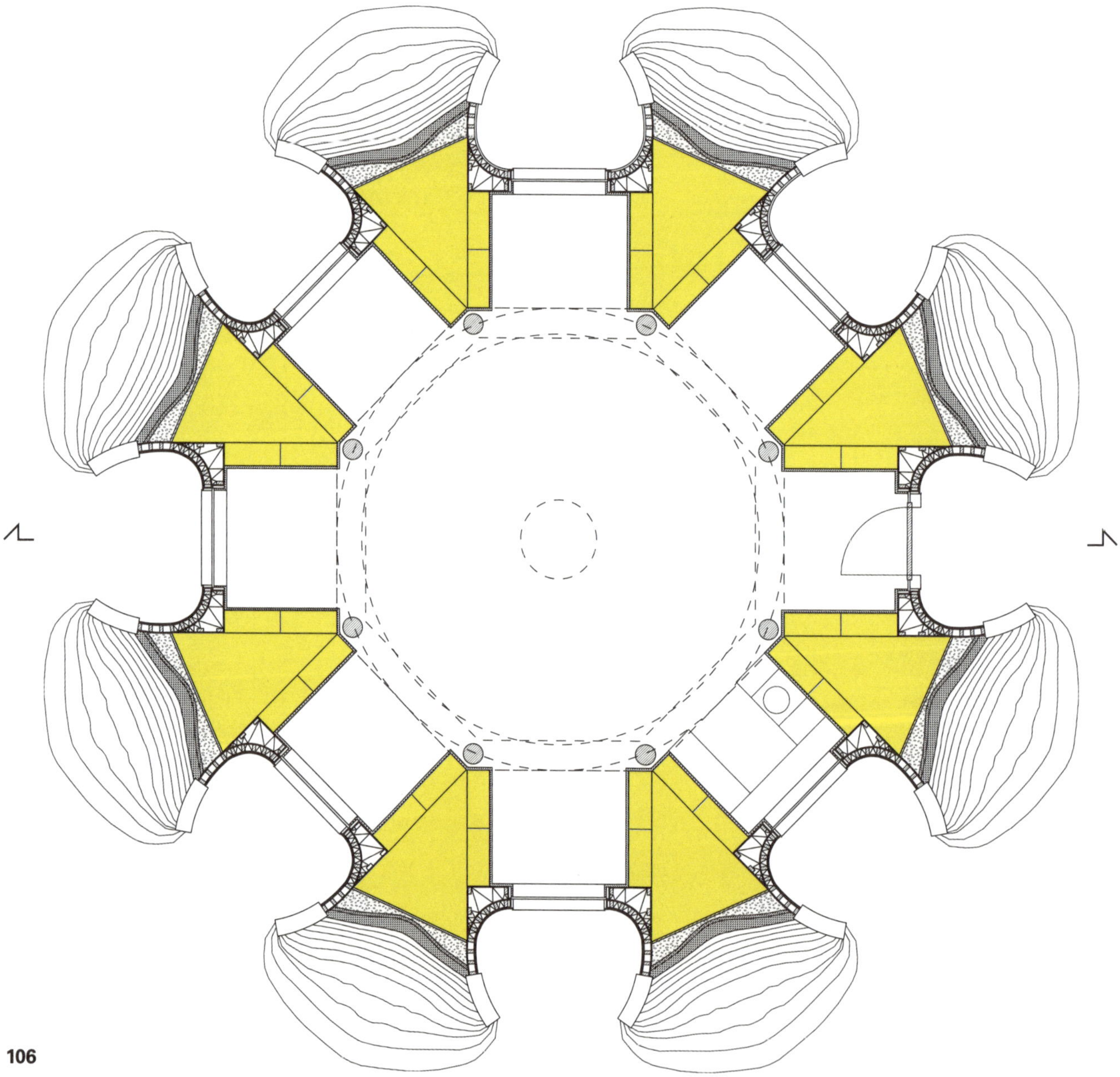

[→■4]
Section and plan,
scale 1:100

[→■5]

such as with earth and straw bales, through various initiatives like providing information, participating in trade fairs, and offering conferences, seminars, and workshops.

Minke designed the building as a coffee shop to be erected in Spain. Kierulf—who is particularly concerned with building physics—modified and adapted Minke's design to meet the conditions of the Slovak climate; he also directed the work at the building site. Kierulfová drew up the plans required to obtain building permits.
The building was erected in the summer of 2010 during two educational workshops, each two weeks long, organised by ArTUR as part of the Leonardo da Vinci project "European Learning Partnership for Strawbale Building" funded by the European Commission. [→B371] This helped defray the total cost of Createrra's construction, which amounted to about 45,000 € (725 €/m^2).

One cannot help but notice the green-mound form of the building emerging from amidst the wild vegetation growing around it. [→■3] The layout is very simple, not so much because of its small size as because of the choice to employ load-bearing straw bales. The result is a central domed space, with a diameter of 6 m and a height of about 5.5 m, surrounded by eight lower vaulted spaces, for a total of 65 m^2. [→■4] The interior is an unpartitioned, articulated environment, where the central space under the dome has a table for meetings and serves multiple functions, including hosting exhibitions, while the eight niches in the perimeter act as a vestibule, a kitchen with a counter

[→■6]

[→■7]

[→■8]

[→■9]

and sink, a corner with a sofa reserved for relaxation, and five workstations with computer desks for Kierulf and his staff. [→■5]

As is typical for a Minke building, there is no underfloor cavity, nor the usual kind of foundations: the entire structure rests on a 400 mm-base of cellular-glass gravel spread over a geotextile sheet, compacted from 2 to 1.3 volumes and levelled. The cellular glass layer is deeper along the perimeter of the building to increase drainage. Pits were temporarily created in the cellular glass bed to accommodate eight round columns of solid Slovak oak timber. The columns are supported by cast-concrete pad foundations. Once firmly placed, the boxes forming the pits were removed and the space was filled with more cellular glass gravel. The ground floor was then stabilised with a walkable raw earth layer added above it, creating something like an insulating raft.
The top ends of the timber columns are connected by a ring beam that supports the dome; this beam has a double-box section, the outer cavity acts as a ventilation duct (corners were sealed with adhesive tape to ensure airtightness), the inner one is used for running the cables.
The straw was supplied loose and was baled on site to a high density (120 kg/m^3) with equipment created by Minke. The bales were superimposed and pinned by wooden stakes, also to avoid movement during construction. The bales of the eight perimeter vaults were set on centrings, while the position of the dome bales was defined with the aid of a rotational guide that Minke had already been using for some time to erect adobe domes. [→B201] [→■6,7,8] This is not the first building ever to be covered with load-bearing straw bales (the first was built by Minke himself in Tamera, Portugal), [→B78] but this building is probably the first in which bales were cut to precise dimensions like ashlars, to optimise the shape to the stress conditions and to bring the compressive force to the centre of each element. This was obtained with another simple machine designed by Minke: parallelepiped bales were given a trapezoid shape (α=3.8°) by cutting them on two sides with a device including two saws, specially developed at the FEB. The saws can be rotated; the cut generates flat and very resistant surfaces, "much stronger than uncut ones," Minke explained. [→B198:287] The last bale, which can be compared to a keystone, was inserted by using cardboard panels to reduce friction and then hit with a wooden hammer to press against the others.
According to Kierulf, to encourage use of natural materials in the construction sector, prefabrication should be promoted. In the past several years, various prefabricated wooden frame and straw infill elements have been developed in Europe by companies like the Lithuania-based EcoCocon, with which Kierulf works closely. For the eight perimeter niches at Createrra, prefabricated elements, insulated with cellulose were employed.

[→■10]

[→■11]

[→■12]

Once the vaults and dome were complete, the bales were compacted by tying them with belts and then trimmed to obtain smoother surfaces. The inner and outer surfaces were then covered with two plaster layers; an earth mixture was sprayed onto the external surface with pumps, while different premixes from a local company were laid onto the inner surface by experts from Latvia, obtaining a sort of catalogue of finishes and colours. [→■9,10,11] The flooring is made of pure clay treated with linseed oil and wax.
Above the entire construction is an EPDM waterproofing membrane; after placing bagged cellular glass to fill the saddles and create a smoothly curved slope, jute bags filled with substrate for green roofs mixed with seeds of drought-resistant plants were laid on the roof. [→■12] The bags were held together by geotextile, but this was not enough to prevent water to make them slide down during a particularly rainy autumn night. Although there was an imbalance in the loads, no cracks were formed, and the bags were later put back up. Minke observed that the local earth is a little too fat; adding some sand would make it firmer. A lush vegetation—mainly succulents to the south, drought resistant grasses to the north—has since grown on the artificial mound.
Howard Liddell observed that "green roofs belie an attitude that any form of human construction is an affront to a natural setting, and that therefore buildings should be hidden away". [→B178:37] Minke may possibly share such attitude towards human construction or he may side with Malcolm Wells in thinking that "architecture, even the good stuff, has always seemed somehow brittle and naked to me" [→B18:103; see also B335] and that "only in the most ancient and overgrown of [cities] did the buildings begin to take on that vine-and-wildflower kind of adornment you might call planetary appropriateness". [→B18:104] What is clear, however, is that Minke's green-roofed buildings are sometimes hard to discern, as is the case, for example, with the Am Wasserturm eco-settlement in Kassel. [→■2] He has indeed dedicated an entire book to defending the reasons for adopting green roofs and to discussing the methods for building them. [→B202; see also B131,146]

[→■13]

The small portions of the perimeter wall, corresponding to the eight smaller rooms, are clad with locally sourced, untreated oak boards. Apart from the one in which the entrance door opens, each room has a fixed round window, consisting of three sheets of glass joined at the perimeter, without a frame both to keep costs down and to avoid thermal bridges. [→■12] If a window is to be replaced, the portion of raw-earth plaster that acts as a glazing bead inside will be demolished: it might then be easily remade, even reusing the same material. The fixed windows and the oculus at the top of the dome, which can be opened, provide plenty of natural light to the interior space, and a variety of views. It matters little in what position the sun is, as there are windows all around. Ventilation is ensured by a system that extracts the stale air from the kitchen and the entrance, and distributes the fresh air through a wooden duct in the beam ring at the dome's base and through vents that open in the perimeter vaults.
Summer cooling is achieved by creating a current of air between an opening in the entrance door and the oculus. The 360-mm-thick straw envelope insulates the building well, and the 40+40 mm of plaster guarantee airtightness. The whole also acts as a thermal mass. When passive performance is not enough, heat is provided by electrical resistances (1900 W) positioned in the walls, in the plaster layer. During the first winter the outdoor temperature reached -7°C, while indoors it was around 17°C; there was

no sign of snow melting, an indication of good insulation. [→■13] According to Kierulf's measurements, the ground temperature under the cellular glass was 14.5°C (in the centre of the dome) and 12.2°C (under the windows) and remained stable. The annual heat consumption is about 700 MJ; performance is being monitored by sensors embedded in the building envelope. Relative humidity at the centre of the bales fell during the first year from 89% to 36% with the support of large fans and a dehumidifier that were used to speed up the drying process of the plaster.
The building is connected to the water mains, but not to the sewage system or septic tank, and is not equipped with a toilet; the bathroom at the Kierulfs's house next door is available. There is no food production on the lot; Zuzana's parents have a vegetable garden nearby and provide the Kjerulfs with all they need.

Gartist

Werner Schmidt's motive for choosing straw bales as his typical building material is mainly that he wants to build houses without ordinary heating systems. Basically, it is an issue of energy self-sufficiency. With super-insulation, just 1 m^3 of firewood can be enough to heat up the entire house for a whole year (as proven by such cases as the Wegmann-Gasser house which, by the way, is very large). "I like the idea that walking in the woods and just picking a piece of wood every time is enough for the winter," says Schmidt.
He shares with most designers whose work is shown in this book the conviction that in addition to finding ways to reduce a building's operational energy and to using renewable energy sources, the overall ecological impact should be considered. As Schmidt sees it, if the embodied environmental impacts (both in the production and at the end-of-life phases) were a criteria for choosing building materials and construction techniques, straw bale houses would be at the top in terms of sustainability. Some of his recent experimental designs revolve around the attempt to reduce the use of wood. "There are enough people who are just building with wood, so I find it interesting to experiment with other construction methods," he explains.

The concept of the straw bale perimeter wall plus container ('wonder box') epitomises Schmidt's idea of the self-sufficient house. Such a house should have an envelope with a high insulation performance and a 'wonder box' that accommodates the wet areas and services for energy, water, and air management. The building envelope can be of simple construction, even with low-technology methods, while the prefabricated unit includes elements that need to be built with precision, such as stairs, cooking implements, and bath. Bathrooms and kitchens should not be adjacent to the perimeter wall of straw bales. [→B44:175]
The low-tech envelope envisaged by Schmidt for such buildings would be made of load-bearing straw bale walls plus a false dome. His favourite reference is the *bories* village in Gordes, Vaucluse; [→B172] similar constructions are also traditional in regions such as Apulia and the Balearic Islands. Schmidt would, of course, replace stone with straw and stack the bales so that they protrude gradually towards the centre until they meet, without creating thrust. This would allow a very basic installation and just need two to eight weeks to settle and assume its final shape. Schmidt has been working for a few years on this concept and in 2009 proposed it as part of an unrealised design for guest rooms at a country hotel in Ronda, Andalusia. In that case, 'junior' and 'senior' suites would have been made of *trulli*-like units with a circular plan crowned by a pitched false dome; they would have a skylight rather than windows. In such a hot climate the *trullo* shape is appropriate because warm air tends to move to the upper part of the volume: if one leaves the door open, warm air can be extracted through the skylight. Moreover, structures with such a form are earthquake-proof. According to a principle proposed by Peter Braun—the structural engineer with whom Schmidt often works, who also performed the calculations for the Gartist building—if you turn the ground plane by 15° and the walls can still stand straight, then the structure will withstand earthquakes. This explains why buildings constructed by the ancient Maya and Inca have endured for centuries.

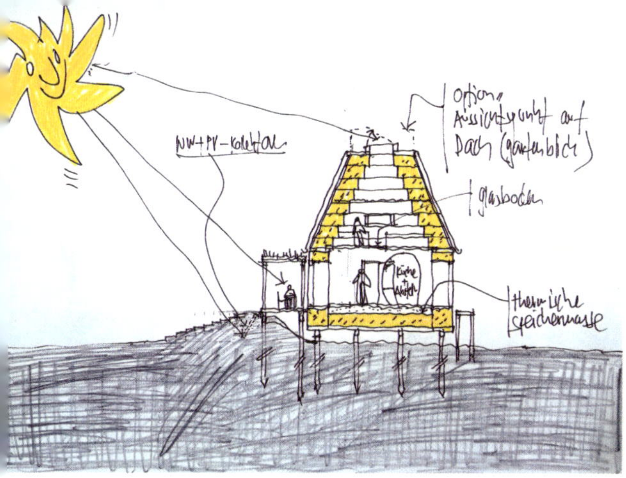

[→■14]

[→■15]

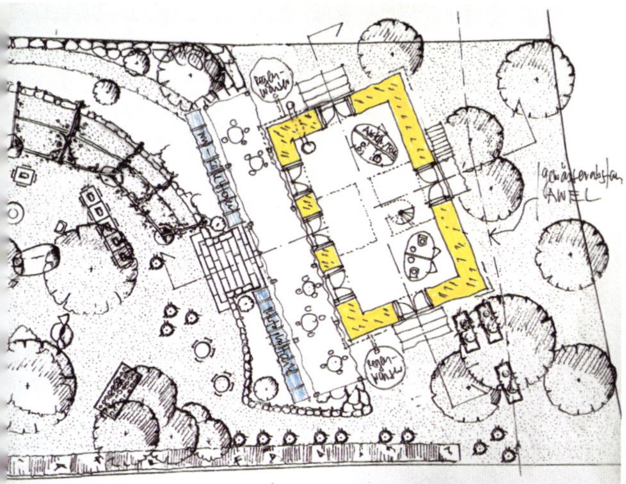

[→■16]

[→■17]

One of the drawbacks of this technique is the difficulty it poses for creating openings, thus limiting the amount of natural lighting and the relationship between interior and exterior more generally. Only zenithal light comes through easily, unless the tall volume is horizontally partitioned. [→■14]

Schmidt was finally able to realise a building according to these principles in 2016-17 for the company Gartist GmbH. [→B360] The building stands in a small industrial area at the outskirts of Bubikon/ZH, among sheds that host a building firm, a meat factory, a dance school, and a church dome. [→■15] The plot has a rectangular shape; it is accessed from the northwest corner and accommodates a warehouse to store tools and a space called 'Grotto' covered by a rigid canopy opposite to it, after which a piazza opens at the centre of the plot. [→■16] The 11.5-m high building stands at the far end with a slightly turned aspect. [→■17] This positioning allows it to take more advantage of the sun and not appear frontally to the visitor. The whole outdoor space is a showpiece landscaped by the clients: Debora Kunz is an herbalist and dietician and her husband, Joel, is a landscape architect. Gartist, their company, designs, constructs, and maintains gardens. With the help of a carpenter, the young couple also built the warehouse and the canopy. A 35-m long, clay-rendered wall defines the south border of the plot and is used as an open-air art gallery; other works of art by the owners are scattered throughout the premises. The garden is aimed at immersing the visitors in a botanical journey through edible flowers, aromatic herbs, and healing plants. The whole facility is used to host courses and seminars as well as outdoor events and can be rented for parties and weddings.

The building was initially designed by Schmidt to serve as a showroom and exhibition space open to the public, as an office for the company, and as a venue for events. But as Debora revealed to us, they found the building so appealing that they immediately decided that they wanted to live there. This affected the organisation of the space: [→■18] the ground floor stayed an unpartitioned large room (76 m²) containing two smaller spaces (a bathroom and a kitchen cum storage) in egg-like constructions—a reminder of a long series of eggs Schmidt has been

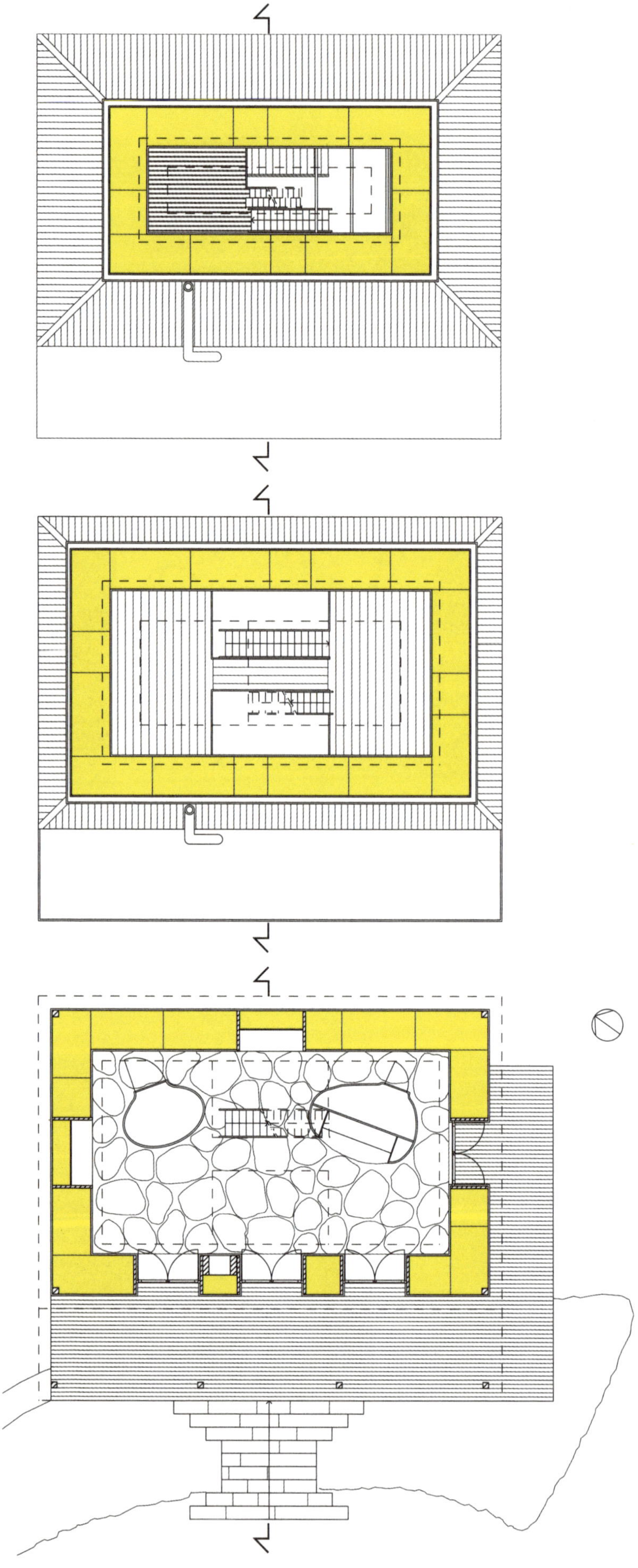

[→■18]
Second, first and ground floor plans, scale 1:200

[→■19]

[→■20]

[→■21]

[→■22]

[→■23]

[→■24]

constructing over the course of his career. [→B44,351] [→■19] The mezzanine is an intermediate environment dedicated to office work, while an additional top level accommodates a bedroom and lounge area. [→■20,21] They also added a very steep staircase leading to the skylight that swings open, providing access to the roof, which can be used as a terrace.

A total of thirteen people worked on the site, including Schmidt, his team, and Debora and Joel Kunz.
Since the land was formerly a swamp, it was necessary to use micropile foundations, 15 m long. The foundations emerge from the ground at about 400 mm keeping the building raised from the moist ground and creating a crawl space where the rainwater collection tank is placed; it is also useful for natural cooling in summer. HEA 200 beams laying on the concrete piles support the ground floor. This is a construction of transversal *Brettstapel* timber elements lying next to each other with a small gap in between them to allow ventilation of the straw infill, on which stands a grid of blockboard panels (*Tischlerplatten*) filled with straw bales, and closed at the top by more panels; this construction was covered with a 500-mm layer of crushed stone in which the underfloor heating pipes were laid; the crushed stone layer was then machine-compressed and covered by large, rounded slabs obtained by cutting conglomerate rock boulders in 50–70-mm-thick slices that constitute a heavy, heat-storing flooring. [→■22] Such gargantuan tiles are called "Discus" and were suggested by the Kunzs, whose company also markets them. They also selected the stone. [→■23]
The first step in the erection of the walls was the positioning of large window boxes onto which the triple-glazed windows and doors were later fixed. For the wall and roof as well as for the ground floor, Schmidt employed 'jumbo' bales (2.50x1.20x0.70 m), as he has in many of his projects. The total number of straw bales is 182, which were used both whole and cut into ½, ⅓, and ¼. To lay the 'jumbo' bales, they had to use a crane, and work on the structure was complete within five days, including installing the skylight, as shown in the time-lapse video. [→B15] [→■24] The roof slopes are interrupted at two planes by ring plates made of 80-mm-thick, cross-laminated timber panels, and one more closes the straw bale construction at the top: these rings evenly distribute the load on the whole perimeter and are connected to solid timber cross beams that support the first and second floors and the roof terrace, and they help stiffen the construction by bracing the horizontal loads. [→■25]
After completion, the structure was left to settle for approximately one month. The roof was connected to the foundation to secure it against strong wind: two ropes near the corners on both sides were spanned from the top to the foundations before placing the roofing. A single layer of lime-based render, approximately 15 mm thick, was sprayed onto the bales to achieve sufficient resistance to fire, insects, and other agents that can affect the straw's durability.
In the interior, three layers of clay plaster were laid following the sinuous lines of the bales, which resulted in a sculputural effect of great beauty. [→■27] "I prefer to show the material as it is, with all its imperfections. The edges are not straight, we could have done it straight, but we were not looking for that. I think it is fine. You can understand how the straw bales were put together," explained Schmidt. [→B253:93] The base coat was applied with a spray gun in order to thoroughly penetrate between the straw stalks, while the next layers were applied by hand.

Schmidt would have preferred a stretched plastic roofing, the sort of which he had used in the vonRoll Pavilion (2010). As he put it, "For me, using only plastic would be the most economical solution ... but fire regulations changed, and the roof had to be a non-flammable surface." Finally, Schmidt opted for a corrugated steel sheet (*Trapezblech*), which is attached to the timber ring plates at three points. [→■25,26] Between the metal roofing and the straw bale structure, Schmidt created a ventilation gap about 300 mm wide. Then, to avoid problems related to condensation, he placed a felt layer at the connections between the metal flashings and the timber plates.
The roof culminates in a skylight that has a timber-based frame and three glazings, the middle one of which can be opened; it has the function of both illuminating the room below and of permitting the exchange of air. It also gives access to the roof

[→■25]
Section, scale1:50

1 corrugated metal roof sheet; 40–310 mm ventilation gap; 10 mm earth plaster; 1,120 mm straw bales; 50 mm earth plaster; lime wash

2 15 mm sprayed lime render; 1,120 mm straw bales; 50 mm earth plaster; lime wash

3 100 mm soapstone slabs + cement mortar bedding; 360 mm gravel; 41.5 mm blockboard; 700 mm straw bale; 200 mm Brettstapel deck

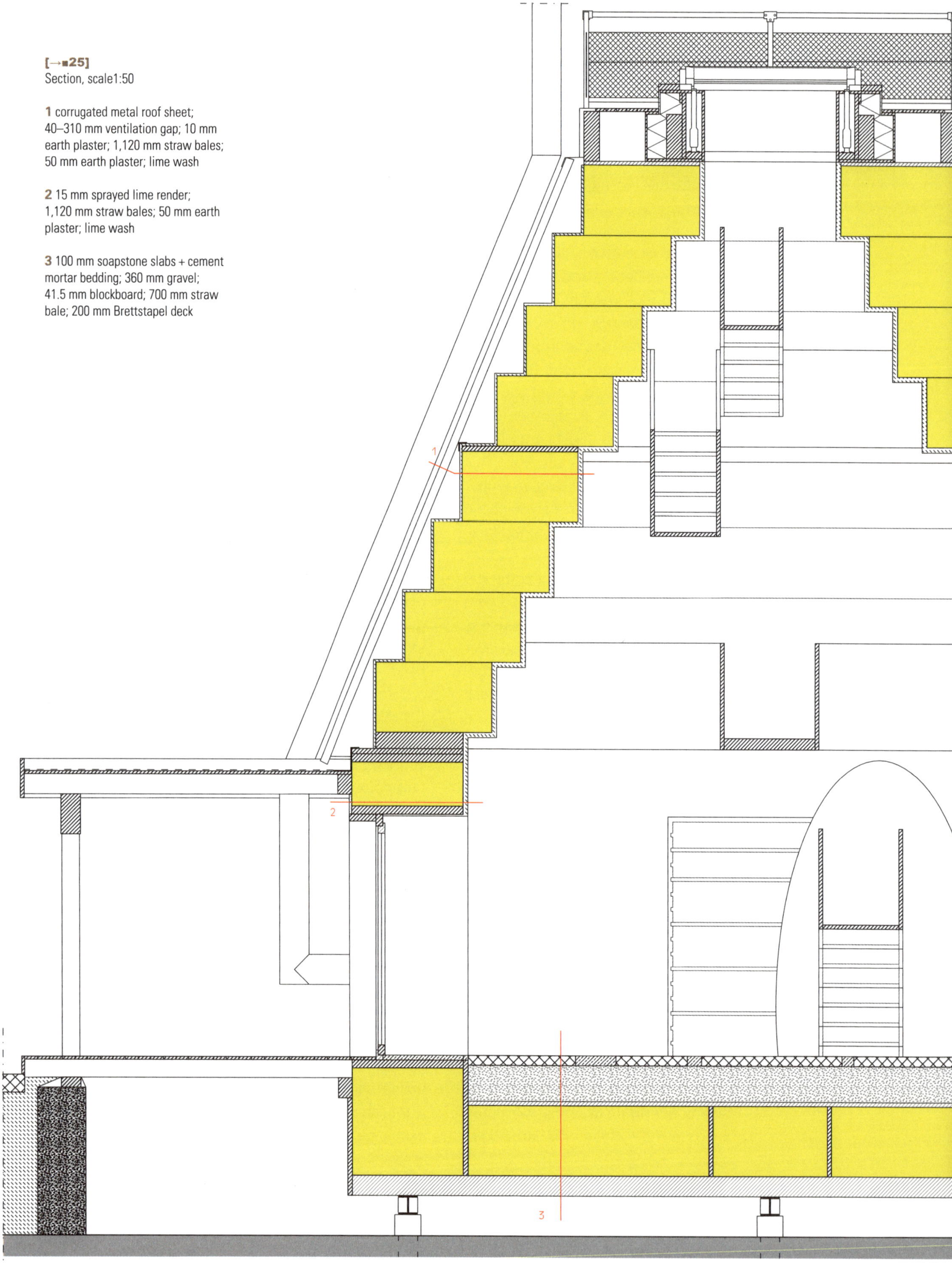

[→■26]

[→■27]

[→■28]

deck, consisting of roughly 100-mm-wide boards, butted. Lighting issues are arguably inherent to this staggered way of building, but at Gartist one of the office spaces on the first floor has particularly serious issues related to its location under the platform (now bedroom) that provides access to the terrace.

The porch was added last. It has a simple timber frame structure and a gravel layer on top of the flat roof. **[→■17]**

The shape of the two "Dracheneier" ('dragon eggs'), i.e., the curvy shapes that contain a kitchen and a bathroom on the ground floor, was moulded by spraying a cement coat onto perforated metal sheets and onto reinforcement layers of fine mesh. **[→■28]** While this was a quick and strong solution, it nevertheless ran counter to the goal of keeping the embodied energy low; a similar but much lower-impact solution can be seen for instance in the walk-in earth sculpture that Anna Heringer built using the *zabur* technique at the 15th Biennale di Venezia. The sculpture was shaped layer-by-layer, using only hands as a tool; **[→B32:88–91]** it is questionable, however, whether such a technique could allow covering a significantly larger span.

Schmidt explained that for him the egg shape is "a beautiful shape. If you make a round shape it is simply a thing that you put there, while the shape of the egg has a meaning in itself". According to Guillermo Ráfales Sancho, they "are symbols of freedom in formal expression. [They] mean intimacy, protection, shelter, but also life and energy". **[→B253:108]**

The smell of open-pore, sawn timber boards inspires a pleasant feeling, as soon as you enter. The way sounds are gentled and toned down by the massive envelope contributes to the sense of healing and relaxation. Noise interrupts thought, disrupts sleep, and harms digestion, **[→B71:204,205]** thus causing stress. And stress can trigger many illnesses. **[→B72:182]** Schmidt makes only modest claims for the potential health benefits of straw bale construction, merely pointing out: "In non-straw-bale houses, stress is removed less easily." In many of his buildings, 'feeling just right' is an immediately perceivable, immersive sensation. This stems partly from the non-straight lines and thick walls, which convey a feeling of security and comfort. Day stresses the importance of conveying such a psychological sense of safety, arguing that "similar buildings convey the sense that they are 'strong' enough to still be there when you again need" them and can therefore strengthen self-reliance and immunity against illness. **[→B72:222,230]** Schmidt's buildings all possess warm interior surfaces and suggest comfort, if not cosiness: floors **[→B5:233]** and walls have a soft and pleasant surface feel thanks to the use of granular materials (such as hand-finished plaster) and their natural texture (such as exposed wood). **[→B72:235]** Among others, Thiis-Evensen has noted that "a space with smooth walls seems colder than a comparable space with finely textured wall surfaces". **[→B302:173]**

In winter the large thermal mass of the ground floor is heated by means of underfloor pipes located in the gravel layer; the water running inside them is heated by vacuum tube solar collectors located on the south side of the building (vacuum tubes were chosen because they work with diffuse light as well: Bubikon is a foggy location). This underfloor heating system is complemented by a firewood-burning backup stove and an emergency electrical heater. Located to the left of the entrance door, the stove is inserted into the perimeter wall, while the stainless-steel chimney remains outside to avoid degradation in the case of malfunction. According to the Kunzs, they burnt approximately 800 kg firewood during the winter of 2017/18. This amount might be reduced if the building was used the way it was originally intended.

The crawlspace is about 400 mm high and is always cold due to the evaporation from the wet ground. Regardless of the outside temperature, it remains at roughly 6–8°C most of the time. In hot weather, a small electrical extractor, similar to those used in kitchens, is turned on (it can be controlled manually). It sucks the cold air from beneath the house and then releases it through a slot inside the kitchen egg at a height of about 1.5 m. This flow of cold air is coupled with opening the skylight, allowing hot air to escape while fresh air is pulled in. The building is very tall, so the stack effect is facilitated and the heavier cold air stays on the ground level. The thermal mass of the ground floor is very useful in summer too, because the cold air from below the building is circulated into it, keeping the inside temperature cool.

[→■29]

[→■30]

The cost of the building was 250,000 CHF for foundations plus envelope; the total cost was about 450,000 CHF (3,500 CHF/m^2, about 3,100 €/m^2, a sum that might seem outrageous by European Union standards, but is the norm in Switzerland).
The false-dome system should allow for a significant reduction of timber, except where indispensable, such as in window frames and beams. The false dome should also give the building a lower environmental impact overall, thanks to the low embodied energy of the straw bales: for a discussion of these statements [→§13].
To further examine the benefits and drawbacks of the false-dome system, it would be necessary to consider the impact of applying such a system to more complex schemes, such as multi-storey and multi-apartment buildings without renouncing spatial and architectural qualities.

In term of the production of food, the Kunzs tried to set up a diminutive 'closed-loop' production cycle à la John Todd. [→B309] On the south side of the building, they set up tanks for breeding freshwater fish, to which they feed worms. The tanks also have the benefit of producing food for ducks, as water lentils proliferate within them. In addition, the Kunzs also tend hens and rabbits, grow herbs for teas, and have a small hydroponic vegetable garden. [→■29] During catered events, they use edible flowers grown on their property. [→■30]

Framed structure: Bamboo Ark

Andrea Bocco Guarneri

Toki Hirokazu 陶器浩一 is a structural engineer and professor at the University of Shiga Prefecture 滋賀県立大学. He was the first person in Japan to earn a Ph.D. in environmental science. He has been experimenting with unconventional structural solutions in several materials, including a three-dimensional spatial grid made of small-section dimensional timbers, and an innovative joint design that conjoins metal plates through use of thermal expansion. In 2011, when the Tōhoku earthquake and tsunami struck, he and assistant professor Nagai Takuo 永井拓生 had just started experimenting with bamboo structures, designing a temporary installation for the "Osaka City of Water" festival according to the same principles that he would later adopt for the Bamboo Ark. **[→B287]**
One month after the catastrophe, Toki visited Oyakaigan 大谷海岸, a coastal fishing and aquaculture port in Motoyoshi-cho 本吉町, Kesennuma City 気仙沼市 (Miyagi prefecture 宮城県) and met a childhood friend, Takahashi Kazushi 高橋和志, who had lost his father and house in the tsunami. Takahashi is the president of the Takahashi Kogyo Company 高橋工業, which is known for the production and construction of curved and three-dimensional steel structures using shipbuilding technology. He also owns the local fishing port. Takahashi offered to provide some land on a mound that overlooks the Pacific Ocean at about 11 m a.m.s.l., a space that had served as a gathering place for the community for centuries. Takahashi asked Toki to design a temporary structure that would provide locals, especially children, with a place to gather, and where rehearsals for the traditional *tora-mai* 虎舞 (tiger dance) and the related annual festival could take place. **[→B14,19,287]** **[→▪1]** Some fifty children and older members of the community used to rehearse in the local Kō-min-kan 公民館 (a public building run by the local government that offers various bureaucratic services and usually contains large spaces that locals can use), but it had been destroyed by the tsunami.

The Bamboo Ark was born as a humanitarian project and bamboo was chosen as a structural material primarily because after the tsunami hit, it was the only material available in abundance: bamboo culms could be harvested from a forest near the site.

[→■1]

Though it began life as a project aimed at serving the community, [→B218] it soon became a research project as well, centred on form-finding, structural modelling, testing durability, designing for emergencies, and a host of other issues as well. The Japanese Building Standards Law does not define the characteristics of bamboo, and up to the construction of the Bamboo Ark, it had only rarely been used as a structural material. [→B95,101] Toki, however, sees bamboo as a wasted resource. Throughout Japan, he observes, wild bamboo forests grow that could easily be harvested and transported.

Toki and Nagai began by studying the local bamboos. They found that the cold climate significantly restrained their growth; their useful length was about 6 m. [→B214] There were two kinds of bamboo available: *madake* 真竹 (*Phyllostachys bambusoides*) and *mōsō* 孟宗竹 (*Phyllostachys edulis*). The change in the cross-section diameter is roughly linear over the length of the cane. For *mōsō* the average wall thickness was roughly 11% of the diameter, for *madake* roughly 7%.

Before entering the design phase, Toki and Nagai oversaw the performance of hundreds of tests on potential joints and on bamboos growing in Shiga and Kesennuma. Using an Amsura universal testing machine, they found that not origin but species determines the difference in characteristics. *Mōsō* is thicker than *madake*, so members which would need to withstand more bending and axial force were to be made of *mōsō*. With this use in mind, they therefore examined *mōsō*'s bending and tensile strength thoroughly, while compression and shear strength tests were omitted, as it was supposed that compression and shear loads would be small and bamboo would fail because of bending load. All the *mōsō* specimens were at least three years old and were tested within two weeks after harvesting. Because of the urgent nature of the construction, they had to harvest the bamboo in September, when it contains a lot of sap. For durability, a winter harvest would have been better. The moisture content of the specimens was 60 to 80%. For a more permanent structure, well-seasoned bamboo would of course have been preferred. Toki and Nagai chose not to attempt removing vegetable oils from the bamboo, since it would have been difficult to eliminate them in full-length culms; moreover, the building was to be temporary. This allowed them to test the durability of the untreated bamboo. Since for *madake* members joint strength was more critical than the bamboo's own strength, tests on *madake* were omitted.

They ascertained the design strength by subtracting the standard deviation from the average value of the maximum admissible load. This corresponds to a 30% reduction, which is quite conservative compared with the 5% generally used for wood materials. Long-term and short-term allowable stress levels were set to one-third (38.0 N/mm^2 for bending, 55.2 N/mm^2 for tension) and two-thirds of the reference strength (114.1 N/mm^2 for bending, 165.6 N/mm^2 for tension), respectively. Arch members, columns, and the upper and lower chords of foundation trusses have a slenderness ratio of about 60 to 100. For the compression axial load of such members, they used the Euler elastic buckling load as the reference strength. Based on Tanaka et al., **[→B300]** one-third of it was set as a long-term allowable compression axial load, and two-thirds for short-term load.

Most of the Bamboo Ark construction work had to be conducted by students and volunteers who lacked training in construction, making use of limited material and labour. Toki and Nagai therefore had to develop a joining method which could provide sufficient structural strength and stiffness without the aid of special equipment or machines. They also decided to design joints that would not pierce the bamboo, since splitting is likely to occur if screws or bolts are driven into the unreinforced, round bamboo. After consulting with local farmers and fishermen over how to make the joints, Toki and Nagai adopted a particular method of rope binding. **[→■2]** They determined that the strength of such joints depends on the friction between the round bamboos and on the material used for fastening them. Several tests were performed on four kinds of ties: a) 3-mm wire; b) three-strand 3-mm polyester rope (it was chosen because it is easy to tie and does not loosen easily); c) the same type of rope + heat-resistant and water-resistant cloth tape, 75 mm wide, to increase friction; d) the same as above, but with a notch of about one third of the diameter carved into one bamboo. **[→■3]** Both solutions c) and d) were based on suggestions made by students.

Test results showed a dramatic difference between the strengths of various tie solutions, ranging from 0.50 to 4.56 kN. Strength also depended on the species of bamboo. They ascertained the design strength of joints by subtracting the standard deviation from the average value of the test results, and, as above, the long-term and short-term strengths were set to one-third and two-thirds of that. They selected solutions d) and c); the latter is much weaker, but they chose to adopt it because of its excellent deformation performance. They also found that the joint strength is relatively insensitive to errors in winding the rope, and that, even with inexperienced workers, quality can be considered uniform. **[→B214]** Possibly, with expert labour, ties constructed only from rope might have been sufficient: see for instance the community learning centre designed in Ujung-Alang by Eko Prawoto, where only *ijuk* rope was used. **[→B174]**

The Bamboo Ark project was based on the assumption that most of the process—from procurement of materials to construction work—would be carried out manually by students and volunteers, minimising the use of either special techniques or large machinery. **[→B311,312]** In addition, they would seek to avoid performing construction work at potentially dangerous heights. They would also leave the bamboo elements exposed. To meet these various aims, Toki and Nagai developed a simple and structurally viable method of construction.

[→■2]

J1A (A1+FB1およびA1+FB2接合部) FB1材、FB2材の地組時上側に切り欠き	図面ハッチング	ロープの長さ 7m	ガムテープ 柱有 梁無	テープの色 赤色
J2A (A1+A2接合部)	図面ハッチング	ロープの長さ 6m	ガムテープ 有	テープの色 青色
J2B (A1+A2+A4接合部)	図面ハッチング	ロープの長さ 6m × 2	ガムテープ 有	テープの色 青色

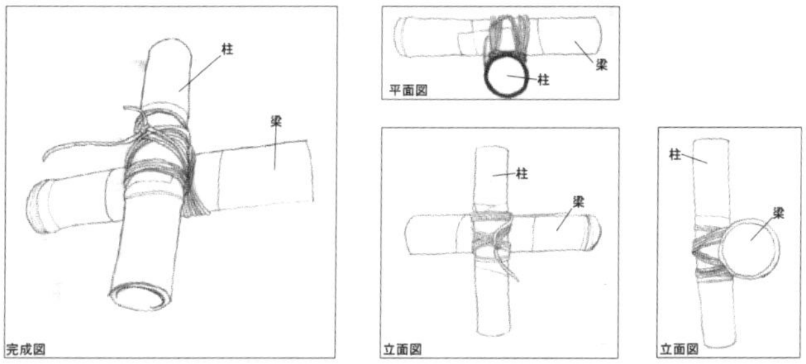

■製作過程

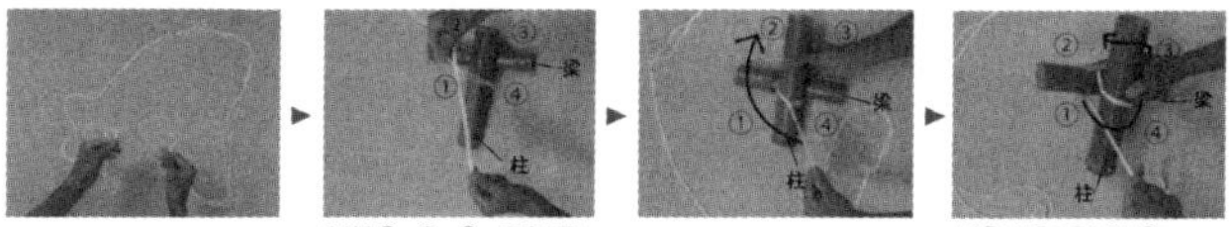

二重にする。

先端を④→裏→②→手前に通し、中心で二重にして作った輪にに先端を通す。

④に強く引き、②の方へ。

(1)②から梁の裏を通し①へ
(2)①から柱の手前を通し④へ
(3)④から梁の裏を通し③へ
(4)③から柱の手前を通し②へ

ロープをクロス方向に二重ずつ二方向に巻く。
(1)②から梁の裏を通し①へ
(2)①から柱の手前を通し③へ
(3)③から梁の裏を通し①へ
(4)(2)(3)をもう一度

(1)①から柱の手前を通し④へ
(2)④から梁の裏を通し②へ
(3)②から柱の手前を通し④へ
(4)(2)(3)をもう一度

割りを入れる。
(1)④から柱の裏を通し①へ
(2)①から梁の手前を通し②へ
(3)②から柱の裏を通し③へ
(4)③から梁の手前を通し④へ
(5)(1)〜(4)を巻けるだけ

ロープを1本ずつにし、片方を①(②)の方へ、もう片方を③(④)に持ってくる。かた結びをする。

J3 (A1+A3およびA2+A3接合部)	図面ハッチング	ロープの長さ 4m	ガムテープ 有	テープの色 黄色

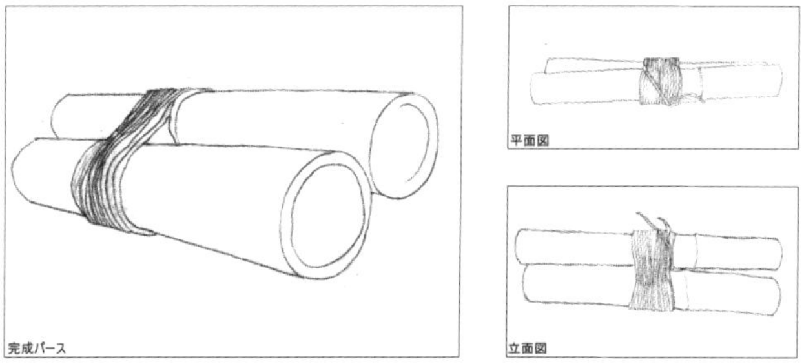

■製作過程

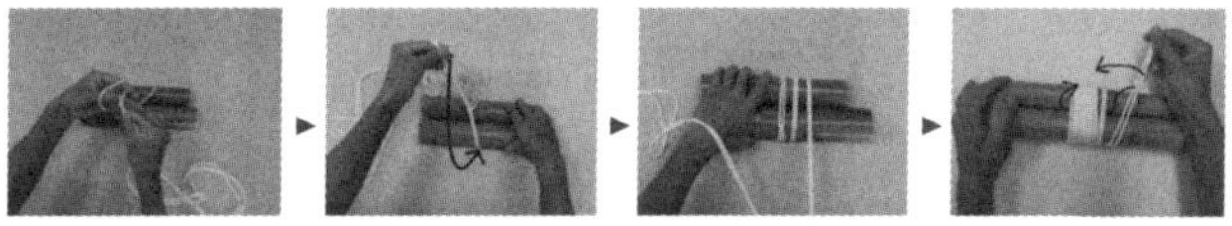

二重にした輪に先端をを通す。

上側に強く引き、下の方向へ。

部材にロープを6〜7周巻いていく。

片方のロープを巻いたロープの下にくぐらせる。

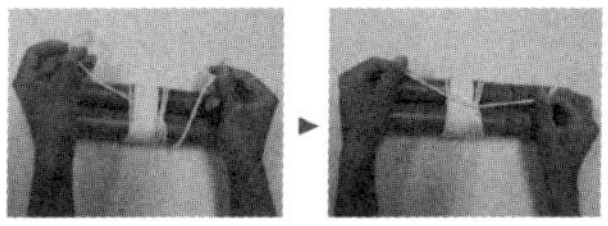

お互いのロープを結ぶ。

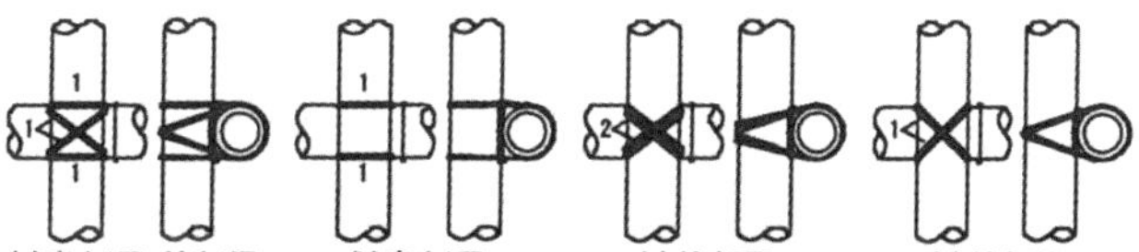

(a) 直交1回+斜め1回　(b) 直交1回　(c) 斜め2回　(d) 斜め1回

図10　ロープの巻き回数を変えた試験体

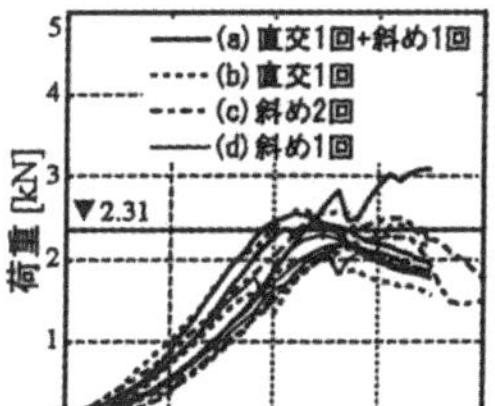

図11　荷重ー変形関係

表5　各巻き方の耐力（()内は COV)

巻き方	平均値[kN]	標準偏差[kN]
(a)	2.69	0.29 (10.6%)
(b)	2.31	0.15 (6.4 %)
(c)	2.40	0.24 (10.2%)
(d)	2.19	0.07 (3.2%)
全体	2.40	0.28 (11.5%)

[→■3]

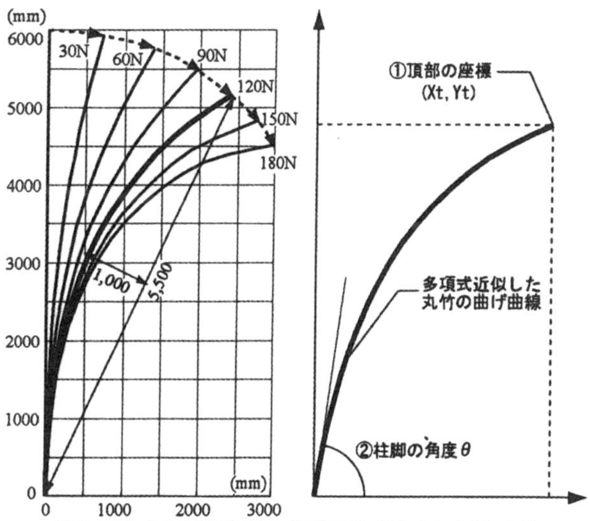

※モウソウチク（元口径 60 〜末口径 D30, 長さ 6m）を例に作図

(a) 丸竹の曲げ形状解析結果　(b) アーチ形状の作図方法

図5　モウソウチクの曲げ形状解析およびアーチ形状

[→■4]

[→■4] An example of bending deformation of bamboo. The bending stress of the arch member is about ½ of the long-term allowable bending stress (38.0 N/mm²) and the shear force at the column base is the joint long-term proof stress (1.22 kN). In this model, the load is 120 N and the rise is about 1 m against a length of 5.5 m.

Ordinarily, bamboo structures are designed to take only axial loads. But in some cases, when they need to be stiff enough to withstand bending stress, they may be bundled. [→B188] In other situations, in order to improve the structure's in-plane rigidity, the bamboo is bent to form arches. [→B312] (A combination of both bundling and arched shapes can be seen in the work of Canyaviva.) [→B353] As a result of repeated field tests, experiments, and discussions, Toki and Nagai decided to form arc-shaped frames by tying the top ends of two or three pieces of bamboo and creating self-balanced, two-dimensional structures. [→▪4,6]

They obtained the shape of the frames by conducting a geometrical nonlinear analysis, which they based on two-dimensional elements and on the cross section and the characteristics of the *mōsō* bamboo that they actually used. In the model, the deformation is generated by a concentrated load to the tip, but the coordinates of the tip were updated at each increase in load so that the load vector was always orthogonal to the axis of the bamboo tip. This is similar to the way that a bamboo cane is bent by human power. [→B312]

They performed a similar analysis on several lengths of bamboo, and a polynomial that approximates the bending shape was obtained whose parameters are the angle at the base of the column and the coordinates of the top end. It was therefore possible to describe forty-eight different arched frames with three basic patterns, arranged radially at 7.5° angles; changes in the two parameters are continuous from position 01 to position 48 so that the three-dimensional surface formed was smoothly curved. Among other advantages, this feature makes it possible to avoid the potential occurrence of locally excessive stress in the membrane that envelopes the construction.

Stress analysis was performed on a three-dimensional framework model that considers the cross-section variation from the base to the top end of the bamboo members. In an article on the subject, Toki and Nagai describe the equations they used. [→B312] The plan was spiral-shaped with continuously changing height and span; one side had an overhang somewhat similar to the visor of a cap, leaving an opened section below that faced the sea; access was through the gap between the coils of the spiral. [→▪5] The total floor area was 176 m^2 with a maximum height of 6.88 m.

The density of the bamboo employed was about 220 kg/m^3 immediately after harvesting (it was used fresh), and as it dried it decreased to 120 kg/m^3 in about one month; then asymptotically. If a density of 120 kg/m^3 is assumed, the total weight of the building is about 4,800 kg, i.e. about 28 kg/m^2: much less than in ordinary buildings.

In terms of seismic behaviour, the Bamboo Ark can be regarded as a single-mass system. The translational and rotational degrees of freedom are the dominant modes in the earthquake response; in any case, the building is very efficient since it is very elastic and constitutes a highly dissipative system. Because of its extremely low weight, the structure's performance in the event of storm is a crucial design issue. The horizontal component of the wind pressure was calculated at 69.39 kN and the total at 225 kN, compared against an extremely rare earthquake force of 11.67 kN. This called for the specification of a heavy ballast to resist the potential force of wind.

Mōsō is larger in diameter than *madake* and has thick walls, which give it a high bending modulus. In addition, cracks are less likely to occur in it. It was therefore specified for members that are subject to bending, like those that form the arch frames (A1, A2, A4, C1), as well as those that need to bear a high axial load, such as the upper and lower chords of the foundation trusses (FB1, FB2). Because of its thinner walls, compared with *mōsō*, *madake* is easier to work with. The diameter decreases gently from root to tip—the diameter and wall thickness are almost the same over 4 m or more—, so a given cross section is easy to obtain. In the Bamboo Ark it was used for joists, as a flooring material, and for truss webs (FT1, FT2) that only need to bear axial loads.

A life-size mock-up was built on campus to check and test everything, and to give the students the opportunity to practice; students also experimented with bending the bamboo and working with the ropes. [→▪6]

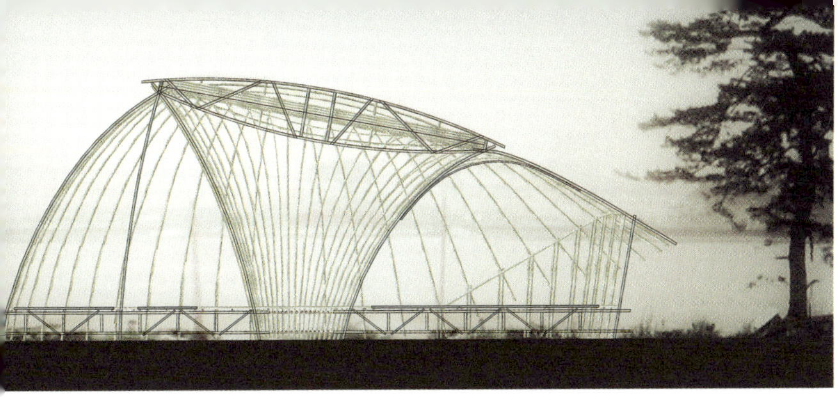

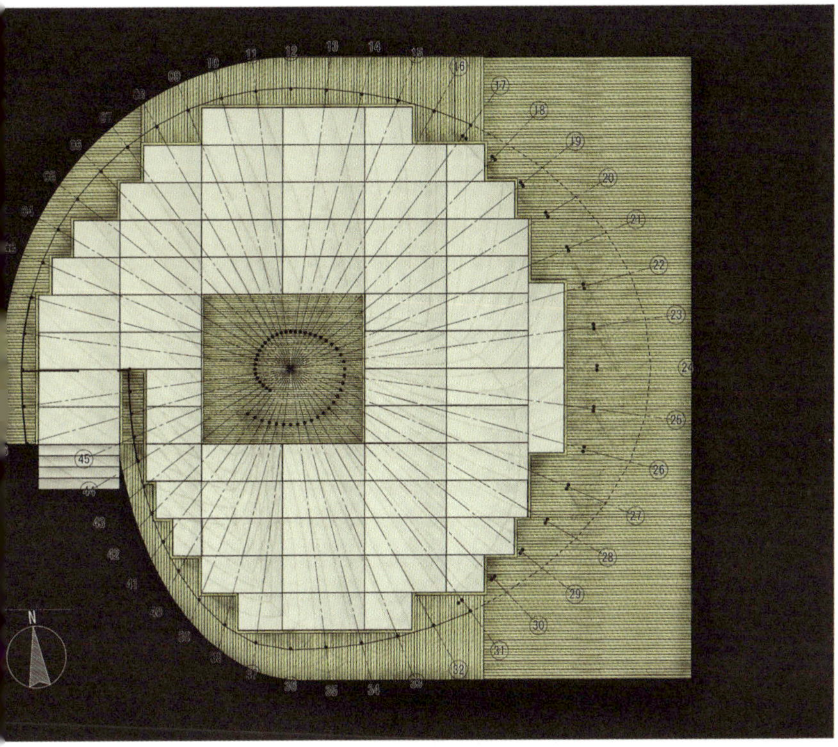

[→■5]
Section and plan,
scale 1:200

[→■6]

[→■7]

《接合部 凡例》

- J1 A (赤) :A1+FB1 / 切り欠き+ロープ 6m
- J1 B (赤) :C+FB1+C / 切り欠き+ロープ 12m
- J2 A (青) :A1+A2 / ガムテープ+ロープ 6m
- J2 B (青) :A1+A4+A2 / ガムテープ+ロープ 6m×2
- J3 (黄) :A1+A3&A2+A3 / ガムテープ+ロープ 4m
- J4 (緑) :FB1+FT2&FB2+FT2 / ガムテープ+ロープ 6m
- J5 (白) :C1+A2+C / ガムテープ+ロープ 12m
- ▼ :FT2の位置を表す(マジックによるマーキングを行う)

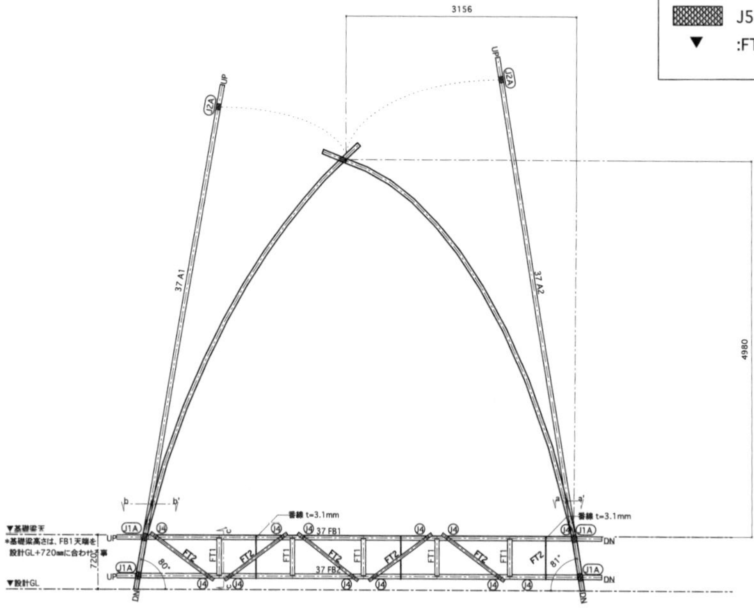

Arch 37

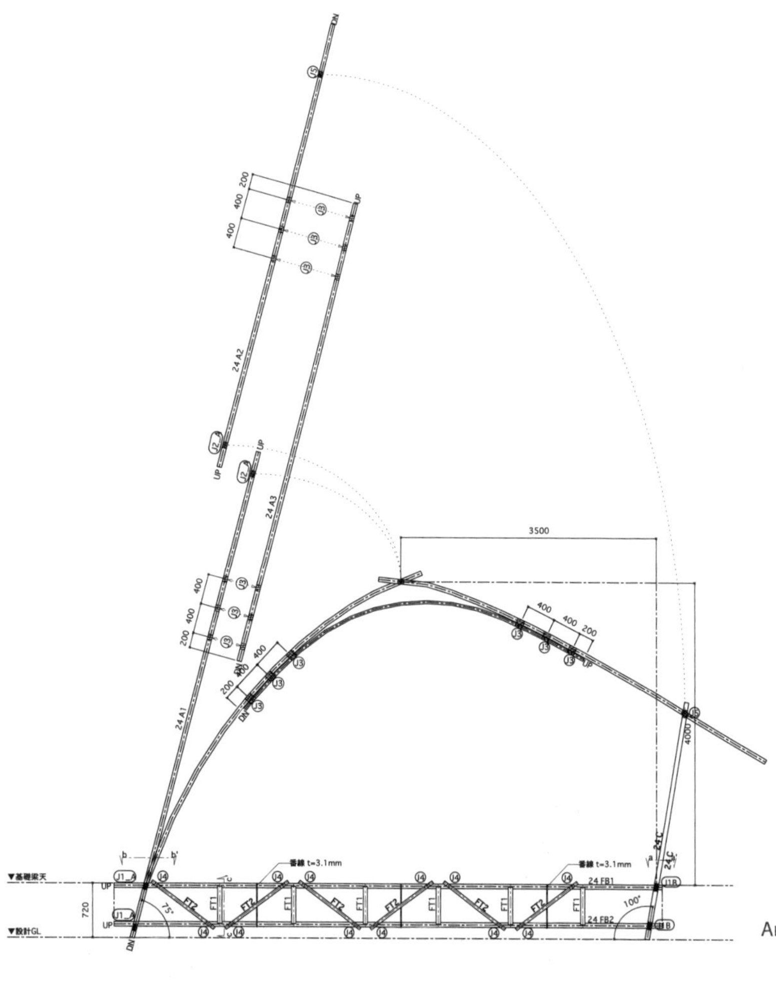

Arch 24

[→■8] scale 1:100
Assembly diagrams of two of the main types of frames, and shapes taken by such assemblies after bending.
Bamboo members have an average thickness of 60 mm. Original bamboo member directions are expressed by DN (bottom end) and UP (upper end).
Foundation beam height is FB1 top edge; design to fit GL + 720 mm (A1, A2, and A3 junction core is the top edge of FB1–30 mm).
The joints legend represents the colour of the marking tape at the time of scribing.
The axis drawing is counter-clockwise from 00 to 47.
The upper/lower relation of ground setting is A1, A2, and A4 on FB1 and FB2.

The project was compliant with the safety level requested for temporary buildings by the Building Standard Law. The prefectural government therefore issued a permit for four years; the civil servant in charge took responsibility for not forwarding the application to the national government as well. After its expiration, the permit was renewed for another three-and-a-half years. Apparently, the Bamboo Ark is thus far the only example of a load-bearing bamboo structure that has been granted a construction permit in Japan.

To build the Ark, Toki spent about 800,000 yen (roughly 6,000 €) from his own research funds. Formally, the owner of the building was Toki's university lab. An agreement with the landlord was never signed as there was a relationship of trust between them. Volunteers offered their labour and others donated some material, such as the fabric that envelopes the structure and the sandwich panels. Two construction workshops were held, the first from 9 to 25 September and the second from 15 to 26 October 2011. About seventy people joined the workshops, including graduate students and social workers, for a total of 403 days.

The first step was to remove the debris from the site, and to level the ground with picks and shovels. No underground foundation was specified as it was not possible to use concrete foundations; instead, compression-resistant metal sandwich panels (500x500 mm) were placed below both ends of the base trusses, i.e., at the foot of the main columns. The elements used for the foundation were chosen by occasion: they are thermal insulators for refrigerators (two double-sided galvanised barium steel plates with urethane insulation in between) that were intended to be thrown away as industrial waste, but were instead donated to Toki's team. Any other slab with a certain stiffness would have been fine for the task.

The structure consists of forty-eight radially arranged frames, composed of a base truss (later covered by a floor) [→■7] and of a vertical structure that consists of arches. Each is different in shape but based on three configurations: two arched members (A1+A2); three arched members (A1+A4+A2); or two arched members (A1+A2) connected by an under-arch tie in split bamboo (A3) to form a longer span and supported at one end by a column (C1). [→■8] The split bamboo element A3 is juxtaposed to the round bamboo member A1 or A2 so that their curvatures match; they are then tied tightly with rope. By adjusting the position of the notch in the base truss upper and lower chord members, the incline of the columns and arches which had been determined in advance was obtained. The notched joint—joint type d) described above—was used only at these 192 places, because carving a half fishmouth requires precision and labour. It was nonetheless necessary to prevent slippage and increase strength and stiffness at a joint which bears a non-negligible reaction force (0.7–0.9 kN) due to the initial bending process. In fact, after joining the arch members and the column (if any) to the base truss, the arch elements were bent toward a predetermined intersection point and joined in such a position. The whole process was performed with the frame lying flat on the ground where the calculated curve had been marked. Since *mōsō* tends to warp and bend, it was sometimes difficult to accurately reproduce the shape as designed. The tolerance was set at 50 mm; priority was given to reproducing the framework shape precisely at the perimeter of the building to create a continuous surface for the membrane.

The assembled frames were sequentially placed at predetermined positions, and the base trusses of adjacent frames were connected to each other at the outer end, using additional reticular elements in *madake* to prevent them from tipping over. [→■9] Each truss was then ballasted with twelve bags, each containing 30 kg of dirt. [→■10]

Except those at the base truss, all joints between round bamboos were type c) described above; the total number of these joints was over 3,500, each employing 6 to 8 m of rope depending on the diameter of the bamboos. Tape was only used where slippage could occur.

The apexes of all frames lie on a flat surface that has a certain angle of inclination from the horizontal; on such plane a lenticular truss frame was laid, which constitutes the top of the building. This 'roof' has a distorted circular shape and is constituted by truss structures in both X and Y directions; the upper and

[→■9]

[→■10]

[→■11]

lower chords of these trusses are bent into arches. The trusses are held together by a perimeter ring consisting of a double reciprocal structure made of 2-m-long elements. The span of the trusses increases from the centre to the sides at a 1.6 ratio at each step. [→■11] Since the membrane at the top of the roof was poor in stretchability and because it was difficult to introduce tension, they arranged four rows of stainless-steel strands at 45° angles in order to brace the roof structure. The structure was then assembled on the ground, a waterproof membrane was added, and finally it was craned up in place so as to connect with the intersections at the apexes of each frame. [→■12]

In the second workshop, *madake* joists were used to level out the unevenness of the foundation trusses, and then a floor was created by screwing the same sandwich panels used for the foundation plates onto these joists. [→■13] In the central and the peripheral parts of the building, as well as on the deck protruding on the east side, floors were made of round bamboo canes. [→■15] The floor was located at 0.8 m above the ground.

A highly stretchable polyester fibre membrane—a single sheet 40 m long and 6 m wide and weighing 90 kg—was tied at 300-mm intervals to the frame at the top (the membrane is sewn back on itself, forming a hem, and has eyelets through which a rope can pass), then unfolded from the middle to both sides and stretched until it was possible to fix it to the lower edge of the frame so as to wrap the entire building. [→■14] The membrane was then attached to each arch with a series of plastic snap buttons fixed to webbings that had been sewn on in advance at regular intervals. [→■17] There were, obviously, differences between nominal and real dimensions, but these differences remained tolerable and adjustable thanks to the flexibility of the membrane and the bamboo.

The membrane, in addition to filtering the light, had a structural role; indeed, from a structural point of view, the building was not complete without it. In fact, the cutting pattern was designed 10% smaller than the surface that it was meant to cover, such that by fixing it a predetermined tension (100 N/m) was introduced, stiffening the whole structure. The frames of the Ark could only take planar loads; loads from every direction were borne by each of the forty-eight frames according to their position and distributed in the whole structure. If the entire building was subject to rotation, such stress was resisted by the in-plane rigidity of the outer tension sheet.

The reaction force at both ends of the tensile membrane was borne by two panels made of split bamboos intertwined in an oblique lattice pattern. [→■9,16] Each panel spanned four frames and was fixed to them with wire and rope.

The Ark was essentially a pavilion, unheated and unequipped with water. The initial intention to build a small complex around it was cancelled, both because it was not really indispensable and to avoid the burden of maintenance. During the seven-and-a-half years of its service life, Toki and his students went there two or three times a year to monitor and maintain it, especially in the aftermath of typhoons or heavy snowfalls. They did not worry about protecting the bamboo; instead, they carried out periodic maintenance activities, replacing the damaged parts if needed. The need for repairs increased over time. In the first four years one or two repairs were carried out. In the fifth, it was ten. From the sixth year on, many bamboos at the base of the arches had broken. By the end, about half of the arch elements had been reinforced. The damaged members were strengthened by adjoining green new bamboo pieces extending 1 m in each direction from the fracture, or by juxtaposing split bamboo pieces, without removing the broken ones. In some cases it was deemed sufficient to reinforce elements with longitudinal cracks by wrapping them in cloth tape. In addition, they found that the tape itself deteriorated over time. However, this did not necessarily lead to a reduction in structural performance. The ends of the horizontal bamboo used for the decking, which protrude and get wet, had often deteriorated. Finally, after seven years, the bamboo members of the frames had begun to sag, which meant that the membrane no longer stretched tautly across it.

While there are many studies of the strength of bamboo, there are few related to examining its durability. Toki and Nagai carried out tests on the material

[→■12]

[→■13]

[→■14]

[→■15]

[→■17]

[→■16]

obtained from disassembly, which they then compiled into reports. [→B213] They regularly performed tests to investigate the changes in structural performance of the replaced elements and compared the results with those obtained in previous years. In the undamaged parts, the material did not show a significant decrease in tensile strength. Horn beetles damaged sections of the bamboo, however, and the parts that were exposed directly to sunlight had dried excessively, causing cracks. [→B312] In addition, the dismantling of the Ark offered the rare occasion to perform destructive tests on the standing structure: the building was loaded and pulled with a crane to understand the change in performance.

After the reconstruction of the Kō-min-kan community centre in 2017, the dancers went to rehearse there again, so the Ark was used just occasionally. And while the local community had developed an affection for it, they nonetheless always associated the Ark with the tsunami. Thus, when it was finally dismantled, they were glad to no longer live with a reminder of the catastrophe. From the outset, Toki had envisioned the Ark as a temporary structure. One section did, however, remain. At the request of the community, they preserved the deck, which had been extended to provide more space for outdoor gatherings.

About 2 km from the Bamboo Ark, in 2012 Toki and his crew built the Bamboo Ark # 2, another open-stage construction with a port location. It was disassembled after four years. [→B81] Moreover, since 2013 Toki and his students have been designing and constructing a Bamboo Park in Bodaiji 菩提寺 (Konan City 湖南市, Shiga prefecture 滋賀県). Plans for the park grew out of a project related to managing, with the aid of older residents, a community-owned bamboo forest. The Park goes on enriching itself with playful structures which create a small collection of experiments in bamboo construction located along walking paths. Some of them, such as the 'Dragon' or 'Bamboo House' and the 'Bamboo House II' are supported by living bamboo piles, which means that when a cane is dead and no longer offers reliable support, it is simply replaced by another one, which has grown nearby in the meantime. [→■18] The joints employed in the Bamboo Park are the same as those in the Bamboo Ark. The Bamboo Park also requires maintenance, but in this case the local community participates in its upkeep. [→■19] In addition to older members of the community, students from grade school on also join in, as do Toki lab students, since the park is not too far from the University of Shiga Prefecture campus.

Toki cares a great deal about the social impact of these constructions. He conceives of them as tools for supporting local communities. For him, continuous activities of and with the local people count more than the buildings themselves. This is the reason why he is not particularly interested in building more bamboo structures. Such a focus would decrease the intensity and quality of his contribution to the community.

Now, Toki's main aim is to apply the experience with the Bamboo Ark to the design of a permanent structure. His team has just started a five-year research programme on a bamboo structure that anybody could build. He is developing a new type of joint that will be free to slip and change the shape of the structure. Neither rope nor bolts will be used. He also plans to establish a protocol for the structure's maintenance, since durability is the most relevant requirement in bamboo structures, and a maintenance-free bamboo construction is not possible.

[→■18]

[→■19]

Passive performance: Biestøa

Andrea Bocco Guarneri and Giuseppe Salomone

Gaia group, a team of ecological architects, was established in 1983. The architects' families began to buy old, unoccupied farmhouses and land in Lista, a peninsula along the southern Norwegian coast, laying the foundations for a small community. One of the founding principles of the group was the insistence on 'breathing' constructions and on natural ventilation; another was that the group could not only design houses, but also build them, as it included architects/carpenters such as Rolf Jacobsen and Dag Roalkvam. In 1990, the Gaia group (later, Gaia Lista) **[→B359]** initiated Gaia international to form a broader group made up of ecological designers from thirteen countries, **[→B239]** among whom were David Pearson, Declan and Margrit Kennedy, Howard Liddell, Varis Bokalders, **[→B47]** and Joachim Eble.
Bjørn Berge is one of the founders of the Gaia group. He has developed a specialised knowledge about building with natural materials. He is the author of the most authoritative book on the subject, *The Ecology of Building Materials*, whose first Norwegian edition appeared in 1992. **[→B25]** Among Berge's basic principles is avoiding proprietary systems and product-based solutions in general, which do not serve ecological objectives but economic ones. He is not interested in doing research for companies nor in developing products and patents.

Moreover, he has been conducting research on alternative techniques for the *Passivhaus* as commonly understood, also borrowing concepts from traditional houses, such as the stratification of layers; a warm central core; and the contraction and expansion of the inhabited area depending on the season. His most advanced research piece on the subject is titled "Absolute passive energy design. Achieving passive house level by utilising hygrothermal properties of wood", or helTREnkelt ('simply wood') for short. **[→B27]** The research was a response to new Norwegian regulations which stipulate that all new buildings must comply with *Passivhaus* energy standards. To meet these, thermal insulation, airtightness and thermal bridges have to be taken into account. The new regulations also require buildings to have a mechanical ventilation system with heat recovery. This model is the only one being considered.

Berge and his research partners wanted to see whether the *Passivhaus* standard could be achieved through passive, unconventional measures, the sort of which are not included in mainstream methodologies for energy consumption assessment. In their opinion, the advantages of limiting technical installations would be many: robustness (no moving parts, independence from energy supply), low embodied energy (limited use of metals and plastics), user friendliness (a noise-free and adaptable system, with reduced monitoring and maintenance needs), low construction and maintenance costs. **[→B27:6]**

The design methodology proposed is based on what Berge dubs the "Lima pyramid", comprising four phases:

- Adapt: measures that can be applied to use, divert or redirect environmental energy flows, e.g., by exploiting latent heat from moisture in the air, and wind for cooling;
- Reduce: measures for further reduction of energy demand that cannot be met through adaptation, e.g., locating rooms requiring a lower temperature level adjacent to the perimeter walls;
- Stabilise: optimising the energy flows in relation to daytime use and local climate patterns, e.g., evening out the indoor temperature and humidity levels by using effective materials and layout;
- Select system: heating and ventilation systems are considered to meet the needs not addressed by the steps above, e.g., ventilation and energy distribution based on differences in wind, pressure, and temperature.

According to Berge's concept, as already affirmed by Per Krusche, **[→B168]** the building will be composed of several room 'layers'. A first building envelope protects against wind and weather. A second is the boundary between heated and unheated volume. This makes it possible to avoid negative pressure areas. In addition, there should be large ventilation openings in the outer envelope, but not in the inner one. Thanks to the materials used, the inner envelope should nonetheless be very permeable to vapour.

One of the main measures considered in helTREnkelt is the use of timber's hygrothermal storage properties, of its ability "to stabilise the moisture level in the indoor air, and prevent moisture loads on surfaces and structures." **[→B27:5]** In addition, he notes that porous materials allow to take advantage of latent heat in water vapour. This energy can be recovered by condensation in hygroscopic surface materials instead of being expelled through the ventilation exhausts. The process raises both the air temperature in the room and the surface temperature of the material. The reverse process can be used for cooling. **[→B27:25]** Hygroscopic materials are nine times more effective than mechanical ventilation at dealing with indoor humidity. **[→B178:34]**

Hygrothermal mass can also be used to capture and temporarily store solar energy. The efficiency and duration of the process will increase inversely with the timber's ability to dry out. This solution is efficient if the building is equipped with a separate 'conditioning' room that will supply the building with air, such as a south-facing conservatory with large hygroscopic capacity where leafy plants provide moisture as the temperature increases. This, in turn, binds large amounts of energy that can be used to heat the remaining rooms after sunset. **[→B27:47,48]** This principle is applied in one of Berge's most recent works, a house in Nordhassel, close to Borhaug **[→▪1]**, and will eventually appear in Biestøa too, where the clients are building a conservatory.

[→▪1]

HelTREnkelt research stopped at the end of the first phase, and this is why only the first report is available. For one reason or another, pilot buildings were

[→■2]

not built. Industry and, consequently, the Norwegian state have not shown an interest in funding research or promoting systems that do without machines and other things that can be marketed. Sustainability is fine, but economic growth is more important.

The quality of indoor air in airtight buildings is often poor because of chemical and synthetic products, toxins, radon, and positive ions, which mechanical ventilation does not always eliminate effectively. Long-term consequences range from allergies to metabolic disorders and even cancer. Breathable materials of natural origin help prevent such risks by introducing dynamic insulation or the 'pore-ventilation' method, which makes the roof work like a gigantic heat exchanger, whose U-value is close to 0. Liddell, a long-time friend of Berge, explained that air is drawn into a room from above the ceiling through a fine, waterproof, yet breathable membrane and through the thermal insulation in the roof:

> As this air enters the room through the whole ceiling area—almost as a fine, slow-moving aerosol—it has already taken up the heat that was going out through the ceiling and has also dehumidified. While the natural stack effect at the extract end can be used to induce the air to go through the membrane, this system usually comprises both an input and output very low-power fans. **[→B178:83]**

Such a system is in operation both in Biestøa and in the recent extension of Berge's own house, Farahuset, in Jølle.

Berge is also convinced that living in a homogeneous Passivhaus indoor environment is not good for one's health: the body is made to withstand different strains, and the immune system is stimulated if it has to cope with temperature differences even within a house. In his words, "Health is the power to react ... to all environmental changes ... [it] is the result of resilience, of the ability to adapt: to cold, to hunger, to different foods". **[→B29:43,258]** Berge recognises such positive value of differences and therefore details parietal surfaces and floors so that the body can perceive them, even when moving within the same room.
He is also interested in knowing how his buildings behave over time. He maintains relationships with homeowners and pupils to know if the houses and schools he has designed work well. In his opinion, effectiveness lies in people's behaviour, more than in technological solutions.

Pearson, another of Berge's friends, recounted that at Lista, "farmers discovered that a tree planted at the rear of the house grew into a shape that helped the wind flow past more easily". **[→B239:90]** **[→■3]** This can be seen at the west end of Farahuset. Careful observation of the extremely windy location and the intro-

[→■3]

duction of measures inspired by the vernacular tradition helped Berge develop a capacity to design with the wind which is in my opinion unsurpassed at any latitude. Berge makes impressive use of extremely low-tech, yet effective simulation tools to study the interaction between the building and the wind. His masterpiece is without doubt the Trekkfuglbu på Lista fyr, a cabin built for the observation of migratory birds that sits just beneath the Lista firehouse. **[→■2]** The cabin is open towards the sea, which means it faces against the prevailing wind which can be really strong there. The framed timber construction offers a perfect shelter against it: the form of the roof and deflective panels at the sides create turbulences that divert the wind and make it 'jump' over the cabin.

The house under consideration in this chapter is located in Grimstad, a maritime town of about 23,000 inhabitants on the Skagerrak, in the county of Aust-Adger, about 50 km northeast of Kristiansand.

[→■4]

The owners, Roar Ousland and Marit Grinaker Smith, are not originally from the area. They were drawn to it because of the relatively low real estate prices, compared to the main urban areas in Norway: despite the gorgeous location along the coast, Grimstad is too far from Oslo to come for just the weekend.
The couple are an ordinary, middle-class family, not particularly wealthy; their home contains two apartments: they occupy the upper one and during the school year, they rent out the one below, in the basement, to university students, and during the summer to tourists.
Ousland and Grinaker Smith played an integral role in the creation of the building. They were involved at all stages, from design to construction. They not only worked closely with the architect and monitored the construction work, but they also carried out some minor tasks themselves, thereby reducing the costs of construction, if only slightly. [→B377]
Energy efficiency was not their main concern; they wanted foremost to maximise the use of natural materials (to minimise embodied energy and toxicity), and to employ low-tech solutions (to minimise maintenance work and to be able to directly control the systems). In response to their requests, Berge adopted the helTREnkelt approach.

The house is not far from the town centre, on a site called Biestøa where a small group of houses stands a short distance from the sea. [→■4] The building—along with its access courtyard, garage, and western terrace—occupies the northern half of a small plot (759 m^2). It sits at about 14 m a.m.s.l. on a gentle slope, which is why the basement is underground on the north and west sides, while the south and east façades overlook an unfenced garden. On this side, the borders between different properties are almost unnoticeable. The garden is richly planted with apple trees, berry bushes, and herbs, and there is also a vegetable garden. [→■5] As is the local custom, neighbours freely enjoy each other's green spaces, even gathering and picking plants growing on their properties. Grinaker Smith is an agronomist by training and takes care of the garden; she also dries some of the produce—her dried strawberries are just delightful. [→■6]
The composition of the volumes stems from the need to shield the house from the prevailing winds that blow from different directions depending on the season, and to maximise southern exposure, granting access to the best view. Essentially, the house is rectangular in plan and has a single-pitched roof with a slope of 28°. To this main volume are added smaller constructions that provide a variety of functions. To the north and northeast, lower volumes contain storage spaces and a place to lay out the linen and are also covered with a single pitch roof sloping to the north. In the southeastern corner a loggia progressively opens up towards the sun. A garage adjoins the house on the north side, with a narrow passage sandwiched in between; its roof looks like the continuation of the storage rooms' roofs, which are located on the other side of the passageway. [→■8] The combination of such elementary volumes creates a pleasant and original assembly. [→■7]
The cold winds from the northeast are opposed by the volume of the garage, which is shaped and positioned to deflect them. The buffer spaces are also juxtaposed to the northeast side of the building, acting as windshields. On the eastern façade, the balcony, and thus the entire house, is protected by a semi-open diaphragm consisting of timber laths. [→■9] This solution, as simple as it is effective, is the result of Berge's studies, who came to the conclusion that a fence with a closed/open ratio equal to 70/30% can nullify the wind almost entirely. To the

[→■5]

west, at the plot's boundary, there is a low beautiful wooden fence that deflects the wind, making the terrace more enjoyable and providing a sense of intimacy. [→■7,11]
In spite of the measures to protect it from the wind, the building is all but introverted; its front façade is exposed to the true south, allowing it to take full advantage of the heat from the sun; [→■10] the balcony and several windows—larger to the south, progressively smaller to the north—afford views in all directions.
Solar irradiation passively heats the indoor environment thanks to the large windows on the south façade. [→■12] In intermediate seasons occasional overheating actually occurs, but opening the two French windows on the east and west façades for some time is enough to dissipate it. At the moment,

[→■6]

no shading device has been implemented yet. The partition wall on the north side of the living room is directly hit by the sun during winter and is soon to be doubled with an unfired brick leaf to function as a thermal storage mass. The bricks are neatly stacked in the living room and already partially perform their function of mass accumulation. A small greenhouse is about to be built against the basement's south wall, which will make it possible to grow flowers and herbs and to preheat the air coming in from outside.

The layout of the rooms balances functionality, usability, flexibility, and energy efficiency. The house consists of two floors above ground (75 m^2 on the first floor, 35 m^2 on the second) where the owners live, and a basement containing a mechanical room and a small apartment (41 m^2). [→■13]
The main access is to the north, in a hollow carved out of the rather compact volume, under a balcony. A small buffer precedes a hallway, where the staircase is and from where the bathroom and the full-height living room can be accessed. [→■14] The living room, which also contains the kitchen at the east end, is the core of the house and has an almost fully glazed south wall (according to the owners, the kitchen is the room to stay, but the space for food preparation is very small, so they had it one with the living room, without partitions and with the same wooden flooring). To the northeast is a room for music and TV which serves also as a guestroom and loom room; the absence of a door makes it more a nook of the living room than an autonomous space. This room might easily be adapted into the master bedroom with direct access from the staircase, which would be useful if the owners had reduced mobility and could not easily climb the stairs anymore. Another feature introduced upon demand of the clients is a sliding, mirrored wall that gives direct access to the laundry room from the bathroom. Here is where the linen cycle begins with the sorting by colour and washing temperature; clothes and stuff are then taken and washed in the laundry, and after that laid out in the laundry itself or in the adjoining double-height buffer space, where it dries; [→■15] a system of pulleys allows to hoist up the linen which is taken down from the walk-in closet upstairs, where it is stored.

[→■7]

[→■8]

[→■9]

[→■10]

[→■11]

[→■12]

[→■13]
Second, first and ground floor plans, scale 1:200

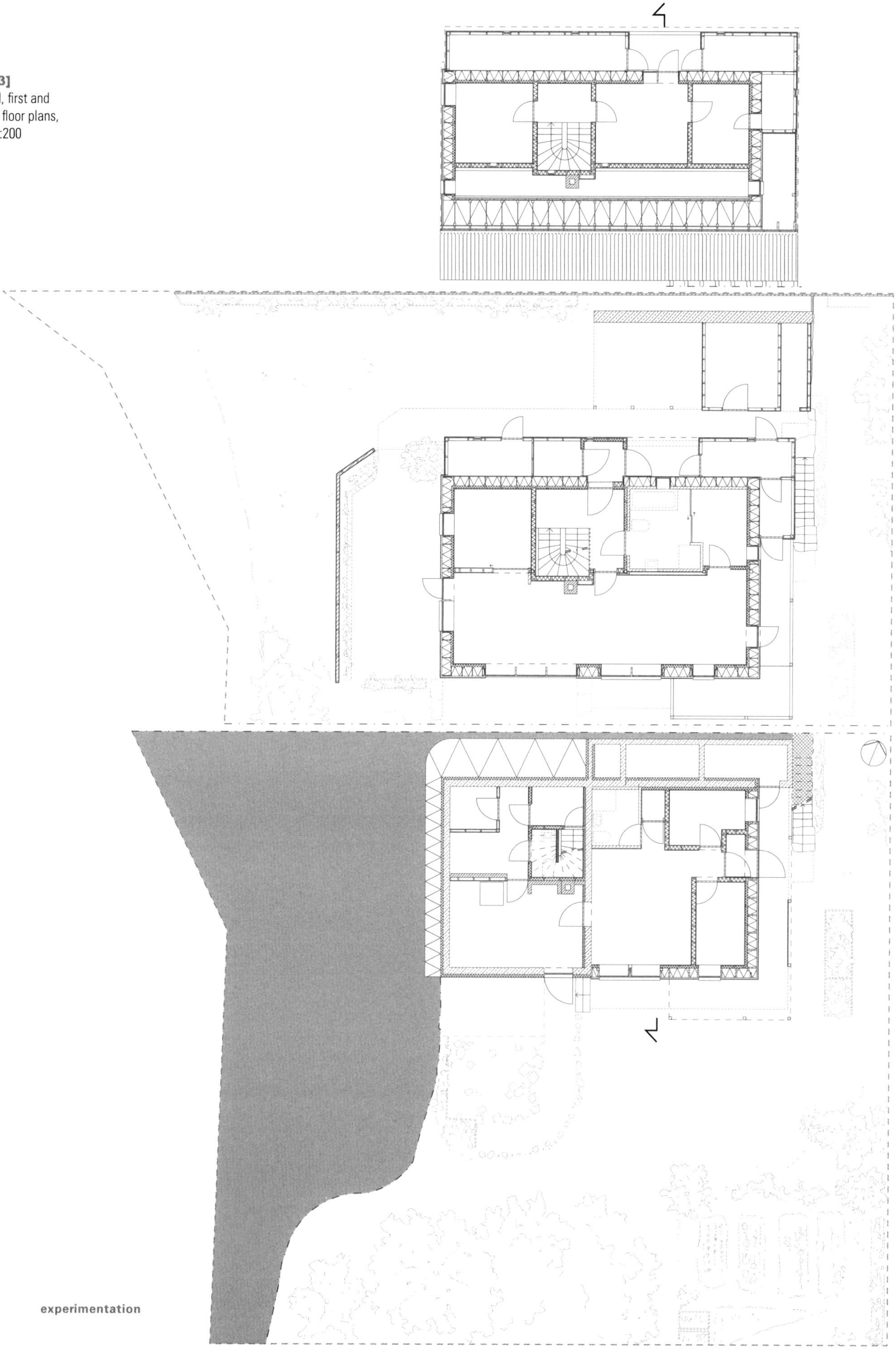

Upstairs are a study, the master bedroom and a walk-in closet connected to it; the first two have diminutive windows facing the living room, essentially for ventilation purposes. [→■16] The bedroom is connected to a balcony above the entrance.
While the plan may appear simple, the house offers an extraordinary wealth of niches and nooks, both indoors and out. Not even in a house designed by Gio Ponti could one find such an abundance of intimate spaces. [→B177] In addition, the Biestøa House offers a lot of spaces for storage, some of them very tiny.
The small apartment on the ground floor sleeps five and consists of a living room with a kitchen, two bedrooms, a bathroom, and a closet. It has raw concrete walls and a polished concrete floor.

The inconsistency of the soil in the south east corner required use of 12-m-deep pile foundations. This issue led to increased costs and to delays in the date of completion.
The underground walls are blocks made of expanded clay, which are separated from the ground by a layer of loose expanded clay. This was meant to limit the heat loss and improve water drainage. Both the walls and the floor are insulated with a 100-mm stone wool layer.
The structure is a timber frame with the exception of a few steel beams, a change introduced by the contractor who did not trust the original structural calculations. [→■17]
Walls are clad in high-quality spruce, acquired from a local sawmill: the vertical planks were obtained from the heartwood of selected mature plants (more than 100 years old) grown under difficult conditions that result in timber with a very fine grain and close growth rings. No treatment or varnish were used; the durability of untreated wood is enhanced by the marine environment, as salty wind impregnates it. To facilitate the evaporation of rain water, the cladding is spaced 100 mm from the perimeter walls, while the minimum distance between the lower edge of the planks and the ground is 0.3 m. The periodic tightening of the screws is the only maintenance required on the façade.
Under the ventilation gap lies a wood fibre layer impregnated with asphalt (12 mm). The insulation is loose wood fibre, blown to a relatively high density (it is assumed not to settle) in the 350-mm cavity between the perimeter wall. This space contains the load-bearing structure. The internal wall is made of wood fibre boards (100 mm), a gypsum board that acts as a vapour barrier (6.5 mm), and of internal pine cladding (14 mm). The roof has a similar layering, but the insulation is 500 mm thick; the ceiling consists of high-density gypsum and vegetal fibre panels (100 mm), which are plastered with gypsum and finished with a silicate paint; the roofing is made of fifty-year-old slates recovered from an abandoned building. [→■18]
The decks of the west terrace and the balconies are pine boards (heartwood only), impregnated with their own resin. This treatment costs about as much as wood treated with synthetic substances and guarantees durability.
The house has an impressive amount of windows, some of which are very small. [→■19,20] They are high-efficiency windows (U=0.7 W/m^{2}K) and, in a typical Berge touch, the frames were painted a bright orange, making them stand out next to the timber cladding that quickly turns grey. Some windows are split into two panes and are provided with both vertical and horizontal hinges to allow air to flow towards the ceiling without causing downward indoor currents. Window sills are protected by metal flashings. The gaps between the counterframe and the load-bearing structure were filled with cellulose fibre in rolls.
With the exception of the ceiling and the walls of the bathroom, internal surfaces are pine wood; the wall boards are arranged vertically to avoid the accumulation of dust at the joints and to make cleaning easier. The wood has been impregnated with linseed oil and whitened with lime lye (NaOH): it protects it and makes the indoor space lighter without closing the wood's pores. The systematic use of breathable surface materials, namely timber, brings a number of benefits to the indoor environment of the Biestøa House, as theorised in the helTREnkelt report:

- The capacity of wood to quickly absorb moisture while emitting heat when water changes from a gaseous to a liquid state is particularly useful for heating bathrooms. A higher temperature is actually needed just immediately after showering, and a temporary increase of 2–5°C

[→■14]

[→■15]

[→■16]

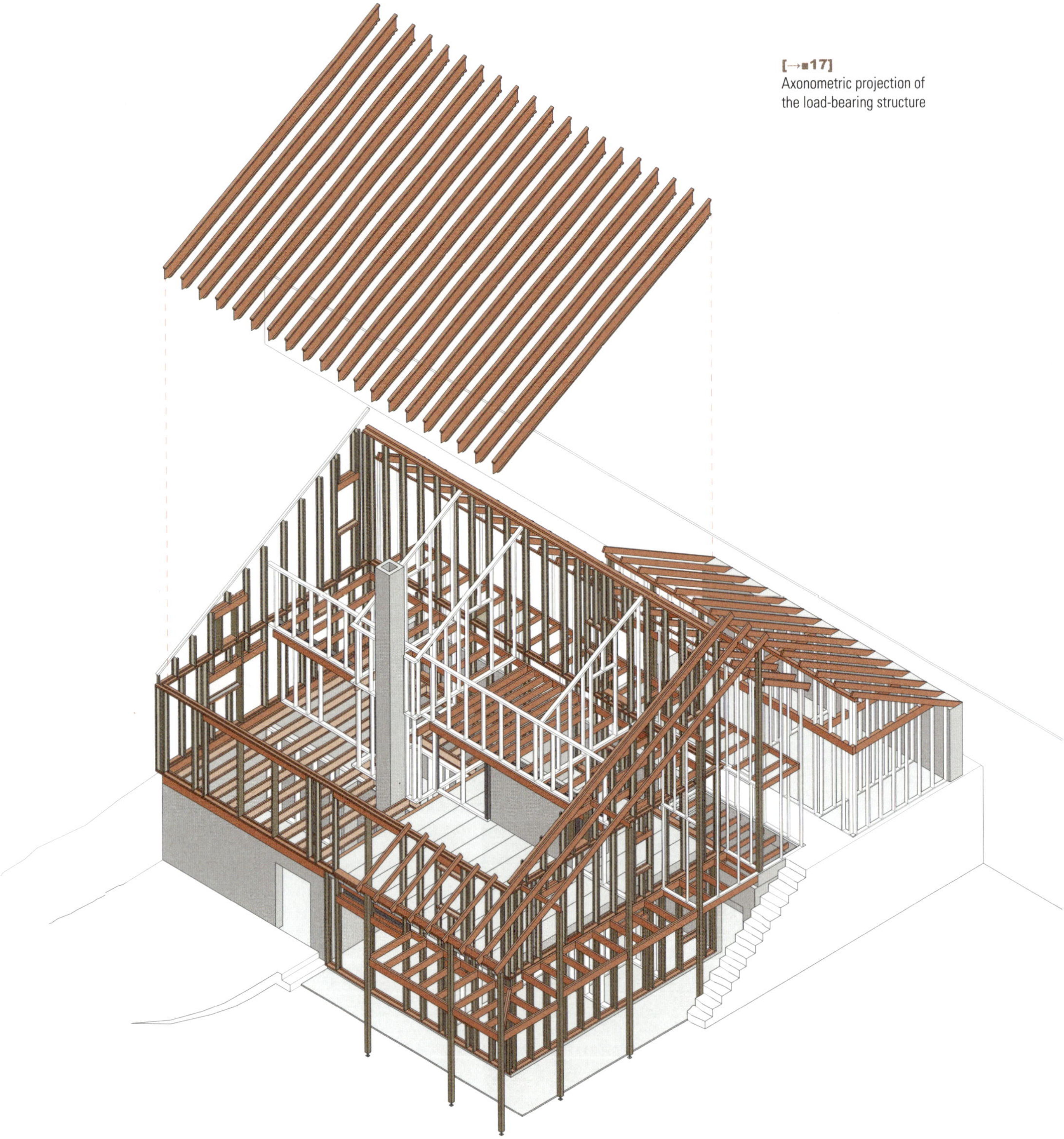

[→■17]
Axonometric projection of the load-bearing structure

can be achieved at that time thanks to the latent heat released by the timber cladding. [→B164:46]

- In humid environments, wood has a significant heat storage capacity; only the outermost part of the wood is moistened; the backside of the material works as an insulator and ensures that the energy is mainly radiated back into the room. [→B27:46]
- By stabilising the indoor air humidity, timber surfaces reduce ventilation requirements and the risk of mould formation. The RH decrease improves air quality perception: this property is

particularly effective in bedrooms, where humidity can reach very high levels.

Construction costs were higher than estimated, due to the introduction of pile foundations and the underestimation of the time needed on the contractor's side, as well as his bad organisation. There were also mistakes in the implementation, some of them risky (cladding on the west façade was too low; the waterproof membrane was not turned up at the edge of the slopes ...). There was a dispute, won by the clients (the contractor asked for 1 million NOK more); and the contractor had to fix some flaws at his own expense. The final construction cost was around 4 million NOK (roughly 410,000 €).

The only heated rooms are the bathroom, equipped with underfloor heating, and the living room where a small, 200W electric heater is occasionally used in winter. The owners would love to have a fireplace or a stove, but have not yet installed it, also because they fear overheating.
The winter temperature of the living room is maintained between 20 and 22°C, while in the bedroom the temperature does not exceed 16°C for explicit choice of the residents. Even in mid-winter they sleep with the window open or at least ajar (they use heavy duvets). This allows the evacuation of CO_2 but has negative consequences on the energy behaviour of the house, even if the interior walls are insulated and the door is kept closed. A worst-case test was carried out by a group of students at the University of Grimstad. They kept the door, vent, and window closed, while two people slept for seven hours in the room. CO_2 levels went up from 368 to 3571 ppm, with a temperature increase from 15.3 to 19.6°C, but RH just rose from 42.3 to 49.6%, demonstrating the cladding's thermohygroscopic capacity. **[→B254,223]**
As a consequence of temperature stratification, if one opens the tiny windows at the top of the partition wall, warm air is taken from the top of the living room and is introduced into the bedroom and study on the upper floor: the living area thus acts as a sort of conservatory for the rest of the house.
The ventilation of the rooms is entrusted entirely to the control of the users by opening the windows and the management of a natural ventilation system through a series of adjustable valves located in all rooms. The indoor ventilation system takes up fresh air on the southern façade. The rising air is delivered into the living room through a manually adjustable vent, and from there it flows to the other rooms. Vents extract stale air from the mechanical room and the bathroom in the basement, the laundry and the bathroom on the ground floor, and the study and the bedroom on the upper floor; air is expelled through ducts that come out of the roof near the ridge. The laundry room is equipped with an additional pair of nozzles which allow to ventilate it even when the door is closed. This system is sufficient to dispose of excess humidity, even in the moister rooms, without having to open the windows.
The height of the living room removes the stale air and the pollutants contained in it; two windows are strategically placed high on the eastern and western walls to allow for a rapid air exchange.
In sum, everything works manually, without energy input and noise. The other side of the coin is that the occupants have to assume an active and conscious control of the house, and the lack of sensors means they must learn how to perceive the changing environmental conditions and react accordingly, as it happens when you steer a sailboat, borrowing Glenn Murcutt's words. **[→B90]** Over the years, the owners have fine-tuned their understanding of the house and adapted their use of it accordingly. For example, they found that opening downstairs for 5' while brushing their teeth before going to sleep produces healthier air quality, especially in winter, and does not affect thermal comfort as the heat is contained in the building, not in the air.

The 850-l tank in the basement, supplied by 24 m^2 solar collectors on the roof as long as the sun allows (from March to October), feeds the domestic hot water system and the underfloor heating system of the bathroom and the living unit in the basement. In summer the heat is used perhaps for one-and-a-half hours; for the rest of the day, the hot water produced by the collectors is discharged. A larger tank would have been allowed to store more water but would have cost more and would have entailed risks of overheating. The system does not work under pressure

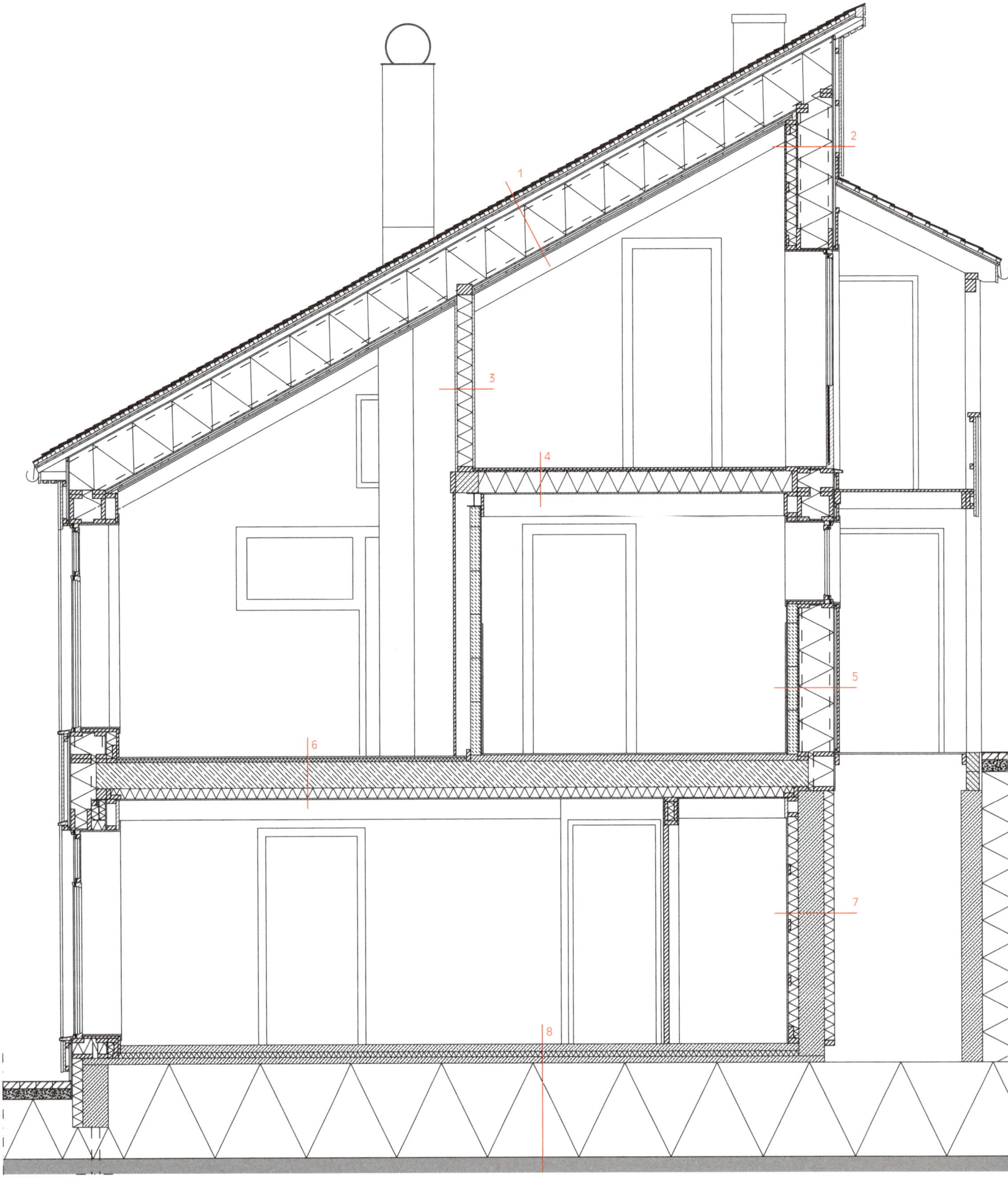
1
2
3
4
5
6
7
8

[→■19]

[→■18] left page
Section, scale 1:50

1 10 mm slates ; 30/48 mm battens; 18/18 mm counterbattens; felt; 15 mm board decking; 48/48 mm battens; 12 mm asphalt membrane; windproof sheet; 400 mm I-beams + 370–400 mm wood fibre flakes insulation; windproof sheet; 12 mm wood fibre panels; 18/120 mm laths; 18/120 mm laths; 2x15 mm fibreglass panels; silicate paint

2 22 mm vertical wood strips on joints; 22 mm untreated timber siding; 36/48 mm battens; 18/36 mm furring strip; 12 mm asphalt membrane; windproof sheet; 300 mm I-beams + 270–300 mm wood fibre flakes insulation; 12 mm wood fibre panels; windproof sheet; 50/100 mm battens + 25/100 mm counterbattens + 100 mm wood fibre flakes insulation; kraft paper; 14 mm timber cladding

3 14 mm timber siding; kraft paper; 150/50 mm studs + 150 wood fibre flakes insulation; kraft paper; 14 mm timber cladding

4 21 mm timber floorboards; kraft paper; 15/50 mm @ 65 mm lathing; 200/48 mm @ 300 mm joists + 200 mm wood fibre flakes insulation; windproof sheet; 12 mm timber cladding, planed

5 22 mm untreated timber cladding; 18/36 mm battens; 18/36 mm counterbattens;12 mm asphalt membrane; windproof sheet; 300 mm I-beams + 270–300 mm wood fibre flakes insulation; 12 mm wood fibre panels; windproof sheet; polyethylene radon barrier; 100 mm aerated cement block; 10 mm hydraulic lime; 12 mm glazed ceramic tiles

6 14 mm timber floorboards; 36 mm woodfibre panels; polyethylene radon barrier; 250 mm expanded clay concrete beams; 100 mm wood fibre flakes insulation; windproof sheet; 12 mm timber cladding, planed

7 100 mm stonewool; 250 mm reinforced concrete wall; 100/50 mm battens + 25/100 mm counterbattens + 100 mm wood fibre flakes insulation; windproof sheet; 12 mm timber cladding

8 70 mm cement screed + electrowelded wire mesh + underfloor heating; polyethylene radon barrier; 50 mm stonewool; 60mm reinforced concrete slab; non-woven fabric; 900 mm expanded clay

and empties automatically when the tank fills up. This means they can avoid using antifreeze additives.
The electrical system is left visible; wires pass between the ventilation pipes in the middle wall of the house, then under the boards at the top of the wall cladding. This necessitates a greater extension of the network, but modifications and inspections are very easy this way: it is sufficient to remove the boards to access the wires.

[→■20]

Analyses carried out in the first two years after construction showed an energy consumption of 80.2 kWh/m^2 in 2013 and 94.5 kWh/m^2 in 2014, which is above the 60 kWh/m^2 threshold for a *Passivhaus*. [→B220] The main causes were: excessive temperature in the rented apartment and in the bathroom; excessive ventilation; the fact that the wood fibre was so dry when purchased that it filled up with moisture when installed and much energy was wasted in the drying process; and dispersion from the hot water tank and some pipes.
Over the next few years, the owners adapted to the house in ways that enabled them to reduce its energy consumption. In 2016 and 2017, the overall annual consumption (heating, hot water, lighting) was around 50 kWh/m^2. These figures refer to the entire house, i.e. they include the rented apartment. Because of the thermal leakage there and the succession of different tenants, perhaps not always sensitive to energy saving, this unit weighs heavily on the general performance.

Food economy system: Kamiyama Food Hub

Andrea Bocco Guarneri

Kamiyama, in Tokushima prefecture 徳島県 (Shikoku island), is a town extending on a surface of 173 km^2 and is made up mostly of hills and low mountains. 86% of the surface is forested, and 70% of the forests are *sugi* 杉 (*Cryptomeria japonica*) and *hinoki* 檜 (*Chamaecyparis obtusa*) trees plantations. Yorii 寄居 and Uetsuno 上角 are the largest settlements and are surrounded by ranges which isolate the municipality from its neighbours. **[→■1,2]** Yorii, where the town hall is located, lies at an altitude of 147 m a.m.s.l. Kamiyama is famous as a producer of *sudachi* citrus fruits (*Citrus sudachi* 酢橘) and plums. Similar to virtually every mountain village in Japan, coniferous tree plantations established after World War II have become unprofitable. It is cheaper to import timber from Canada than to process the local one. In Kamiyama, as in most places, the artificial forests are located on sloping land that is often quite steep and, since they have not been properly managed, are way too thick and have overgrown. At present, less than fifty people are employed in forestry and just 5,000 to 6,000 m^3 of timber are felled annually, while the annual growth rate is 60,000 m^3. A potentially profitable use would be as fuel, rather than for carpentry or furniture-making. There are many deserted houses, but, as is the case throughout Japan, they are rarely made available to newcomers. **[→■4]** The problem is such that a council housing scheme is now under construction. Called the Daejeon Apartment Housing, it was expressly conceived to accommodate young immigrant families. The project is making abundant use of local resources in terms of labour and materials.

The decline in forestry, which had been its main industry, has encouraged emigration, leaving behind an aging population. The population of Kamiyama has fallen to 5,300, about one-fourth of the 1955 population, and the proportion of elderly people is 49%. According to government estimates, the population will fall to 3,000 by 2035, of which the elderly will make up 54%. This echoes a national trend: Japan's population peaked at around 128 million in 2004 and is predicted to fall to 90 million by 2055. **[→B372]** The population is increasingly concentrated in Tokyo, and 896 municipalities are projected to vanish by 2040. **[→B364]** In response to these trends, a "creative depopulation" strategy has been implemented piece-

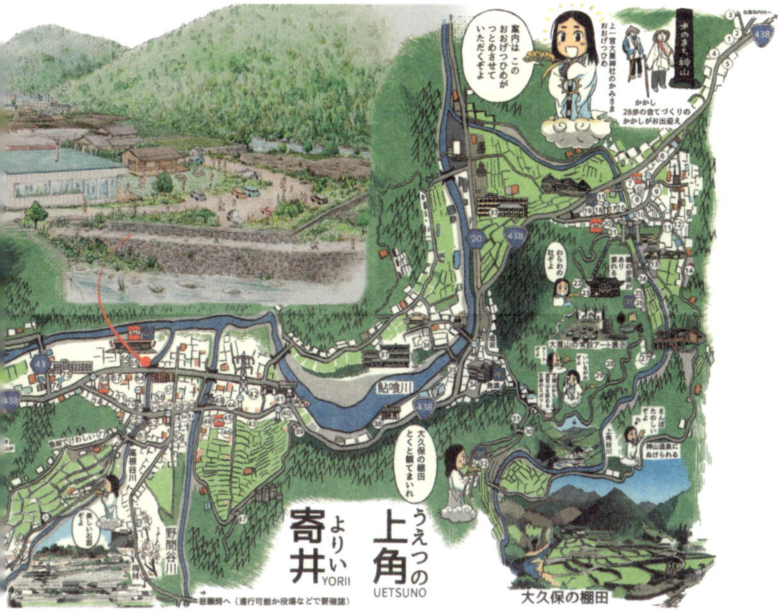
案内は このおおげつひめがつとめさせていただくぞよ
上一宮大粟神社のかみさま おおげつひめ
かかし
28歩の舍てづくりのかかしがお出迎え
鮎喰川
大久保の棚田とくと観てまいれ
神山温泉にぬけられる
上角谷川
大久保の棚田
うえつの
上角
UETSUNO
よりい
寄井
YORII
（通行可能か役場などで要確認）

[→■1]

[→■2]

[→■3]

[→■4]

meal in Kamiyama for the past twenty years under the direction of Ōminami Shinya 大南信也. A study conducted by Tokushima University has shown that in order to keep the elementary school running, five households (of two parents and two children) will have to move to the area every year, and several measures have been adopted to attract new residents. [→B343,362]

Historically, most revitalisation initiatives in Japan have been directed by prefectural and municipal governments. In Kamiyama, however, ambitious initiatives have been conceived and managed from the bottom-up. These measures began in 1992, when a group of concerned citizens established a non-profit organisation (NPO) called Kamiyama International Exchange Association. They launched KAIR, an artists-in-residence programme, which continues to thrive to this day. [→■3] KAIR was successful in putting Kamiyama on the cultural map, and its renown has increasingly spread within Japan and beyond its borders, even outside of the contemporary art circles. Yet, the project remains small enough to be managed by a grassroots organisation.

In 2004, the International Exchange Association established an NPO called Green Valley (now Green Valley, Inc.), which later started a website to attract prospective residents. Yoshimoto Mitsuhiro 吉本光宏 aptly observed that if it were run by a local government, such an initiative would typically limit itself to asking about the size of the family and the kind of house they were looking for and trying to find matching properties. Green Valley, by contrast, proactively sought specific profiles deemed necessary for the town's future and invited people who fit those profiles to come to Kamiyama and start their businesses.

Bandō Kōsuke 坂東幸輔 and Suma Issei 須磨一清 are two young architects who were recruited by Green Valley to remodel vacant buildings to accommodate such businesses. In 2010, they refurbished a workspace for web designers and IT programmers. Several such businesses, like Engawa 縁側, moved to Kamiyama over the following years. [→■5] The partnership Bandō and Suma established, Bus Architects バスアーキテクツ, was soon commissioned to manage several renovation projects and to design a new guesthouse called WEEK. They were also selected to be among the Japanese representatives at the 15th Biennale di Venezia. [→B32] "Food-related businesses that show care in selecting natural ingredients have also taken root." [→B343] A pizza restaurant, a delicatessen, a French bistro, a coffee roastery, a beer brewery, and shops selling organic food have all opened in recent years. Many other creative, craft-based businesses—from custom-made shoes for people with special orthopaedic needs to fabrics dyed with natural pigments—have also opened.

Yoshimoto suggests that such diverse and talented people were "attracted by the 'creative atmosphere'. ... They began businesses one would not normally expect to be possible in a small mountain town. This kind of accumulation has given Kamiyama a creative magnetism where 'people bring more people'." This description perfectly fits Sasaki Masayuki's 佐々木雅幸 definition of a creative village:

> a farming village which is rich in 'creative spaces', where global issues ... are addressed by implementing creative solutions that emerge from the autonomy and originality of residents and provide for the local economy as a self-sustaining cycle, by nurturing unique aspects of the culture while preserving the abundance of the natural ecosystem; introducing new art, science, and technology; and combining artisan-like small manufacture with farming and forestry. [→B271]

[→■5]

[→■6]

[→■6] From far left, clockwise: *wasabi-na* (wasabi leaves), *aka-karashi-na* (red brassica), *mizu-na* (potherb mustard), *komatsu-na* (mustard spinach)

It is worth noting that the Green Valley approach to local regeneration had no specific ecological focus, only a demographic one. And whereas in many places tourism and cultural events were set as instruments for local revitalisation, in Kamiyama priority was given to self-supporting, permanent activities.

In 2015, the municipality of Kamiyama established focus groups devoted to such issues as energy, housing, training, and food to discuss the future of the town. The participants in the food focus group formulated a revitalisation plan called the "Machi wo Shōrai Sedai ni Tsunagu Project" まちを将来世代につなぐプロジェクト or Project to Connect the Town to Future Generations. The Kamiyama Tsunagu Corporation 神山つなぐ公社 was established in 2016 to implement the project.

In addition, an independent company, Food Hub Project Co., Ltd., [→B358] was established in 2016 by the Kamiyama town office, the Kamiyama Tsunagu Corporation, and Monosasu, Inc. モノサス, a company based in Tokyo, which holds the largest share (67%). The Food Hub Project is an agricultural company and represents one of the best examples of 'circular' economy one may find in a marginal settlement. The director, Manabe Taichi 真鍋太一, explains that he had already formulated the concept before he discovered that organisations built on the "farm local, eat local" principle were thriving in the USA. The concept was originally endorsed by the United States Department of Agriculture. [→B1]

The Food Hub Project operates farming, food-processing facilities, a restaurant ('Kamaya' かま屋), and a bakery ('Kama Pan & Store' かまパン&ストア),

[→■7]

[→■8]

and conducts food-education-related activities; in other words, it provides a full range of possibilities for locally managing the food cycle and organising production with respect to local consumption patterns. All of these activities were started simultaneously. "A food circulation system connecting small things to small things" is the motto of chief farmer, Shiramomo Kaoru 白桃薫. Such a local food system, based on small quantities and a circular economy, makes the community richer and less dependent.
The farming team grows rice, vegetables, wheat, fruit trees on a total area of 3.5 ha. Some vegetables are grown in unheated polytunnels. **[→■6]** The production of vegetables, wheat, and fruit is organic: pesticides are avoided and only organic fertiliser—local *shiitake* 椎茸 waste dried and pressed into briquettes—is used. In rice cultivation, organic fertilisers are also used, but a limited amount of pesticide is allowed when there is a possibility that the yield will be significantly reduced.
The production of the Food Hub agricultural team is supplemented by that of the Satoyama no Kai 里山の会, an informal group of retired farmers who sell their surplus, however small, to the Corporation, thus supplementing their pensions. Their names are painted on wooden tablets resting on the edge of the Kamaya kitchen hood. On average, the Food Hub spends about 250,000 yen (2,000 €) per month to buy produce from small local farmers.

The farming industry in Kamiyama is centred on the professional production of highly appreciated *sudachi* and plums, which are very popular and marketed nationwide. These products are considered 'typical' and belong to the local tradition, but such specialisation is also the result of the policies of JA (*Nōkyō* 農協), the powerful monopolistic organisation of Japanese farmers. Decades ago it was decided which product each region was to provide to the national wholesale supply chain, and even when to supply it. Such 'efficiency' principles have seriously eroded the self-sufficiency of individual regions in terms of their food supply as well as reduced biodiversity, since only those cultivars that can be harvested prematurely, handled intensively, and transported over long distances were selected. Until a few decades ago, in Japan (and everywhere else) people used to eat—and to build a food culture around—what was grown locally. In Kamiyama, there is still enough subsistence production of rice, often on small plots and highly subsidised, to meet local needs, and many residents have vegetable gardens. **[→■7]** However, lack of next-generation farmers and the aging of the current generation is leading to the abandonment of the land in most farming communities in Japan's marginal regions. Currently, the average age of Kamiyama farmers is 70.5 years (the Japanese average is 66.4). The ramifications of the impending disappearance of farming on both landscape and the structure of the local society and economy are obvious. It is therefore urgent to connect the older generation, many of whom are still farming and leading a traditional lifestyle based on a high degree of self-sufficiency and thrift, with a new generation of farmers, many of whom are very likely immigrants. The Food Hub Project has put in place a programme to attract young farmers to Kamiyama and provides a paid two-year training course to two people per year who would farm in a way that is adapted to the local context.
(The cultural landscape of Kamiyama—particularly with respect to local features that reflect the ingenuity of elderly peasants—has been studied since 2016 by professor Ishikawa Hajime 石川初, and a group of students, at the Keio University 慶應大学.) **[→B142]**

The Food Hub Projects' centre of operations is in Yorii, next to the National Road no. 438, which runs through the valley. Two buildings form a small complex around a landscaped open space and parking lot. **[→■1]**
At the Kama Pan & Store, bread is baked in front of the customer and sold alongside traditional Kamiyama products (spices, sauces, and sake produced from local ingredients), carefully selected organic vegetables from all over Shikoku Island, hand-crafted *miso*, soy sauce, and other ingredients used at Kamaya restaurant, as well as tableware and culinary utensils. **[→■8]**
The small new building (63 m^2) was designed by Shimazu Takashi 島津臣志. It was built by a local carpenter according to the conventional construction method based on a structural grid of Kamiyama *sugi* timber columns at 1-m centres lengthwise and 4-m

[→■9]

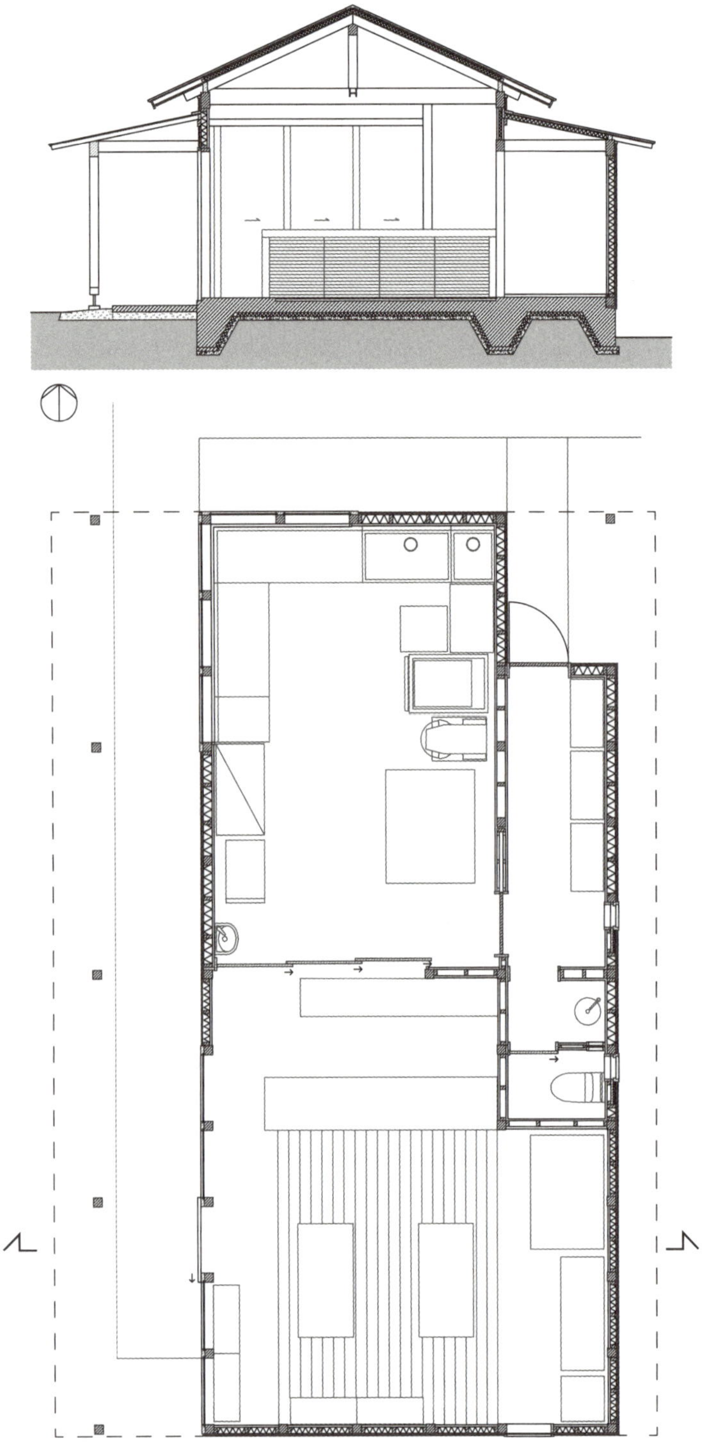

[→■10]
Section and plan, scale 1:100

[→■11]

[→■12]

crosswise. [→■9,10] The main body of the building measures 4x12 m and has a gabled roof; its larger sides abut two lower volumes, each 1.5 m deep, with single-pitch roofs. The one to the east is an open porch, which serves as an entrance.

The interior space is divided in two halves: the south part houses the bakery workshop and has an annex to the west, which contains a changing room and restroom; the north part contains the shop, which extends into the northwest corner, where some columns have been omitted to create an unobstructed sales area.

The walls are externally clad with vertical timber boards, interrupted by numerous windows that allow observers to view the bakery from the outside and provide a view of the mountains on the other side of the valley from the inside. The roofing is made of white-coated corrugated sheets.

The head of the baking department is Sasagawa Daisuke 笹川大輔, who moved here with his family from Tokyo to take part in the start of the Food Hub Project. [→■11] He currently bakes several kinds of bread using homemade yeast, including *pain de campagne*, square loaves, baguettes, and Kamiyama loaves flavoured with seasonal vegetables. [→B216]

The wheat used is produced in Hokkaido and in Kagawa prefecture. A small fraction (less than 1%) is locally produced in Kamiyama, which is nevertheless significant because it comes from an autochthonous cultivar that has been grown for generations by the Shiramomo family. [→■12] They used it for many years to produce *miso* and soy sauce, but in recent years they had been growing it just to preserve the seed. Its flour was originally deemed too weak for bread-making, but after Sasagawa mixed it with stronger flour and adjusted the amount of water and rising time, the Kamiyama *pain de campagne* was born. He is delighted by the idea that bread consumed by local people may induce local farmers to sow wheat again and save fields.

The Kamaya restaurant next door was opened in 2017; [→■13] hours are from late morning to evening, serving meals at lunch and operating as a café the rest of the time. They serve eighty meals per day on average (a few *bento* 弁当 boxes are also prepared every day and taken to elderly people who cannot easily make their way to the restaurant). In the beginning, they also served dinner, but it was discontinued due to a lack of customers. The name comes from the local dialect and refers to the area in the *doma* where the oven (*kama[do]*) stood and where neighbours stayed to chat and drinking tea with the owners of the house. Reminiscent of this tradition, the restaurant kitchen was placed at the centre of the tavern and is open on all sides, highlighted by a hood-like black metal plate box hanging from the ceiling. As Nakano Koji 中野晃治 observed, "The position is totally intentional as it is literally at the centre between production and consumption: it is the place that makes both sides of the food process visible, connects them, and gives them meaning". [→B216] The centrepiece of the kitchen is a traditional earthen stove, where rice is cooked with spring water.

Unlike the Kama Pan & Store, the Kamaya building predates the Food Hub; it was built about twenty-five years ago and used as a factory for producing electronic components. It has a steel structure on a 4x10-m grid and a flat roof. The conversion was designed by a team lead by Nakahara Shinichiro 中原慎一郎. The easternmost bay was demolished to create greater access to the courtyard. The resulting building measures 236 m^2, almost perfectly split in two halves, each of which is three bays long. The eastern one (116 m^2) accommodates the fully glazed dining room, while the western half contains a second kitchen, which is used as a food-processing lab and for activities related to food education, a food storage area, an office, and restrooms for customers accessed from outside. The whole dining room was given an everyday, homely character. Steel members and ties were painted white, and most surfaces, including the floor, were clad with timber boards. [→■14]

Every week the percentage of ingredients produced within the municipality that are served at Kamaya restaurant is published on the Food Hub website. Such percentage usually ranges in the 50s and 60s; the annual average is 54%. These numbers can be confusing because they do not express the amount of local ingredients in weight—one gram of a local spice will count as much as the imported, main ingredient of a certain dish. For instance, in week 6, 2019, the amount of local ingredients was 55%.

[→■13]

[→■14]

[→■15]

[→■16]

[→■15] Recipe for *miso* soup: prepare *dashi* (broth): boiling water in 44 cm diameter casserole with 10 g dried kelp and 100 g bonito, high heat until almost bubbling. Turn down the flame, wait until bonito settles, skim; 5' later remove all kelp and bonito out of *dashi*: the soup base is thus obtained. Now add vegetables: first *daikon* and other root vegetables if any (which take longer), *shiitake*, then leaf vegetables (Chinese cabbage). Cook a while, turn off the heat, and finally add homemade *miso* paste. Stir & serve.

For lunch, on 8 February, they served fried *sagoshi* fish 青箭魚 with *shogoin daikon* 聖護院大根; tempura with sweet potato and salted kelp; sesame with steamed *daikon* and kohlrabi; cabbage and fried tofu; farm salad; sweet potato rice; purple carrots *kinpira* 金平 (stirred with sesame oil); and *miso* soup 味噌汁. [→■15] The local ingredients in that day's menu were leek, *sudachi* vinegar, sweet potato, daikon, kohlrabi, garlic, ginger, lettuce, *mizuna* 水菜, *wasabi-na* 山葵菜, *benikururi* 紅くるり (red radish), carrots, purple *mizuna*, purple carrots, *komatsuna* 小松菜, homemade *miso*, *shiitake*, and Chinese cabbage 白菜. Rice is usually local, but on that day it was not. Tofu 豆腐 is locally produced, but the soy beans to make it were not grown in Kamiyama. *Sagoshi* fish came from Tokushima prefecture and the eggs from Tokushima city.

The restaurant offers an abundant variety of dishes that celebrates the taste of many different seasonal vegetables. [→■17] Small quantities of a range of diverse ingredients are used, also to promote a local food culture. In fact, it seems that in recent years people tend to prefer vegetables with a high sugar content, at the expense of the diversity of natural savours. Food Hub chefs and bakers create dishes and breads to bring out the unique flavour of each ingredient. A 'chef-in-residence' programme invites cooks in Kamiyama to develop new dishes based on the region's resources.

The use of local materials is not limited to food. Thanks to the cooperation with Kamiyama's Forestry Activation Council 神山町林業活性化協議会, various objects in Kamaya restaurant are made with local *sugi*. Chairs, stools, and trays were designed by Mr. Umemoto of Studio Khii and made by local joiners at the Wood Works Laboratory. [→■16] The plywood was specially produced by a nearby factory, employing local timber only. Unfortunately, the unexpectedly good quality of such plywood did not cause a new product being offered on the market.

The tabletops and desktops were made by local carpenters and sawmills from solid Kamiyama *sugi* timber. Even the disposable chopsticks (*hashi* 箸) are made of Kamiyama *sugi* timber. As no antiseptics are employed, the texture of the wood remains intact. Used *hashi* are burned for cooking rice.

Dishes were produced locally; the glaze was made from lotus root, rice straw ash, and Ashiya ashes (a waste of indigo dye production). Serving dishes are selected pieces of Shikoku folk art. They also use lacquered soup bowls and dishes donated by local residents.

A nutrition educator is part of the Food Hub Project staff and runs activities in local schools. [→■18,19,21] Children share their discoveries with parents, and

[→■17]

[→■18]

[→■20]

[→■19]

[→■21]

this affects the local society at large. Workshops for adults and farmers are also held. [→■20] A general aim is to nurture relationships between producers and consumers and pass down the diverse agricultural and culinary culture of Kamiyama. A big success in this field was that the Food Hub Project convinced the prefecture to modify the name and the curriculum of the local high school, introducing courses in ecology and agriculture. [→B150]

In 2017/18, the turnover of the Food Hub Project was about 8 million yen (63,700 €). This equals 0.6% of the total turnover of the agricultural sector in Kamiyama, which was 1,310M yen (10.4M €) in the same year. The amount of produce (in weight) is not known. At the moment, the Food Hub Project loses money (no income in the first year; it lost 8 million yen in the second year and 4 million in its third); it is expected that it might reach a balanced budget this year. However, I have had the impression that possible losses of such a limited entity would not trouble much a company like Monosasu. There are no plans to expand the Food Hub company.

Domestic sales (food served at the Kamaya and sold at the Kama Pan & Store) and external sales (raw vegetables and processed food sent to other markets) account for 48% and 52%, respectively, of the revenue. The Food Hub employs twenty-one people, mostly immigrants. Only the Shiramomo father and son, who take care of the farming activity, are local.

The annual energy consumption is 56,640 kWh for electricity (used to run refrigerators, air conditioning, lighting, irrigation equipment) and 3,040 m^3 of gas for cooking.

Despite numerous commendable initiatives, Kamiyama has not yet succeeded in reversing the trend towards demographic decline. However, it is considered a success story at the national level and has been the subject of numerous studies and publications. This attention has produced paradoxical results. In 2017, the Japanese Good Design Award was given to a company that makes beautifully turned glasses in *sugi* wood that sell for 13,400 yen (107 €) each, with the claim that their production "helps to restore a water retention landscape".

Soil and earth: Wangeliner Garten

Andrea Bocco Guarneri

One of the benefits of the German Democratic Republic (GDR) was low unemployment and high job security. Due to the GDR's planned economy, which aimed to utilise the full workforce, eastern Germany was unequipped to handle the rise of unemployment that came after the collapse of the communist state, yet such rise was inevitable, since no capitalist economy functions without it. **[→B262:134]** The liquidation of state-owned firms by the Treuhandanstalt combined with the job losses due to the introduction of capitalist competition led to an abrupt rise in unemployment throughout eastern Germany.

The Verein zur ökologisch-ökonomisch Förderung angemessener Lebensverhältnisse westlich des Plauer Sees (Association for the Promotion of Ecologically and Economically Appropriate Living Conditions in the Area West of Lake Plau, or FAL) **[→B357]** was founded in 1990 by municipalities (now included in Ganzlin, Landkreis Ludwigslust-Parchim), private companies, and committed private persons. Such diversity in the membership is quite exceptional and allowed it to take advantage of both the pioneering spirit of a few idealists and the financial support of five municipalities. **[→B86,91]** Klaus Hirrich, by trade a blacksmith and photographer, moved from Dresden in 1986 with a small group of people and bought land and a house in Wangelin, where he still lives today. "Everyone went to the west, we went north", he explains. Hirrich has been the president of FAL for almost twenty years.

The focus on coupling nature conservation and the economic development of a small rural region is rather unique and might explain why FAL still exists after so many years, while similar initiatives have died out. Other reasons include a remarkable level of commitment to the common cause as well as to sustainability, and a visionary capacity to creatively design for the future through a number of manifold projects. **[→B86,91]** Due to the marginality of the area, FAL was free to experiment. Everything they have been doing is consistent with the ecological-economic approach, even if individual projects have a degree of instrumentality and often arose from occasion. But in the beginning, it was a matter of survival. In the GDR, large agricultural cooperatives were formed in which productivity per worker did not matter. With the collapse of employment in the region after reunification, many people were left without a livelihood, and fear and despair spread. These adversities led the partners who created the FAL to come together and think about solutions to help the unemployed, to create jobs, and to keep people from leaving the region.

Thanks to the GDR Employment Promotion Law passed in 1990, between 75 and 90% of the East German workforce received short-time unemployment benefits. The federal government continued such policies in order to minimise the social impact of the reunification process. **[→B171]**

One of FAL's first projects was planting 50,000 trees throughout the area, including birches, willows, and fruit trees. Trees were planted in rows along country roads, streams, and plot enclosures according to historical pictures. During the GDR, many trees had been removed to facilitate the mechanical processing of the fields. The replanting activity was financed by the federal government to create useful, labour-intensive work for local ABM (*Arbeitsbeschaffungsmaßnahme*, or re-employment programme) workers. In addition, stone walls were reconstructed to fence in village squares and cemeteries, and nesting aids for endangered bird species were built.

As part of the *Aufschwung Ost* (East Recovery) policy, the minister of the environment committed a team of scientists and engineers from federal research institutions to develop ABM actions for nature conservation projects in eastern Germany and to support the creation of independently working GbRs. In 1992, Peter Pretscher, a bioecologist at the Federal Agency for Nature Conservation (*Bundesamt für Naturschutz*), was asked to evaluate the feasibility and design the renaturalisation of the Wangeliner See and the conversion of the Retzow Red Army training area, which at that time was still in operation. The shooting range was cleared of bombs and debris and was transformed into the Marienfließ nature reserve, a 1,200 ha expanse of moorland perfect for hiking and home to many varieties of butterflies, bees, and beetles.

The 200-ha renaturalisation plan for the lake was eventually rejected by the local council in 2017, despite the fact that the government was ready to purchase the land at a reasonable price. Local residents were suspicious of it despite the existence of successful nearby examples of similar initiatives.

When FAL began its work, many village houses were in a state of disrepair. The GDR did not like history, nor did the locals appreciate heritage buildings—on the contrary, they wanted them to be torn down. At that time, one could buy a building for 1 mark per square metre (0.5 €/m^2). The first experience with a heritage building came when FAL had to restore a listed half-timbered building in Retzow, where they wanted to establish the felt workshop Ülepüle. The same materials as in the original were to be used, and this led to the building up of a know-how in the renovation of old houses. They also set up a construction company for earth construction, which no longer exists. FAL also initiated a museum about earth construction as well as the European Educational Centre for Earth Building.

[→■1]

The Clay Museum (*Lehmmuseum*) was established in the Seemannscheune, a dilapidated hayloft in Gnevsdorf, thanks to the support of the LEADER II EU programme. **[→■1,2]** The building permit was issued in 1996 and the museum was opened in 1999. The restoration included the renovation of the thatched roof and of the interior, some landscaping, and the installations. The exhibits include information on the geological origin of clay; samples of different local and international soils; historical information on earth buildings in the region, including *pisé* houses

[→■2]

built in the late eighteenth century; rural houses built after WWII for the refugees from the former eastern territories; and a peculiar local type of round barn made of rammed clay. There are also original fragments of old walls and floors; models showing how half-timbered walls can be insulated; samples of contemporary perimeter walls built with loam, that meet both comfort expectations and demands and thermal-insulation standards; and samples of earth plasters, offering a range of aesthetic possibilities. The space upstairs is dedicated to temporary exhibitions, held one to three times a year, on various facets of building with clay in Germany and abroad. The museum publishes a series of booklets on the work of prominent earth-building designers. [→B366]

The idea of building affordable earthen houses developed into the Europäische Bildungsstätte für Lehmbau (European Educational Centre for Earth Building). [→B367] Its headquarters is in Wangelin next to the botanical garden and includes the workshop obtained from the former village dance hall, which was still in operation when Hirrich arrived. It has just been renovated and dedicated to the memory of Khudadad Khademi, an Afghani earth-building expert who intensively co-operated with FAL. Next to it and scattered on an area of over 6,000 m^2 are a house containing the office of the training centre, a few sheds and a host of small open-air structures made of straw, raw earth, and reused materials. [→■5] These structures are constantly increasing because they are built by volunteers and students during the summer workshops in response to their own practical needs (such as temporary showers and toilets) or as part of their training (such as wall and clay ovens). On the premises stands also the Lehmkloster ('earth

[→■3]

convent'), a basic yet dignified building for guests that has five bedrooms, a bathroom, and a kitchen-living room. [→■6] This stone masonry house was insulated with straw bales, the ground floor was remade with standing glass bottles topped with self-produced unfired tiles, and the walls have been plastered by the students.

Under the direction of Uta Herz, the centre offers vocational training courses in earth building, clay plastering, rammed earth, clay oven building, earth colours, *tadelakt*, straw bale building, and roof thatching. [→B97,145] Rüger develops the teaching supports for ecological building work camps. The centre is fully integrated in the ECVET global network of earth building training, which is supported by the Leonardo da Vinci EU Lifelong Learning Programme. ECVET certificates are awarded for some of the courses. The most demanding training course is in earth-based plasters, which leads to a professional qualification as 'clay plaster artist' recognised by the German Chamber of Commerce (HWK).

In addition, FAL receives money from the European Social Fund and the German Federal Ministry of the Environment to carry out the 'Wangeliner Workcamps', [→B384] residential workshops lasting from five to ten days, which are offered at no cost to sixteen to twenty-four-year-old trainees living in the former GDR. The overall goal is to transmit an ecological point of view; it is also hoped that some of the participants consider moving to the region. Training mostly focuses on building, but FAL intends to balance this with more gardening.

Another project launched by FAL is Wunderfeld e.G., a company that processes regional food products (herbal teas, herbal vinegar and oils, juices and spreads) next to Ganzlin's former railway station. Both food and art and crafts products are marketed under this label in the association's own shops at the Wangeliner Garten and in Plau am See as well as through e-commerce.

The largest operation managed by FAL is the Wangeliner Garten, [→B383] which extends over 1.6 ha to the northwest of the village. [→■3] The idea of a 'teaching and experience garden' (*Lehr- und Erlebnisgarten*) was one of the first to emerge out of the efforts to attract tourism to the area. Originally a meadow, the area was mulched and enriched with green manure; an irrigation system was laid; paths were dug and filled; and fences were built. A nursery area was created, and cold frames were built. Trees were planted and hedges and living windbreaks were created. Finally, plants were sown with seeds that were procured free of charge through the 'international seed exchange' between botanical gardens. All the work was performed by about twenty ABM workers, according to Pretscher's project. By 1995, the core of the garden had been created, but it was not inaugurated until 1999.

It is organised in nine thematic areas, containing more than 900 species and varieties of plants. **[→■4,7]** Visitors access the botanical garden through the 'farmer's garden' connected to the area dedicated to historical crops. It is followed by the areas dedicated to spectacular displays and sensory stimulation, which include a butterfly garden, magic plants, aromatic and scented plants, as well as plants showing special adaptation features that are sometimes taken as a model by bionics. The largest area is dedicated to plants used in traditional medicine, sorted by disease. The *Naturgarten* was added to the northeast of the core garden in 1997: it is a sparse orchard (*Streuobstwiese*) with varieties of regional fruit trees, a pond, several contemporary artworks made of natural materials, the *Capitulare de villis* area dedicated to the edible and useful crops which were described at the time of Charlemagne, as well as living borders and walls that provide shelter to insects, birds, and small mammals. Due to the great variety of plants, over one hundred different species of bees and wasps have been observed in the garden.

[→■4]

[→■5]

[→■6]

[→■7]

[→■8]

The botanical garden, which is about 6,800 m², is accessed by passing through a reclaimed greenhouse lying against the 22-m long, 4-m high massive rammed-earth south wall of the Lehmhaus ('earth house'), designed by Günter zur Nieden in 2002. [→B2] [→■11] The Lehmhaus originally contained the entrance, a shop, and a café, but these functions were moved to a new building further north. The Lehmhaus is now used by the office that manages the garden, while its large hall hosts seminars and cultural events such as concerts, films, readings, and temporary exhibitions. It is also used by the local community as a space for gatherings. The Lehmhaus was the first earth building on the site. The rammed-earth walls are made from a mix of brick chippings and lean clay; the roof has a timber structure, is insulated with cellulose, and is planted with ruderal vegetation from the Marienfließ nature reserve. [→B65] On the roof are a solar thermal collector and a PV array.
The garden also includes the plant nursery-cum-polytunnel, a living labyrinth, a playground with underground routes through an artificial mound (mostly made with material recovered from the Red Army training field), a clearing for markets and open-air concerts with a living willow stage as well as the new entrance/café and the guest accommodation area. [→B147]
The garden café serves also as a reception area, with a ticket desk and a shop that sells Wunderfeld delicacies, plants from the garden's nursery, birdhouses, and other items. The café is reached by a path from the parking area. [→■9] The building was designed by Gernot Minke in cooperation with Tobias Weyhe and was completed in 2014. It has concrete foundations and a foam glass gravel ground floor. The wall and roof structure is a timber frame. The octagonal plan is covered with a Hogan roof—a technique Minke has employed in several other buildings—supporting a thick layer of soil. [→■10] The walls of the main room are infilled with straw bales. Two additional rooms containing the toilet and kitchen are located at two opposite corners and have walls of aerated concrete blocks similar to the Gästehaus (see below). The building is a testing ground for trainees from the European Educational Centre for Earth Building, and for its collection of decoration materials and techniques based on clay and lime mortar. Several international artists were engaged at various stages in the finishing and ornamentation of the warm-toned exterior; [→■12] the lively, colourful vertical and horizontal interior surfaces; and in some of the furnishings. [→■13] The building is heated with a low-emission Finnish earthen stove, which was built on site.
Following the construction of the garden, a series of buildings have been built over the past few years. Most of the funding has come from public sources, but some has come from FAL, including money made by selling Klein Dammerow, a manor in a neighbouring village that FAL restored and transformed into an accommodation facility for large groups.
The guest accommodations are used by both course attendees and tourists spending a few days in the Mecklenburg Lake District. [→■8] They include a trailer camp, the Steenshaus, the Gärtnerinnenhaus, and

[→■9]

[→■10]

[→■11]

[→■12]

[→■13]

[→■14]

[→■15]

the Gästehaus, which are located next to each other between the garden and the public road.

The camping area, which usually accommodates participants in the Wangeliner Workcamps, provides space for tents and six trailers arranged in a circle.

The Steenshaus takes its name from Athena and Bill Steen, [→B352] who designed and built it in 2015 with load-bearing straw bales plus metal rods to compress them. Recently, the bales had to be carved out on the outside, in order to insert unnecessary wooden posts so that the long-interrupted work could be continued lawfully. It will contain a kitchen for the trailer camp and a tool room.

As the name suggests, the Gärtnerinnenhaus was originally meant to be a small house for the gardeners, but it is now used as accommodation for paying guests; it is located next to the nursery. It was designed by Sabine Sühlo and completed in 2013. This one-room building, with no bathroom, has a prefabricated wooden frame infilled with straw bales in the floor, walls, and roof.

The Gästehaus was created as a manifesto of innovative, sustainable architecture. [→■14] Its simple form gives it a strong, iconic character, and in fact it was later chosen as the logo for the Wangeliner Workcamps. Built according to Minke's plans, the Gästehaus can be compared with two other buildings of his: a house in Bad Schussenried (Germany) and the lodgings in Tamera (Portugal). [→■15] The former, with unfired brick vaults and a green roof, is formally very similar to the Gästehaus. The latter, built in 2007, resembles the Gästehaus not only in shape, but also in terms of technology. Its load-bearing vaults made of straw bales covered with a green roof were built during a workshop. One of the volunteers led the effort to get Minke to design the Gartencafé and the Gästehaus in Wangelin.

Though German law does not allow load-bearing construction made of straw bales, the Gästehaus was granted a regular permit in 2012, which makes it the first and, to my knowledge, the only load-bearing, straw bale building in Germany. It is not clear how

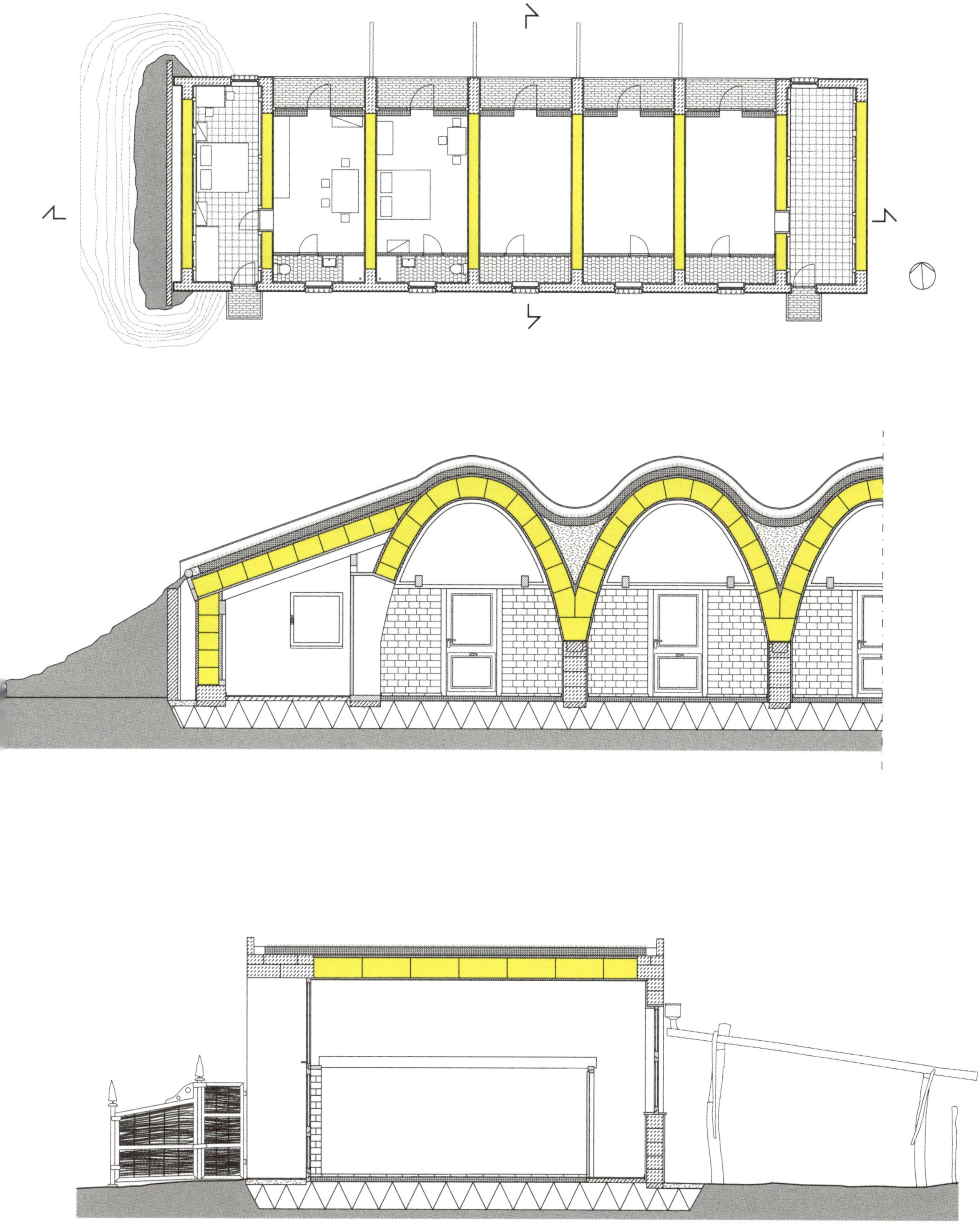

[→■16] Plan, scale 1:200; longitudinal and cross sections, scale 1:100

this happened. In 2016, a decision was made to build more accommodations with the same technique, but to date the municipality has not authorised the project.

The building extends from east to west, next to the northern boundary of the Wangeliner Garten. The five vaults in the middle, a wavy roof, and the two single-pitched rooms at the opposite ends create a perfectly symmetrical façade composition. [→▪16,17] Moving eastwards, one finds a dressing room (16 m²) with showers for campers, four double bedrooms (16 m²), each with an adjoining bathroom (4 m²), a communal living area, an additional bathroom, and a twin bedroom. [→▪18] Each room has a separate entrance from the outside.

Construction began in 2011 with the excavation, levelling, casting of concrete foundations at the base of walls, and the building of a 500-mm deep ventilated underfloor cavity filled with cellular glass gravel. During a two-week workshop organised by the European Educational Centre for Earth Building, a group of twenty-three volunteers, supervised by Minke, Weyhe, Hirrich, and Rüger, built the structural parts of the building. The rest of the building was completed over the following four years.

The north façade, the walls at the foot of the vaults, the east and west walls, the short walls protruding outside the south façade, as well as the south heads of the vaults are all made of autoclaved aerated concrete (AAC) blocks.

As in Hrubý Šur, [→§6] bales (there are 128 of them per vault) were cut to a trapezoidal section and the angle at which each course of bales lies was calculated in advance. [→▪19] Straw bales were superimposed, like the ashlars of a stone vault, making use of centrings and resting on the AAC block walls. [→▪20] Threaded rods connect the blocks and the bales, and belts and ropes were tied to them to pre-compress the vaults so as to avoid subsequent settlement under the load. [→▪21,23] Sixty more straw bales were used as an infill in the wooden frame of the side rooms. [→▪22] A 4-mm waterproofing membrane was laid above the rendered straw bales and covered with 200 mm of earth, on which ruderal vegetation grows.

In the north wall there are large windows, one for each room, which allow light into the bathrooms. The south façade is triple-glazed. Each room has a large arched non-openable window at the top, a door in the middle, and two panels at the sides with raw-earth brick walls that form Trombe walls. Unfired brick walls have also been built to separate the bedrooms and the bathrooms. Timber beams on top of these walls ensure support for furniture, canopies, and lighting fixtures.

A base layer, 25 to 30-mm thick, of earth-lime plaster was sprayed onto the straw bales and the AAC block walls to obtain a flush surface. A subsequent layer of earth-based plaster was applied to the internal walls. Each room has a unique colour scheme. The bathrooms are plastered with *tadelakt*, creating shimmering, slightly wavy surfaces. The floors consist of a 70-mm layer of tamped earth plus a 30-mm finish layer of earth, sand, shredded straw, and linseed oil. The end rooms have ceramic tile floors.

According to Rüger, the building has multiple problems. An excessive amount of linseed oil was used on the floors, causing an unpleasant smell: in the future, the arched windows will be openable to provide additional ventilation. Another issue is that in some Trombe walls, the intermediate glass was broken, for unknown reasons; moreover, the walls do not supply significant heat and require constant cleaning. Finally, condensation occurs at the top of the vaults due to the lack of a ventilation gap underneath the waterproof membrane. The membrane will be removed and a new one will be positioned on battens.

Heat is distributed to the rooms through pipes embedded in the walls. In 2017-18, 5,055 litres of gas were used for heating both the space and water. Water is used not only by the visitors in the guesthouse but also by campers in trailers and tents.

The number of visitors of the garden has increased thanks to inclusion in the International Horticultural Exposition (IGA) in Rostock in 2003 and the Federal Horticultural Show (BUGA) in Schwerin in 2009. It is known today as Mecklenburg's largest herb garden and receives 6,000 to 8,000 visitors per year. It offers seminars, workshops, guided tours, and markets: 250 people participate yearly in its courses and events on topics such as natural gardening, herbs, herbal medicines, and cooking. Both the cultural programme and the public it draws are richly diverse.

[→■17]

[→■19]

[→■18]

[→■20]

[→■21]

[→■22]

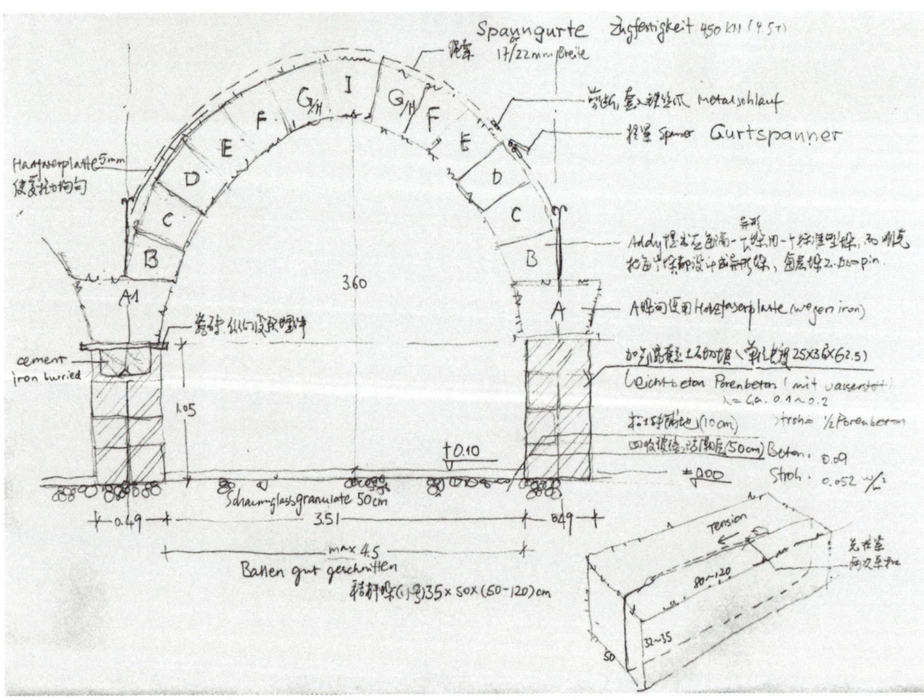

Gurtspanner
A
B
C
D
E
F
G/H
I
3.60
1.05
0.10
cement
iron buried
Leichtbeton Porenbeton
Schaumglassgranulate 50 cm
0.49
3.51
max 4.5
Ballen gut geschnitten
Tension

[→■23]

The garden acts as a magnet, bringing tourists to the community. Thanks to the activities and workshops, in summer the small village teems with life. The garden might be even more attractive if it was served better by public transportation. Its presence has been a decisive factor in the choice of some people and businesses to settle there in the last few years (a tree nursery, an organic building materials shop; a graphic designer, and a number of artists). More people would be willing to move to the region, and Wangelin in particular, if housing was available. People willing to move here have creativity and initiative but hardly any financial resources. FAL would like to develop affordable housing and property models that allow for the cohabitation of different generations, create workspaces, and recover vacant agricultural buildings that could be developed into very sophisticated, sustainable, and cost-effective living spaces. **[→B357]**

Discussions in the 1990s gave rise to many ideas for making the region south of Lake Plau more attractive for tourism and for developing the appropriate infrastructure in Wangelin. FAL thought the organisation would last for only two or three years because at that time, everybody thought that large industrial estates would be built in the area. Nobody predicted that FAL would still exist thirty years later. This is also due to its having been well administered and ultimately self-sustaining, with a significant contribution still being made by the long-term unemployed. In total, there are thirty-five team members; Wangelin has eighty residents. Moreover, FAL is recognised as an educational institution at the European level, and its efforts have been acknowledged by several institutions and studies.

FAL is evolving as a centre for environmentally conscious education and as an interest group for integrated village development. They hope that Wangelin and Gnevsdorf can serve as model villages, breeding grounds for a good life ('Werkstatt des guten Lebens'), in spite of a certain unwillingness of the indigenous people to participate. **[→B86,91] [→■24]**

The Robert Bosch Stiftung supports regional citizen projects in East Germany with the programme *Neulandgewinner—Inventing the Future Locally.* **[→B351]** Behind the local initiatives are committed

[→■24]

people who, in times of rapid social change, want to shape their environment and their neighbourhoods with unconventional ideas. FAL's "Affordable building for the soul in rural areas" project was awarded a grant from the programme. Its main goal was to create practical examples of nature-oriented building. The house built with the Steens was meant as a prototype.

Another goal of the project is to increase the possibility that a local economy survives through the promotion of local products such as timber, fruit, and vegetables. Despite the return of land ownership to smallholders after the German reunification, the land is mostly managed in huge production units dedicated to monocultures such as wheat, corn for fuel, alfalfa. In addition to craftspersons and artists, the FAL would like to attract organic farmers, although long land-lease contracts make it difficult to take over. One push could come from the development of community-supported agriculture (*solidarische Landwirtschaft*) schemes. **[→B173,207]**

The two main goals of this project of FAL echo its two more general themes: building and care for the land. They may have arisen by chance and independently from each other; but subsequently, people at FAL could see how consistent it is to work simultaneously on *Lehmbau* (construction with earth) and *Gartenbau* (gardening), and how much these two topics are interconnected.

Education and inspiration: WISE at CAT

Andrea Bocco Guarneri
and Martina Bocci

Led by Gerard Morgan-Grenville, in 1973 a group of inspired visionaries, moved by the energy crisis and an environmental concern, decided to settle in central Wales. They rented a large abandoned quarry of about 16 ha, a few kilometres from Machynlleth, where the rural economy was based on sheep breeding. It was a desert landscape of slate slabs, some stone buildings, and a nineteenth-century reservoir; there was no connection to electricity or to the water mains. Thanks to donations, they began creating an experimental and energy self-sufficient village, starting with polyurethane foam-sprayed caravans and a hydro turbine. Gradually, they managed to become more technically proficient, **[→B8]** in spite of their "little experience, earnest amateurism". **[→B49:14]**
The history of the Centre for Alternative Technology (CAT) **[→B50,354]**—'alternative technology' is a phrase coined by Peter Harper, one of the founders—was inspired by the ideals of alternative and radical thinkers like Schumacher. **[→B52]** It put these ideals into practice thanks to the cooperation and combined skills of the many volunteers and workers who over the years took part in this utopian community, made up of "toffs, geeks, hippies and deviant locals", as Pat Borer playfully remarked.
CAT's history went through several phases and changed continuously in terms of both technology and community balance. Founded as a countercultural dream, it quickly became apparent that it would be necessary to establish economic independence and to finance itself: in 1975, CAT opened to the public and transformed itself from an experimental community to an information and tourist attraction centre. Admission tickets were one of the main sources of income—at its peak, between 1975 and 1988, the visitor centre attracted 65,000 visitors per year.
Over the years, 2.8 ha were covered with energy-efficient buildings, gardens, and technological experiments. **[→■1]** The area became a demonstration site with the aim of generating interest in alternative ways of doing things. CAT wanted to inspire in the public a desire for change, to inform, and to enable through practical example. **[→B354]** It created a working model of a sustainable community that makes more responsible and better use of natural resources, has a reduced dependence on the industrial production system, and is located far from large urban centres,

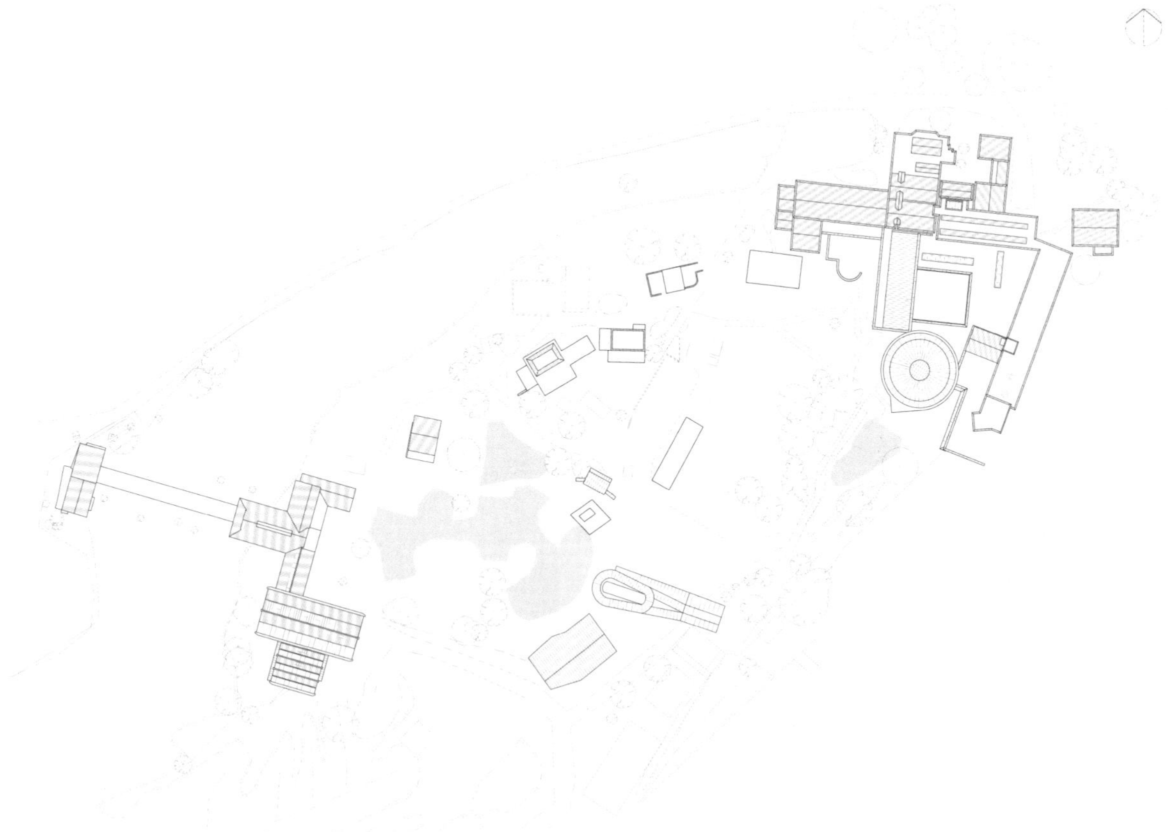

[→■1] CAT plan, scale 1:2000

in order to show that a gentler kind of lifestyle can be feasible and rewarding. **[→B310]**
With the foundation of the legal entities CAT Public Limited Company and CAT Charity Limited, CAT has subsequently become an educational, research, and development centre with a more pragmatic commercial aim that provides a more stable income stream. **[→B123]** In its forty-six years, CAT has contributed to the local economy (around £1.5 million or 1.7 million € per year) and has created a large group of people actively involved in environmental and social protection, many of whom have settled in Machynlleth or nearby villages and have established thriving businesses.
Three million people have visited CAT, and 1,200 students have graduated from courses at least partially offered at CAT's Welsh Institute for Sustainable Education (WISE). **[→B286]** One of the stated aims of CAT is to develop a reflective and critical attitude in students and to make them agents of change for a more environmentally sustainable society. The number of visitors has now decreased to around 20,000 per year, while the number of university and professional courses offered and research projects has been constantly increasing.
The report *An Alternative Energy Strategy for the UK*, published in 1977, **[→B66]** was the first pioneering attempt in what is now one of the crucial activities of CAT. Since 2007, CAT has been working on the research project "Zero Carbon Britain". The project ultimately aims to reduce carbon emissions to zero. Most reports, including *Zero Carbon Britain: Making It Happen*, **[→B67]** are addressed to the British government. A 2018 edition has expanded to include much broader scenarios and analyses at the global, regional, national, and sub-national scales. **[→B68]**

CAT's buildings are full-scale prototypes of green techniques made mainly from local and recycled materials. They include the Whole Home, a superinsulated house funded by Wates Homes (1976); a timber-framed building realised according to the Walter Segal self-build method (1977); **[→■2]** the upper and lower stations of a water-balanced cable

[→■2]

[→■3]

[→■4]

[→■5]

railway (1992), which was built to facilitate access to the centre; the green-roofed off-grid Eco-Cabins guest accommodation (1988); [→■3] the Straw Bale Theatre (2000); [→■4] and the AtEIC, which is an information centre and a shop (2000). [→■5] In 2006, the entire premises were remodelled and the Wind Pavilion—a lightweight structure made of local wood and reused and recycled materials—was also erected. More experiments have been started recently, such as a *Miscanthus* bale house.

"With hard work and a lot of compost" they covered the slate debris left from the former quarry with lush greenery: flowers, a forest garden, an orchard with thirty ancient varieties of apple trees, the Whole Home garden (to show what could be grown on a small suburban plot), and Roger's Field, a 3,000 m^2 plot in front of the Eco-Cabins. [→■6] Cared for over thirty years by Roger McLennan sticking to a method adopted from the beginning, it provides fresh, organic vegetables, including salad, beans, broccoli, cabbage, kale, carrots, beetroot, *daikon*, courgette, squash, and pumpkin (potatoes are not grown, as they are easily available at the local market). McLennan encourages environmentally friendly weeds, plants flowers to attract pollinating insects, and avoids pesticides, herbicides, and fertilisers. He

[→■6]

produces compost from sharp sand, topsoil, dead leaves, and organic waste from the restaurant. For fruit trees and bushes, compost is obtained from dry toilets. Polytunnels are used to grow seedlings.

CAT managed to reconcile practise and theory and to run off-grid only at the very beginning of its existence, when the community members lived with very little electricity. As it offered more and more services, CAT needed to connect to the mains, although they keep generating part of their electricity through photovoltaic and hydro systems (a wind turbine provides energy to the Eco-Cabins). Space heating and hot water are obtained from solar thermal panels and a local combined heat-and-power station that burns biomass. Liquefied gas is used for cooking.

Water comes from a large reservoir above the centre and is also collected from the roofs. This water is used to generate energy, operate the cableway, water the gardens, and for cleaning; it is purified with a chemical-free process for drinking and cooking.

Motivated by environmental ideals, Pat Borer, an English architect, moved to Wales in 1974 and joined CAT in 1976. [→B378] An architect-builder, he was deeply influenced by Walter Segal's method. [→B196] His profession is of a highly practical nature: "You can't design a building without knowing how to build it," he maintains. Over the years, Borer has become the de facto official architect of CAT. In 1990, he moved a little further afield and set up an independent professional studio, with CAT as his main client. Borer has also written, with Cindy Harris, *The Whole House Book*, [→B126] one of the best ecological architecture manuals available. In writing his book, he partly drew on his experience gained through the experiments at CAT.

In an interview, Mason explains that when selecting building materials, Borer does not follow the BRE's Green Guide to Specification and the Inventory of Carbon and Energy (ICE):

> Indeed, he retains a healthy scepticism. ... Pat discriminates positively in favour of natural and then locally available materials, knowing this ensures low embodied energy. He consciously focuses on embodied energy rather than embodied carbon. Pat views using less energy per se as the imperative, rather than diversifying to renewable sources and perhaps seeing that as a license to profligacy. This stance is continued in choosing not just to use timber, as a natural, sustainable and even ethically traded material, but also endeavouring to use less of it. ... Pat also makes the point that "Nowadays everyone seems to be stuffing buildings full of wood because of its carbon sequestration". [→B192]

This point is very relevant to the overall topic of this book. [→§13]

In recent years, Borer has moved away from the timber stud wall and is now keen on materials such as hemp-lime and straw bales, materials that allow one to build a wall that functions both as a structural element and as insulation.

He encourages people to use local materials so that one can see where they come from, and to develop direct relationships with producers and suppliers. As

[→■7]

Borer puts it, "This claim is irrefutable and highlights an everyday, verifiable link between justice and the local. ... As with food, to foster social justice the construction sector should probably be paying more for materials." [→B192:9]

David Lea is another English architect who moved to North Wales in the 1970s. "I wanted to explore the land use and smallholding/agriculture side of things," he recounted to Adam Voelcker. [→B323:29] He was attracted by the commune movement but "wanted a commune where things were done well". After spending six months at John Seymour's, he started his individual experiment with farming and gardening at Ogoronwy in Snowdonia. After all these years, he admits that "living in the woods and mountains of Snowdonia has had a profound effect on my outlook and given me an independence. ... As I got to know more about living in the countryside, things had to work in a really practical way". [→B323:38]

Lea's architectural works express an earnest appreciation for the vernacular tradition and for man's relationship with nature. Among his most notable works are the Royal Agricultural College in Cirencester; Hillier's visitor centre in Romsey; a sports hall in Blaenau Ffestiniog; an artist's studio in Nettlecombe, Somerset, made of saplings, whose form was directly derived from the materials he used; his own house and office at Ogoronwy; and the Segger House at Blaen Camel. [→B37,38,39,40,259,323]

Lea's friend, the architectural critic Peter Blundell Jones, wrote that

> Lea is not only a skilled draftsman ... but has also been all his life a maker, ready with tools to hand, willing to experiment and with a profound feeling for detail. Lea has always been keen on using naked wood, retaining a sense of the tree that it had been instead of crushing the life out of it and imposing a mechanical homogeneity. Lea has consistently promoted the idea of a modest, efficient and humane architecture, with generous daylighting, good way-finding, priority to on-foot, avoidance of unnecessary services and adherence to a small scale. ... Behind all his projects lies the utopian vision of a stable and dignified state of existence, which would be at once generous, resilient and sustainable, making wise use of the earth's bounty. In this there are distinct echoes of William Morris. [→B323:11]

Lea and Borer have worked a lot together, although not many of their projects have been built. [→B42] [→■7] Lea explained: "I was more interested in the formal aspects, the historical context of the buildings,

[→■8]

- wood
- hempcrete
- cellulose
- earth
- stone
- concrete

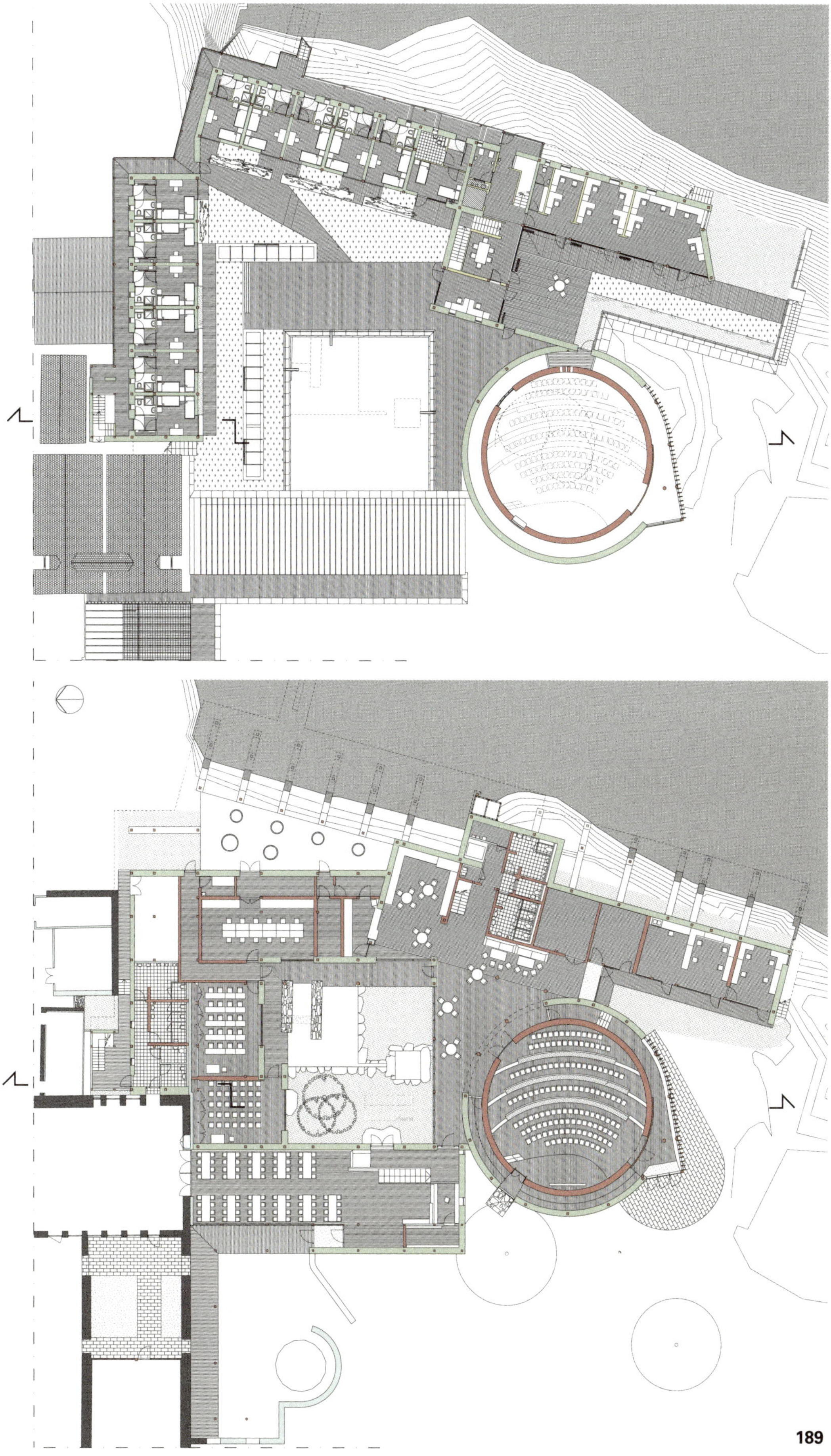

[→■9]
First and ground floor plans, scale 1:500

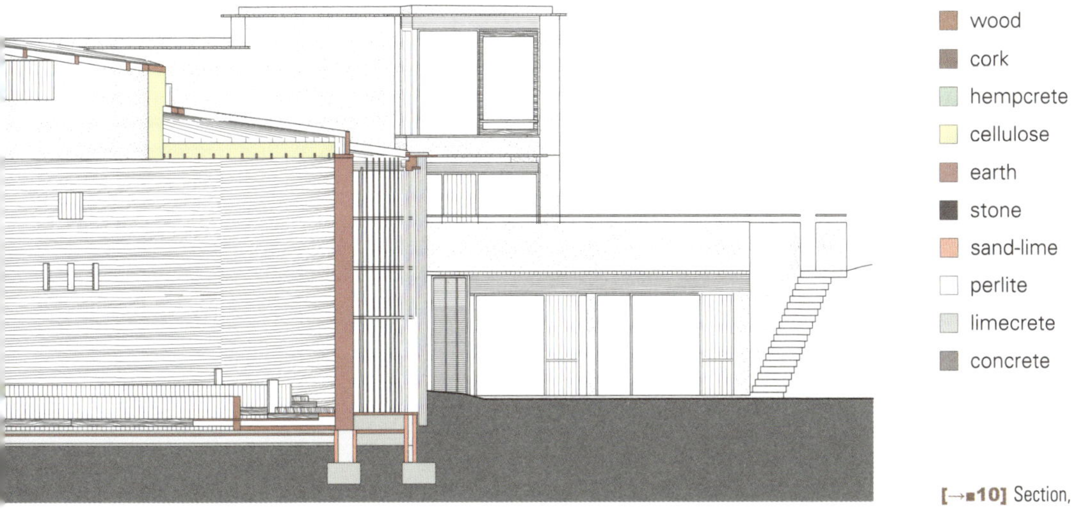

[→■10] Section, scale 1:200

[→■11]

he was more interested in the technology. ... He's an incredibly efficient person, unbelievably productive—the drawings he did for the WISE building are astonishing [because of their quantity and] detail." [→B323:54] (By the way, Borer was already proficient in designing with BIM as early as in 2007). Together, Borer and Lea have designed the most significant buildings at CAT, experimenting with natural materials "in a bid to improve thermal performance, encourage local sourcing, and to reduce energy wastage, always with a sense of direct confrontation with the substance, its capabilities, its smell and texture, its weight, its new possibilities". [→B323:11]

The WISE building represents the best implementation of CAT's approach to date. [→■11] It is a synthesis and at the same time an evolution of everything done before in terms of architecture, but on a larger scale. It is an example of best possible practises, meant as something to examine and learn from—detailed calculation of environmental impacts and permanent performance monitoring were also planned but not implemented. [→B124] It is also the culmination of both architects' careers, a "substantial building complex by Lea [and Borer] that we can [finally] experience in reality". [→B323:12]

The complex was created to ensure a suitable structure to accommodate the many students and activities from a growing number of university courses, as well as residential courses for professionals. Currently, WISE offers five master's programmes, in partner-

[→■12]

[→■13]

[→■14]

[→■15]

[→■16]

ship with the University of East London, focusing on sustainability, architecture, adaptation, and energy. In 2017, a partnership was also established with Liverpool John Moores University, offering three more courses in food, ecology, and behavioural change. In addition to university courses, CAT attracts groups, lifelong learners, and organisations. Short courses cover a variety of topics related to sustainability and green building, with an emphasis on self-construction, the most popular being the "Build a Tiny House" course.

The first drawings of the WISE building date to 2001. In an early proposal, the theatre was in a central position, and the complex had a very compact layout that did not allow adequate views from all rooms. The theatre was subsequently moved out of the centre, and a courtyard was designed in its place. The bedrooms were initially planned on a steep wooded hill to the north of the restaurant, but for financial reasons they were integrated with the areas dedicated to teaching and sociality. [→■8]

There was a very strict sustainability brief in terms of operational and embodied energy, embodied water, procurement of materials, and durability. Energy produced in situ from renewable sources was to be used wherever possible. CAT encouraged experimentation in the building technology; WISE was to be a large-scale demonstration of ecological architecture, an exemplary building whose scope was to show that it is possible to construct a 'mainstreamable'—that is, 'non-alternative'—version of sustainable building.

During the construction work, which started in 2006, a legal dispute arose between CAT and the original

[→■18]

[→■17]

[→■19]

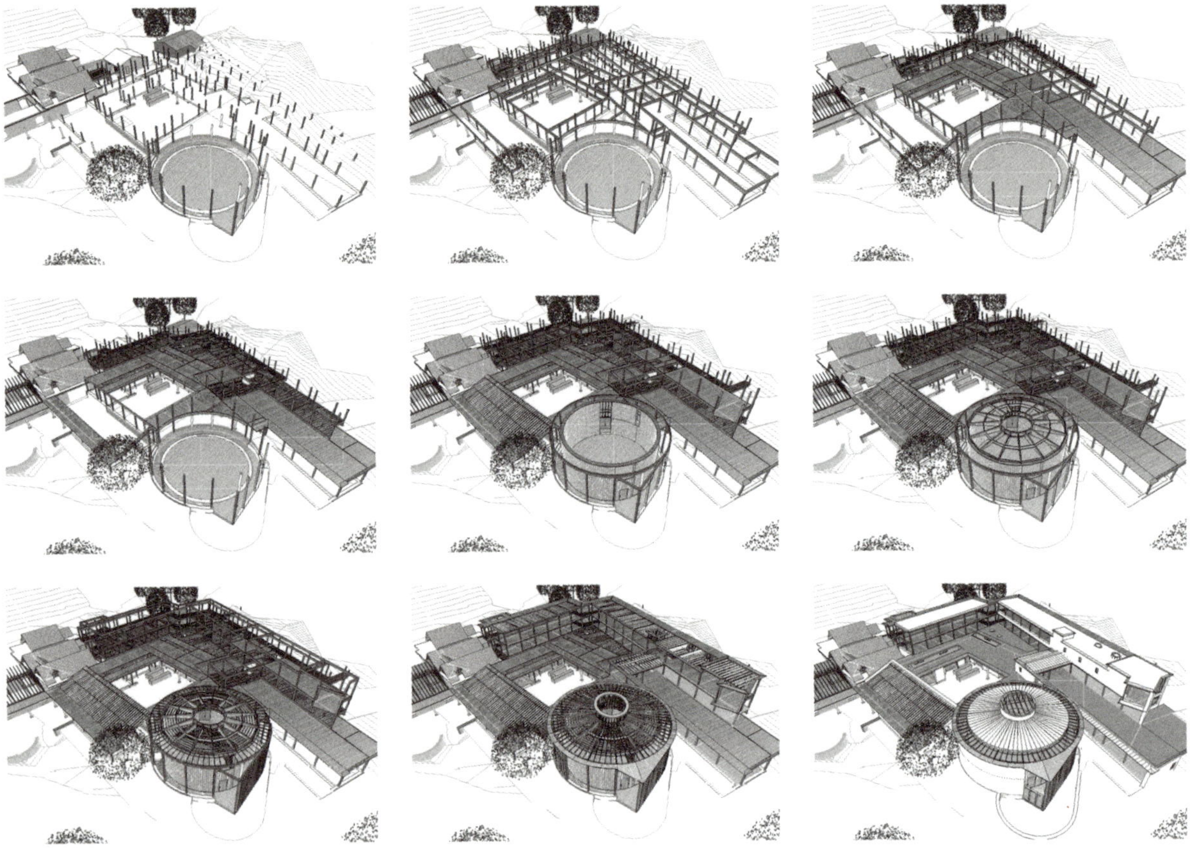

[→■20]

[→■21]

contractor of WISE on account of the numerous structural defects and inadequate protection, which resulted in extensive damages. The contractor went into liquidation immediately after losing the lawsuit, which meant that CAT could not obtain compensation. Fortunately, the cooperation with the new contractor, C. Sneade Construction, was excellent and the damage was repaired, also thanks to the support of many donors—the Sheppard family alone donated £650,000 (750,000 €). WISE was finally inaugurated in 2010.

The huge and partially unexpected costs associated with the realisation of WISE turned out to impose a turning point for the entire centre; CAT Plc was put in creditors voluntary liquidation in 2013, and its activities were absorbed by the charity. It was a hard time for CAT, also due to a continuous decline in visitor numbers. They had to drastically reduce their budget, they let eleven staff members go and shut down the Quarry Shop in Machynlleth. The structure of the enterprise was changed to adopt a clear-cut approach, eliminating the few remaining elements of the original community spirit in favour of a more rigid business system. Decisions were made from the top down, and a lack of transparency and other problems arose. This led to the voluntary retirement of a large part of the staff, and in turn the CEO eventually resigned. [→B124]

Located in the northeast corner of the CAT site, the WISE complex—which extends on 2,212 m² GIA—has incorporated and expanded an old quarry building. It presents a clear sequence of volumes, courtyards, and terraces at different levels on the slope. [→■10,12] The design is such that the visitors move in a gradual spatial progression that alternates between intimate and open spaces and offers ever-changing vistas, with a reflective and contemplative approach that is typical of Lea. [→■9] He said: "Views out to surrounding landscapes can change and unfold in surprising ways as we follow the route from room to room. I want people to experience the beauty of nature, the amazing complexity and harmony of its patterns and its ever-changing effects." [→B323:62] The WISE building is a serene and welcoming place, a monastery for learning that offers a high quality of living to its diverse users.

Next to the restaurant, a larger room was provided that is at the same time a new dining space, a reception area, and an airy lobby. [→■13,14] It is generously glazed towards the arcade that embraces the old and new buildings. The lobby is also illuminated from a skylight next to the back wall. An unassuming door in the southeast corner, which is reached by walking up a flight of steps, gives access to the educational complex.

To the left is the Morgan-Grenville courtyard, which contains the old waterwheel pit and an adjoining shallow pool surrounded by a gravel surface that some visitors find reminiscent of a Zen garden. [→■15] Gargoyles perch on the drains of roofs and terraces, and spout the water running off into the pools. In the time between lectures, this space is populated by students standing barefoot in the slate-lined pools or sitting on a few larger rocks emerging from the gravel. On the east and north sides, a timber-decked, roofed ambulatory defines an outdoor route to the workshops. The south side is fully glazed and visually connects the courtyard with the foyer of the lecture theatre.

The latter is a circular drum of rammed earth that seats 180 people. [→B118,136] [→■22] The theatre is used for lectures and film projections. The stage is set to one side; the zenithal oculus that illuminates it can be closed with a rotating disc. A monumental sliding door to the south provides access to the ambulatory and an outdoor seating area. [→■23] The combination of skylight, double-glazed wall to the south, and rammed-earth wall allows the ambulatory to be seen as a huge Trombe wall system. [→■24] As Blundell Jones observed, the drum is "important for the visual balance of the whole complex and makes a worthy mix to the squareness of the court, subscribing to an old architectural rhetoric of gathering people for a unifying event". [→B42] [→■16] Many feel it recalls a sacred space. In plan, the circular shape of the theatre mediates between the north and west wings which follow the geometry of the old building, the court in the middle, and the east wing, whose axis is slightly twisted. Such twist "opens up the foyer as a kind of crossroads and definitive social centre" of the whole complex. [→B42]

In line with the edge of the court, stairs that overlook the stack of waste slate at the back provide access to the upper floors. [→■17] On the right, the east wing accommodates offices opening onto a large terrace, while the left part of it as well as the whole north wing contains twenty-four en suite double rooms on two floors, which are used by students or rented to tourists. The rooms are accessed from open galleries running behind them, which provide cross-ventilation and give privacy to the rooms. [→■18] The façade is a sequence of opaque, timber-clad walls and large sliding windows that open the rooms to the ample roof terrace and a view of the landscape, giving the lively feeling of a hillside village. [→■19] At the southern end of the east wing, a seminar room with a bay window protrudes towards the valley.

The site was levelled out using more slate debris. [→B127] To minimise the use of cement, wherever possible limecrete—a concrete that uses NHL5 as a binder—foundations were specified. However, due to the poor stability of the slope, reinforced concrete had to be used on the steep east side. [→■21] For this,

[→■22]

[→■23]

[→■24]
Section of the theatre drum wall and ambulatory, scale 1:50

1 terne-coated stainless steel roof sheet; 50 mm timber battens; 18 mm plywood decking; vapour-permeable underlay; air gap + (150/50 mm radial rafters; 350–1045/150mm plywood web radial I-beams); 450 mm cellulose insulation; 150/50 plywood web I-beam + 125/38mm @ 400 mm ceiling joists; vapour control layer; 12.5 mm plasterboard

2 20 mm lime render; 500 mm hemp-lime + 150/50 timber studs; 20 mm lime plaster

3 450 mm rammed earth

4 22.5 mm oak timber decking; 120 mm gravel substrate; single ply EDPM membrane; 19 mm plywood; 250 mm cork panels; vapour control layer in rubber; 12 mm plywood; 50 mm perlite insulation; 12 mm plywood sheathing; 150/50 mm Brett-stapel deck, lower edge planed

5 22.5 mm ash flooring; 19 mm plywood; 36 mm wood fibre + under floor heating pipes; 12 mm plywood; vapour control layer/radon barrier; 50 mm hempcrete levelling screed; 250 mm perlite insulation in bags; 50 mm sand blinding

6 22.5 mm ash flooring; 19 mm plywood; 100/50 mm floor joists; air gap + timber frame; 12 mm plywood; 68 mm hempcrete levelling screed; 200 mm perlite insulation in bags; 50 mm sand blinding

7 protection board; polypropylene waterproof membrane; 215–300 mm sand lime brick (outer leaf painted with cold-applied damp proofing); 300 mm perlite; 102.5 mm sand-lime brick; vapour control layer; skim coat of render

8 50 mm cork insulation; 102.5 sand-lime brick; 300 mm hempcrete; 102.5 sand-lime brick; 50 mm cork insulation

9 22.5 mm ash flooring; 50/48 mm floor joist; 19 mm plywood; 68 mm hempcrete levelling screed; 200 mm perlite insulation in bags; 50 mm sand blinding

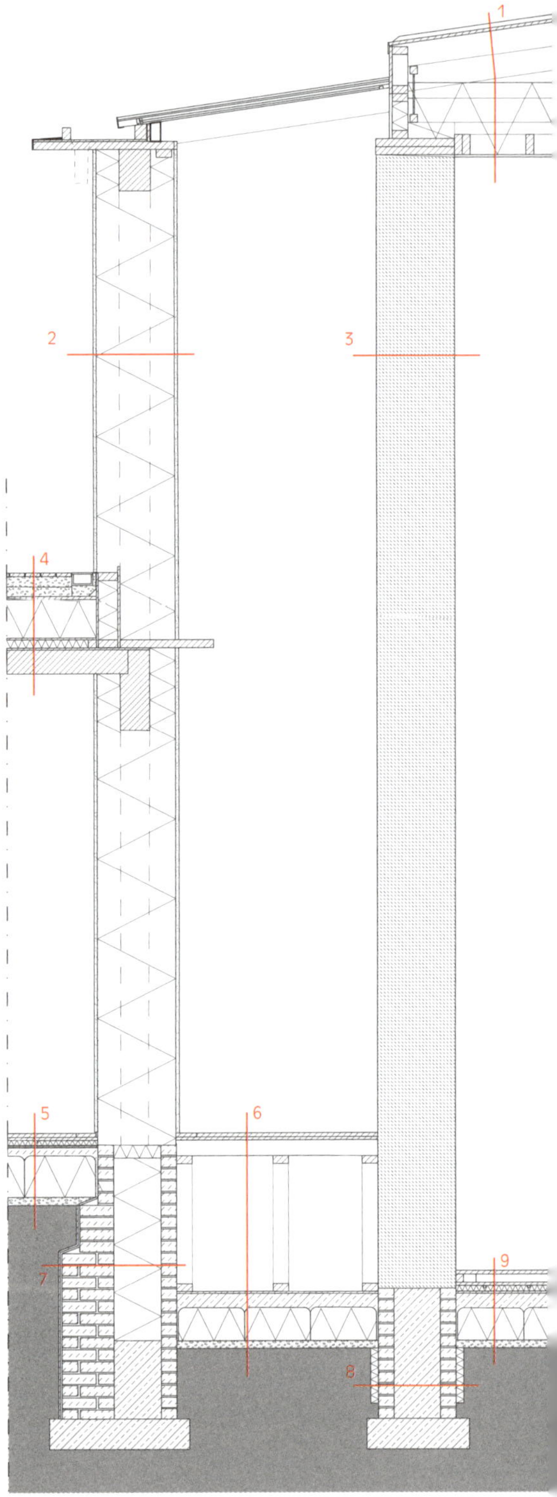

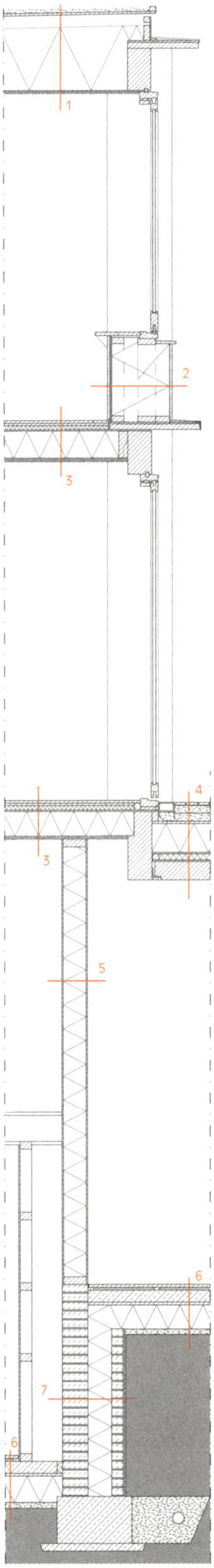

[→■26]
Section of the south façade of the north wing, scale 1:50

1 35 mm gravel; EPDM membrane; 18 mm plywood sheathing; 50/50 counterbattens + ventilation gap; 520–400 mm cellulose insulation; 520–400/47 mm trussed rafter @ 500 mm centres; 12 mm plywood; 12.5 mm plasterboard; skim plaster

2 20 mm two-coat hydraulic lime render; 485 mm hempcrete + 100/50 mm studs @ 600 mm centres; 15 mm wood fibre permanent shutter; 20 mm two-coat hydraulic lime plaster

3 22.5 mm ash flooring; 19 mm plywood; 36 mm wood fibre + under floor heating pipes; 10 mm shadow gap; 220 mm cellulose insulation between joists; 2x12.5 mm plasterboard

4 22.5 mm oak timber decking; 120 mm gravel substrate; single ply EDPM membrane; 250 mm cork; vapour control layer in rubber; 12 mm plywood; 50 mm perlite insulation; 12 mm plywood sheathing; 150/50 mm Brettstapel deck, lower edge planed

5 12 mm plywood boarding; 200 mm cellulose insulation; 12 mm plywood boarding

6 25 mm ash timber flooring; 24 mm wood fibre + under floor heating pipes; 100 mm limecrete slab; vapour control layer; 25 mm softboard; 200 mm perlite insulation; damp proof course; 50 mm sand blinding

7 225 mm sand-lime bricks; 200 mm perlite insulation; 102.5 mm sand-lime bricks; polypropylene waterproof membrane; protection board

[→■25]

[→■27]

[→■28]

50% of the Portland cement was substituted with granulated blast-furnace slag. The perlite-filled cavity plinth walls supporting the timber frame were made of autoclaved calcium silicate bricks. To avoid cold bridging, cork slabs were used at key points of the foundations. The ground-bearing slabs were made with hempcrete on 200 mm of bagged perlite draining insulation with a 25-mm softboard on top and a vapour control/radon barrier of recycled polythene.

Floors are either homegrown ash boards or ceramic tiles dry-laid on plywood and are provided with underfloor heating.

Most of the load-bearing structure consists of glulam timber frames with galvanised steel flitch plate connections, to carry important loads over long spans with a minimum expenditure of material; [→■20] weight and EE are lower than a steel or concrete structure, but a small amount of formaldehyde glue had to be accepted. Freestanding round glulam columns, tapered for visual pleasantness (entasis), have been used in indoor spaces and covered areas, while most of the structure is hidden in the walls.

The frames of the upper storeys and the roof, where loads and spans are smaller, were made of softwood beams. Floors are made of 150x50 mm solid timber joists like in a Brettstapel, maximising the plan's flexibility. The deterioration of the unsheltered timber structure was one of the main factors that led to the change of contractor; the damage was so extensive that the timber could not be left with its natural finish as expected.

The roof slopes were insulated with 400 mm of recycled cellulose fibre between masonite I-beams and covered with 18-mm sheathing plywood, an EPDM waterproofing membrane, and tin-coated stainless-steel sheets. The terrace roofs and flat roofs are insulated with 250-mm cork panels and covered with an EPDM membrane and a cedar decking or gravel or expanded clay and soil on which grass grows.

A total of 790 m^3 of timber was used. Wood was also used for door and window frames, windowsills, and sliding louvered screens on south-facing windows; reveals were made of wood-wool.

The courtyard walls were made with slate from the demolished old quarry building, while the facing cladding of the plinth walls is made from new slate. Internal walls are timber studs with cellulose insulation; some were infilled with unfired and unstabilised clay blocks instead. 2,000 m^2 of perimeter walls were infilled with UK-grown organic hemp shiv and a proprietary lime binder (a mix of pure lime and possibly 15% Portland cement). [→■25,26] The cement is useful for, among other things, giving the initial set, since carbonation takes place over a longer time. Despite the cement content, walls retain breathability. The mono-material, massive, and wet construction removes the necessity for an airtight membrane. William Stanwix and Alex Sparrow claim that "it is possible to combine lightweight insulations with heavy thermal mass materials, but this is not as effective as combining the two into one material [as hemp lime]". [→B292] Walls are 500 mm thick with a U-value of 0.14 W/m^2K, and were rendered with limewashed lime render with a warm, rich ochre pigment.

The lecture theatre has visually attractive load-bearing rammed-earth walls, 500-mm thick (with hindsight, Borer says 600 mm would have been better), left unfinished on both faces. [→■27] They are 7.2 m high and form a circular structure with a diameter of 14.4 m, divided into three sections by two full-height gaps for doors. To construct such an ambitious project required careful control and skilled operation, from the choice of the raw materials onwards; several materials were tested at CICM, University of Bath, and a waste product with specific size, grading, and clay content was chosen. They brought 320 tonnes of earth from a quarry near Oswestry, the same that had supplied earth material for the AtEIC walls. The ramming required 230 working days by four people; earth was laid in 100-mm layers, which were compacted to half-volume to achieve the specified density and strength. [→■28] No lime or cement binder was employed. A proprietary shuttering system, with an adjustable radius, was rented: the rental alone cost more than two-thirds of the total cost of the earthen walls. The final cost was about £800/m² (930 €/m²): at the AtEIC it had been £190/m² (220 €/m²).

During the construction the walls needed to be protected from rain: to use a temporary roof or to build the roof first (as was the case at the AtEIC) would have been possible good practices, but at WISE the contractor decided to use only tarpaulin, thereby slowing down the work. The rammed-earth walls support the roof but are never exposed to the outside and are waterproofed to ensure durability.

Fired-clay pipes have been used throughout for ducts and drains instead of PVC pipes.

The measured therma energy consumption (space heating plus domestic hot water) of the WISE building is remarkably low, about 55 kWh/m²a, thanks to the high level of insulation and thermal mass, the care taken over cold bridges, the airtightness, and the high-efficiency glazing. It was also designed to maximise passive solar gain, natural ventilation through windows and 'casement vents', and daylighting (even the lecture theatre is effectively illuminated by the skylight). Sliding louvered screens help to prevent overheating in the south-facing offices. Air conditioning is avoided, and mechanical ventilation is limited to the lecture theatre (to prevent it from becoming stuffy as carbon dioxide levels increase) and to the bathrooms and toilets. 68 m² of solar thermal collectors on south-facing roofs supply the bedroom showers and feed the central hot-water tank.

The WISE building displays a wide "palette of low-energy, benign, high-performance, robust, 'pre-industrial' construction methods, with a sprinkling of 'industrial vitamins'". [→B51] In the words of Pat Borer, the result is a building basically made of "plants and earth", real materials "humans have grown up with", [→B208] that reveal a vernacular familiarity. Components with a high environmental impact that might be necessary for effective operation have been minimised. Petro-chemical materials and aluminium have been used sparingly; materials produced with little processing and in a sustainable way were preferred. Local and British products, labour, and professional services were prioritised both to reduce the impact of transport and promote the local economy.

The most surprising feature of WISE is its modern identity, which was obtained through the elimination of the inessential and the attempt to move 'green building' away from the hippie stereotype. "We believe that is how green building is going to be accepted, if it is accepted at all, in the world of students—the real architectural world—who won't look at something if it's hairy wood with grass growing on top." [→B192:5] Lea thinks that people "appreciate that it is a modern building that doesn't refer back to the past", albeit it conveys timeless qualities such as serenity, durability, and a harmonious relationship to landscape. [→B323:54]

The building complex also shows that energy efficiency does not necessarily involve architectural compromises. Rather, energy-saving devices can be integrated into the composition. If we compare the specifications of WISE with the best practices theorised by Borer and Harris in their *Whole House Book*, we see that the former faithfully adheres to the latter, probably due to the will of making WISE a sort of permanent exhibition of materials and techniques. The few cases where it deviates are due to structural problems inherent with the site (reinforced foundations) or to the adoption of glulam wood imported from Denmark.

Reconciliation: Maruyama-gumi

Andrea Bocco Guarneri

Yuki Masami 結城正美 explains that, in the narrative of recent decades, *satoyama* 里山 has been "romantically idealized as a place where humans live in harmony with nature, while at the same time [it has been] neglected and left behind in [Japan]'s economic development". **[→B344:279]** However, she recognises that places still exist where (agri)cultural practice, knowledge, and a way of life cannot be easily differentiated, and explicitly refers to Berkes's concept of 'traditional ecological knowledge'—defined as "a cumulative body of knowledge, practice, and belief, evolving by adaptive processes and handed down through generations by cultural transmission, about the relationship of living beings (including humans) with one another and with their environment" **[→B28:7]**—to describe "the place-rooted, close, and complex relationships among residents as well as between humans and the environment" in a *satoyama* system. **[→B344:280]**

Noto-hantō 能登半島 (and in particular Oku Noto 奥能登—'deep Noto', the tip of the peninsula, with a population of about 50,000 and four municipalities) is one of the symbolic territories, at the national level, for *satoyamas*, and has been recognised at a global level in the framework of the following programmes: the Satoyama initiative of the Japanese government and the United Nations University; GIAHS ('globally important agricultural heritage systems') of the FAO; UNESCO World Heritage Sites; UNESCO intangible cultural heritage (the *ae no koto* ritual, あえのこと, dedicated to the divinity of rice fields). **[→B1,79,154,160]** This impressive series of distinctions was bestowed on Noto at least in part thanks to its marginality, which has preserved its cultural landscapes and productive practices. Nevertheless, there is a risk that protection and labelling activities disjointed from local development might give life to "cosmetic agriculturalism" or "superficial agriculturalism". **[→B153]**

A few ecologically minded artisans and farmers are being attracted to the area and a GIAHS label is to appear on local products, yet such initiatives are still too weak to counterbalance economic and demographic marginalisation trends: there is no sign that the polarisation between a rich south and a poor north is diminishing in the prefecture of Ishikawa. **[→B154:283]** **[→■1]** Designations have led to adopting

[→■1]

a policy of 'valorisation' that focuses on fast accessibility (construction of the Noto airport, ongoing extension of the motorway), that is functional to a bite-and-run consumption and to a trivialisation of the 'experience' of the territory. On the contrary, Oku Noto would need a policy focussed on its uniqueness—that is, it should be promoted as a haven for 'slow life', for all those who want to run traditional and innovative businesses based on natural resources and intelligent manual labour, as well as for 'slow' tourists who are willing and able to enjoy such diversity and appreciate it. Such a policy would require creativity, so to provide good welfare services in a rarefied demographic context.

The Kanazawa University's 金沢大学 Noto Satoyama/Satoumi Meister Program 能登里山里海マイスター育成プログラム [→B365] was started in 2007 "to educate new human resources capable of creating an agricultural, forestry and fishing industry that is concerned about the environment and to develop a new *satoyama* and *satoumi* business"; [→B215] in particular, they believe the local development of the peninsula needs to rely on "the power of youth". To this end, Kanazawa University established a satellite branch in Suzu City 珠洲市 at the farthest tip of the Noto peninsula, where most of the Meister training is offered, and began working with communities, local organisations, and residents in order to study how to appropriately exploit local resources. The programme is run in partnership with Suzu City; each of the partners supports it with 20 million yen (160,000 €) per year. Until 2012 it was a two-year programme; it was later shortened to one year for budgetary reasons. The Meister programme's foci are biodiversity, environmentally friendly agriculture, community revitalisation, food safety, creation of added value to local products, eco-tourism and exchange between urban and rural areas, and the continuation of traditional culture and techniques. All of these are holistically understood as mutually dependent and mutually reinforcing. According to Kanazawa University, the ideal student profile encompasses prospective environmentally friendly farmers, business-minded practitioners, and local leaders. One hundred and sixty-five trainees have graduated so far. About one-fifth of the graduates are from big cities, three-fifths from Oku Noto itself, and one-fifth from the rest of the prefecture, meaning that the programme is especially useful for local young people to increase their cultural tools and awareness.

One of the graduates is Hagino Yuki 萩野由紀, who in 2010 launched a learning community called Maruyama-gumi (Team Maruyama) [→B370] with her husband Kiichirō.

Maruyama is the name of a local round-shaped forested hill (maru means round and yama a forested hill or a mountain), located in the township of Mii-machi 三井町, within the city of Wajima 輪島市. All of Mii is made up of linear settlements, each consisting of a single row of houses located at the edge between the forested slope on one side (exploiting the slope for water supply) and the terraced paddy fields on the other: pure *satoyama*! [→■2,3] Until the 1970s, the rice paddies around the Maruyama were small, with a narrow and elongated shape, and were worked by hand. The farmers also tended small vegetable patches, and the levees between the paddies were used to plant soybeans and azuki beans 小豆. After farmland consolidation, though, plots were made larger and square, so as to facilitate mechanised work, and monoculture took over.

In 2009, Hagino Yuki began surveying plants on the Maruyama and its surroundings. A "citizen science programme" supported by the Ministry of the Environment was already in place there at that time as part of the initiative '1000 monitoring sites of Japan'. [→■4] This was the last place on the main islands of the Japanese archipelago where a *toki* 朱鷺 or crested ibis (*Nipponia nippon*) had been observed in 1970 (recently, the *toki* has come back, although

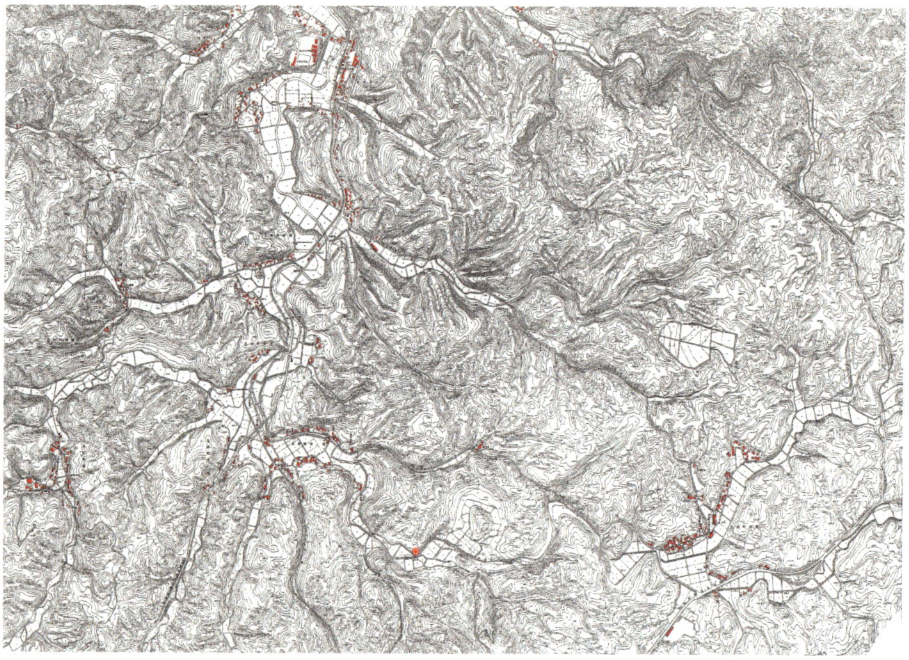

[→■2]

[→■3]

[→■4]

[→■5]

[→■6]

sporadically). The fauna survey initiatives of the very small group mostly relied on the woman who had started them, but she suspended her involvement after she became pregnant. The Haginos, together with professor Itō Koji of Kanazawa University, took over and enlarged the scope of the work, establishing a connection between the people engaged in the survey and the rice farmers tending the neighbouring fields. Moreover, the surveys were shifted from weekdays to weekends to attract more participants. In the first year, Yuki organised eight campaigns, with a total of 299 participants and 252 species recorded. The maximum biodiversity was found in the *kagenagi* かげなぎ, the areas adjacent to a paddy field that farmers are customarily allowed to keep free of shrubs that would shade their plot, even though such areas do not belong to them.

Team Maruyama has been developing as "a loosely knit yet durable network of people" [→B344:282] who want to promote a harmonious use of the territory and who share an interest in the cultural and ecological knowledge in Oku Noto. The team is made up of "farmers, fishermen, craftsmen, architects, designers, intellectuals", [→B154:275] both local and nonlocal. Their goals are mainly to conserve local biodiversity and revitalise the local community, and to establish a locally centred two-way sharing of knowledge and findings between 'foreigners' equipped with a scientific understanding of ecology and residents equipped with traditional knowledge.

Team Maruyama's monthly activities take place on the third Sunday of each month from April to December. They "include the monitoring and observation of plants and animals around the Maruyama and lunches cooperatively prepared by the participants". [→■5,6] [→B344:284] Learning is based on sensory perception, including through food; information on plants and insects is not merely scientific, "but blended with their cultural significance. They explain, for instance, what is edible or poisonous, why particular plants found in the rice fields of natural farming do not exist in conventional rice fields, and which green plant is [mixed] into the *mochi* rice cakes that the whole community enjoys in the winter". [→B344:287]

In addition, Team Maruyama conducts learning programmes for Mii elementary school pupils; scientists and elderly members of the community ten times a year to give them a holistic understanding of the local ecology, which is deeply marked by the rhythm of the seasons. [→■7] These educational efforts are aided by a booklet arranged in the form of a calendar that was drawn and written by Hagino Yuki. [→■9] It is a touching poem dedicated to the local, traditional knowledge of ecological cycles. For each month, a visual guide is offered that shows which plants and animals are found, and where. It also gives tips about their uses and suitability as

[→■7]

food, tools, medicine, toys, or for use in festivals. Information is also provided regarding the plants' and animals' shapes and colours, and about endangered, invasive, and poisonous species. Yuki shows local elementary school pupils and middle school students, both local and from other places, how to make maps of local *satoyama* system issues, drawing on information from senior residents. Awestruck by the richness and vitality of the local ecosystem, Yuki realised that "the divinity of the rice fields is

[→■8]

[→■9]

biodiversity itself". [→B154:276] Now Team Maruyama celebrates a highly original and unconventional *ae no koto* ritual. [→B112] [→■8]

For all the activities mentioned above, Team Maruyama has attracted nationwide attention, winning a Biodiversity Action Award in 2014. The Haginos hope a community will develop spontaneously among participants. Their modesty also reflects their efforts to be accepted by native residents. [→B344:282–284]

One of the team members is Arai Hiroshi 新井寛, an organic rice farmer who is also a Satoyama Meister graduate. [→B369] He was living in Tokyo and looking all over Japan for a place to practise natural agriculture. The municipality of Wajima helped him to settle here. For the first five years he received subsidies. He cultivates twenty-two fields of various sizes for a total of 3 ha. He started with half of that area, but as the elderly farmers retired, they leased more land to him. He sells his rice via the Internet (premium quality at 800 to 1400 yen/kg; rice grown in fields close to those still cultivated using conventional methods is of lower quality).

Arai only grows rice, but on the levees of his paddies members of the Maruyama team grow soy and azuki beans. Arai started with Fukuoka's 福岡 and Kawaguchi's 川口 [→B98,151] no-till methods, but each year his yield decreased. Now he ploughs the paddies at the end of each winter; yet he does not use any fertiliser, not even vegetable fertilisers. Arai claims he is the only professional organic farmer in Oku

Noto (there are two more, but they only grow for personal consumption). There are abandoned fields everywhere on the peninsula, but Arai thinks it is very difficult to cultivate them. It is not clear if he says this because it is difficult to rent fields or because of the poor return considering how much work would be necessary.

The Haginos were both born and raised in Tokyo. Hagino Kiichirō studied architecture at the University of Tokyo 東京大学 and later at the University of Pennsylvania in Philadelphia, where the couple lived between 1993 and 1996. They returned to Japan with an outsider's perspective on the country and had a newfound appreciation for the training, skilfulness, and cooperative attitude in traditional craftsmanship. Kiichirō was employed as a part-time teacher at the Meiji University and other schools, and in 1998 he started his own architectural practice in Tokyo. As they were attracted by plasterers' (*sakan* 左官) and papermakers' crafts, they came to Noto in 2000. The climate and culture shock that greeted them in Wajima, where habits are more old-fashioned, was greater than they had experienced in America.

In 2001, they moved back to Philadelphia but still came to Noto for two months each summer. Yuki learned how to make *washi* 和紙 paper at Tōmi Kazuyuki's 遠見和之 paper mill in Mii according to a special local method, while Kiichirō was enthusiastic

[→■10]

[→■11]

about working on site and reconciling with real materials (he always asks his clients to be involved in the construction of their homes, and his teaching is never disconnected from the practice of construction). This was a place where he could practice this approach and build with natural materials, for instance in the tradition of raw-earth walls, which had been preserved thanks to the isolation of the area. In Wajima they found welcoming people and gorgeous summers, and after a while they were reconciled with Japanese culture.

What made the Haginos decide to settle in Oku Noto is the significance of the "lessons of *satoyama* living: wisdom from the rich natural setting and the farmers' knowledge about how to live in balance with their natural and social setting". Kiichirō would have liked to buy and renovate an old house, but they did not find a suitable one that was available for sale. The paper master, the former principal of the local school, and Takagi Shinji 高木信治—a local architect who designed several brilliant traditional-technology buildings in the area—all helped the Haginos negotiate with local villagers so that they could buy a property. They also facilitated the inclusion of the newly arrived couple into Wajima society.

In the end, the couple bought a small plot (1,580 m²) near the forested hill of Maruyama on a south-facing slope, where *ate* trees had been let to grow during the previous thirty years. **[→▪10]** *Ate* 貴, or *Noto hiba* (*Thujopsis dolabrata*), is a cypress with a very fragrant timber that is flexible yet very water-resistant. Kiichirō hired a local carpenter and started felling the trees and levelling the ground. Due to the powerful earthquake that struck Noto in March 2007, they stopped building for a year: various houses in Wajima had collapsed and Kiichirō contributed to the reconstruction. A contractor was called in to carry out the reinforced concrete work; friends, students, and local artisans helped the family in the construction of the house. No building permit was ever issued (in Japan it is not necessary for buildings outside of designated settlement areas if the floor plan does not exceed 500 m²). The Haginos began living in their new house in 2009.

Kiichirō works as an architect; his architectural office is in a small townhouse just in front of the former Mii railway station. Both of his employees are also Satoyama Meister students. He designed a lot of impressively well-crafted small residential and commercial buildings both for local clients and in the Tokyo area. He is also very active in the preservation and restoration of the earth infill warehouses (*dozō* 土蔵), locally used also as workshops for the lacquerware industry, some of which were damaged by the Noto Peninsula earthquake. The renovation was conducted according to rediscovered vernacular procedures. To remake the earth walls of a *dozō*, he called in a master *sakan* from Kyoto, Kuzumi Akira 久住章, and many people joined the work to learn from him. **[→▪12]** A neighbouring *dozō* was transformed into a permanent site to host earthen techniques workshops. Besides this, Kiichirō teaches at the University of Toyama 富山大学 and maintains a number of international connections. Yuki works as a photographer, essayist, environmental educator, and food creator. **[→B113,114,115,116,117]** **[→▪11]** She also designs packages, websites, and even does the interior design for shops that sell local products. Some of these products are also sold at the famous Wajima morning market, as well as in Kanazawa and Tokyo. In some cases, she not only designed the packaging of a product but also dyed it, making use of weeds. Most of her clients are also Satoyama Meister graduates, whom she is helping to network and team up. She designed a special charcoal burner for the last traditional charcoal-maker in the peninsula, made of fired *keisodo* diatomaceous clay

[→▪12]

[→■13]

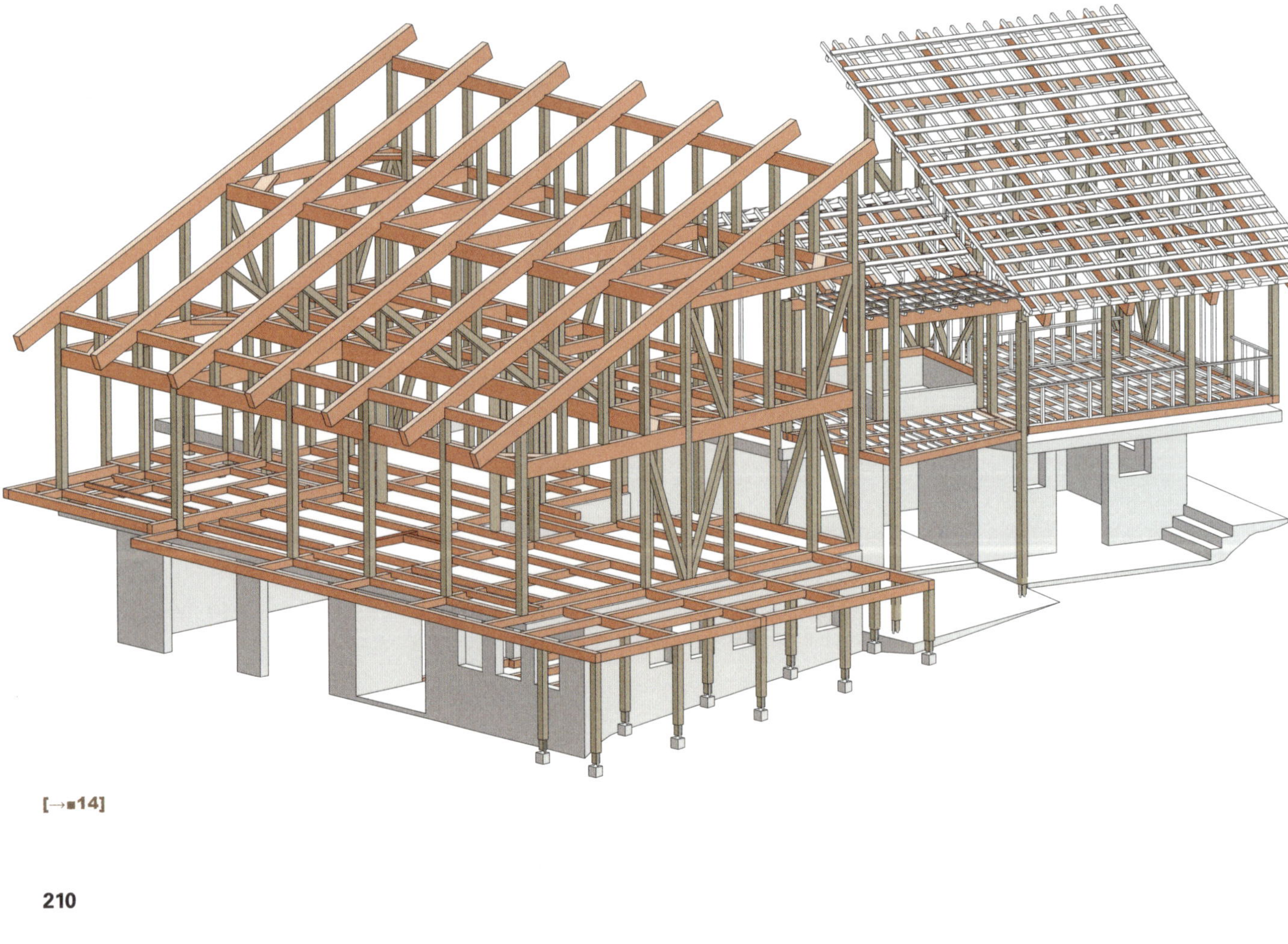

[→■14]

珪藻土. It is a particularly lovely object, radiating a soft glow and a little warmth. It provides an alternative, if only symbolic, market to man-made charcoal, which is otherwise just employed in luxury tea ceremonies. She is now going to start her own sweets shop and café in the basement of their house.

The house lies within the limits of the Noto-hantō Quasi-National Park, at an altitude of 146 m a.m.s.l., and is 800 m away from the small village of Mii-machi Ichinosaka 三井町市の坂. Yuki Masami has argued that this is an expression of

> the new residents' sense of humility toward the traditional village community … [T]he choice of having a home midway between the traditional community and the forested hill seems to imply the Haginos' intention to learn both from the local native people and the local ecosystem. … [T]he location of Team Maruyama is spatially and culturally designed to bridge between tradition and science, natives and non-natives, and humans and the environment. **[→B344:283,284,288] [→▪13]**

The house serves as a base for Team Maruyama activities and was initially designed for a family of five (a couple plus three children). At present, however, the two eldest children have moved to Tokyo, as will the youngest next year.

The total floor area is 197 m² GIA. The house—together with WISE **[→§11]** perhaps the best piece of architecture in this book from a compositional point of view—is two storeys high, with a basement at ground level on the front side and sunken into the slope at the back. The load-bearing structure is reinforced concrete on the bottom level and a timber frame above, that is left exposed inside and clad with horizontal boarding outside. **[→▪14,16]** The structural members are bolted, and threaded tie rods and plates are employed at the base of the posts. Kiichirō did not use plates in the post-beam connections, as is usually done, taking advantage of the fact that a building permit was not required.

The house consists of two wings that meet to form an obtuse angle. **[→▪15,19]** The main one is deeper and contains the kitchen, the full-height living spaces, and a mezzanine that overlooks it. The narrower east wing is offset by half a floor. It contains cellars and storerooms downstairs and the master bedroom and bathroom upstairs. Both wings have single-pitch roofs sloping towards the front and covered with corrugated metal sheets.

The house is accessed from the back. The main floor is just slightly above ground level on this side and is reached by going up a few steps under a porch and an external staircase. The entrance (where the raw concrete slab will eventually be covered by an earth floor) is followed by another buffer space with a timber floor wonderfully textured with an adze (*chōna*) by Amemiya Kunihiro 雨宮国広, a carpenter famous for his involvement in the Kezurō-kai 削ろう会 association promoting international exchanges in wood crafts. **[→▪17,18]** This space gives way to the large, full-height living-cum-dining room, with glazed walls on three sides and a cast-iron stove. **[→▪20]**

Two of the columns supporting the mezzanine are the de-barked trunks of trees felled on the spot. This creates a typically *wabi-sabi* 侘び寂び interaction between the geometrically precise forms and dimensions of most timber elements and the gentle undulations and irregular surfaces of the trunks. Other features in tune with this aesthetics are: preference for simplicity and rawness, removal of superfluousness, acceptance of decay and aging, and of materials patently vulnerable to atmospheric elements and human manipulation. **[→B163]** In fact, natural materials age well and return "to the earth more slowly and with more grace". **[→B83:xv]** Glazing and shutters can be slid to transform the room into something like an open veranda, overcoming the separation between inside and outside. It has been observed that "sitting in this room you feel like you are in a quiet temple in the mountains: the sense of unity with nature is overwhelming". **[→B3] [→▪20]** The dining space is complemented by a wide terrace spanning the whole south front. The floor of the space in the northwest corner was arranged to accommodate tatami flooring, but this was never installed. **[→▪23]**

Going up the stairs, you first reach an intermediate landing that corresponds to the level of the east wing above the *doma*, with its master bedroom (now left unused and unheated in winter) and bathroom, where you can plunge into hot water while looking at the greenery from the large window. **[→▪21,22]** Next to it is a small terrace that enhances your sense of connection with the surrounding space. If you go

[→■15]

[→■16]

[→■17]

[→■18]

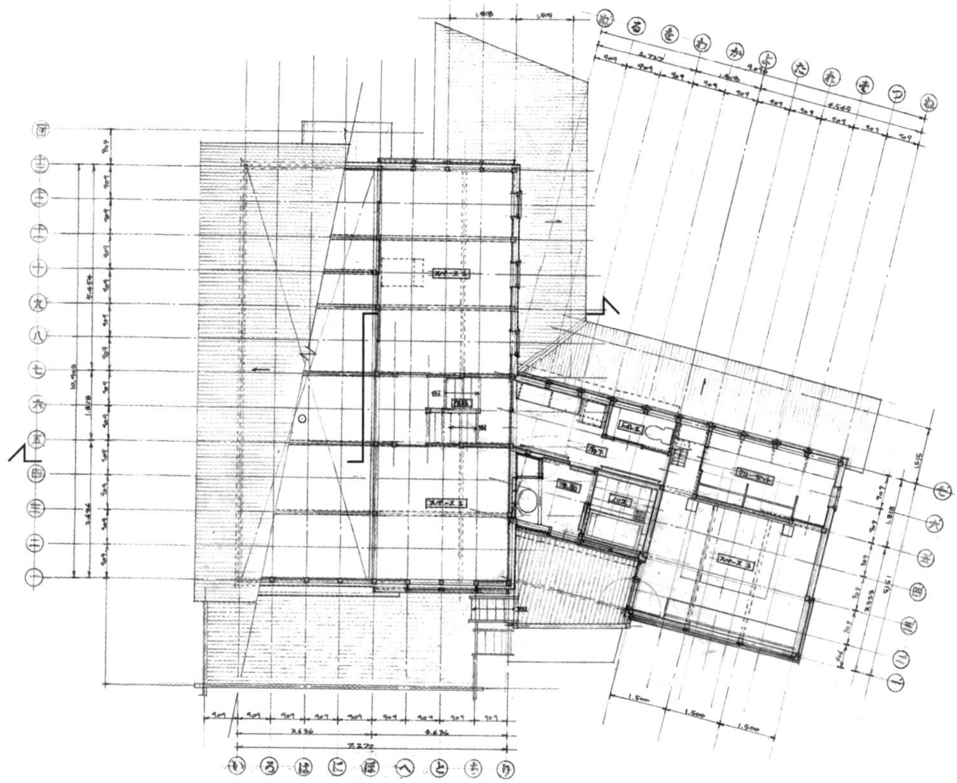

[→■19] Second and first floor plans, scale 1:200

[→■20]

[→■21]

[→■22]

[→■23]

[→■24]

[→■25]

[→■26]

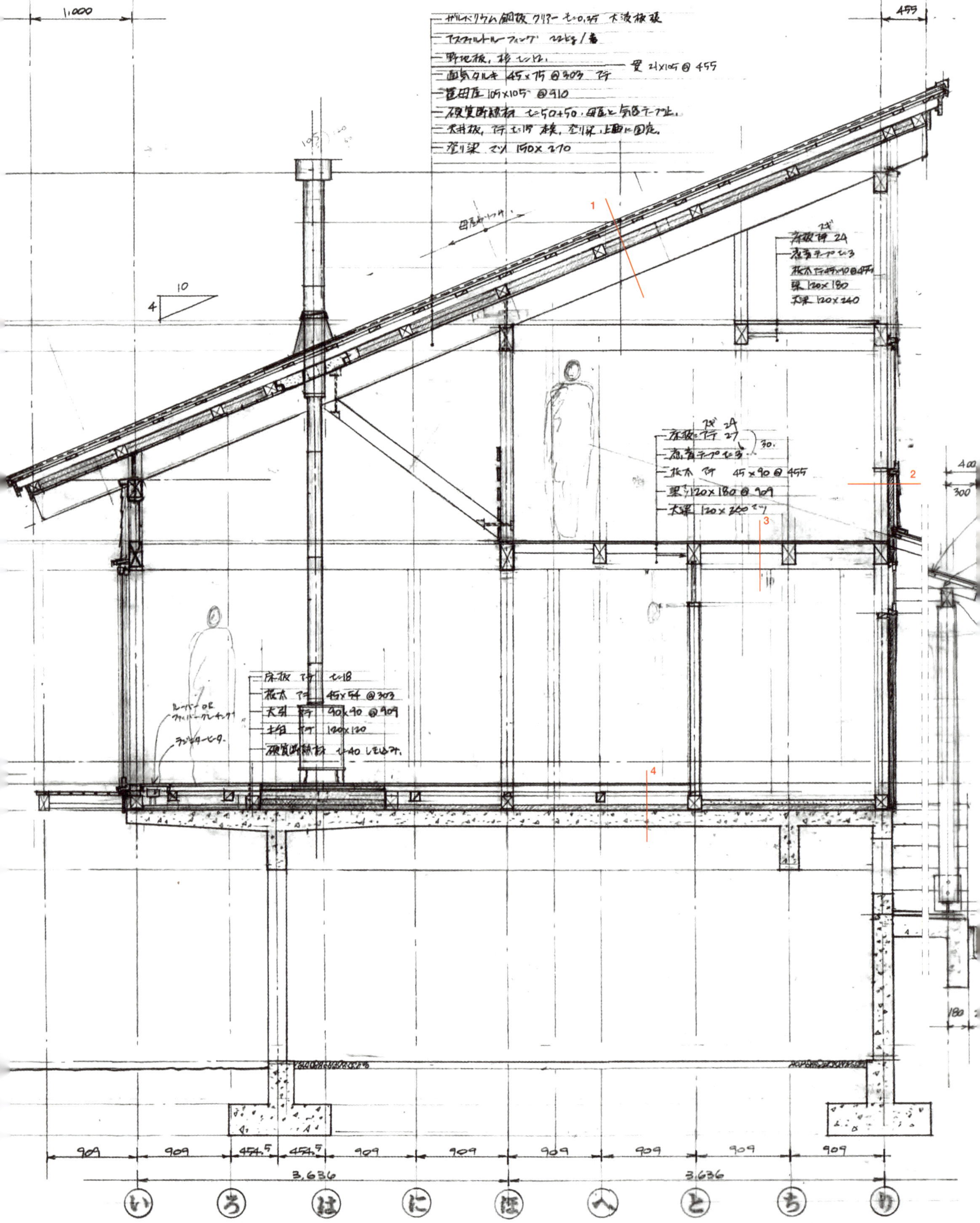

1,000
455
ガルバリウム鋼板 クリアー t=0.35 大波板張
アスファルトルーフィング 22kg/巻
野地板, 杉 t=12
10
4
床板 アテ t=18
根太 アテ 45×54 @303
大引 アテ 90×90 @909
土台 アテ 120×120
根太 アテ 45×90 @455
梁 120×180 @909
400
300
180
1
2
3
4
909
454.5
3,636
い
ろ
は
に
ほ
へ
と
ち
り

[→■27] left page
Section, scale 1:50

1 galvanised steel corrugated sheet; asphalt roof membrane; 12 mm cedar board sheathing; 21/105 battens @ 455 mm centres; 75/45 mm *ate* rafters @ 303 mm centres + ventilation gap; 2x50 mm phenolic-foam insulation panels; 15 mm *ate* board ceiling; 270/150 mm *ate* principal rafters

2 12 mm *ate* boards; waterproof membrane; 21/50 mm *ate* battens; 50 mm phenolic-foam insulation panels; 5,5 mm plywood

3 24 mm cedar flooring; 90/45 mm cedar joists @ 455 mm centres; 180/120 mm beams @ 909 mm centres + (240–300)/120mm girders

4 18 mm *ate* boarding; 54/45 mm *ate* joists @ 303 mm centres; 90/90 mm *ate* garter @ 909 mm centres; 120/120 mm *ate* beams; 50 mm phenolic-foam insulation panels; 150 mm reinforced concrete slab

up a further flight of stairs, you reach the mezzanine that originally accommodated the children's rooms (the larger room is now used as the parents' winter bedroom). [→■24,16]
From the kitchen—a veritable laboratory full of all kinds of utensils and ingredients—you can walk down another half-storey and get to a *doma*-like room with a handmade earthen floor. [→■25,26] This facilitates access to the food-storage space, provides an auxiliary service entrance, and will allow direct access to Yuki's sweets shop.
Most rooms have hand-planed ate boards as flooring and ceilings. The infill panels in the framed walls are plywood—sometimes limewashed, sometimes left unfinished, not an aesthetic choice but because the entire house has never been complete in all of its details. All furniture—beds, desks, bookcases—is handmade. The long table was made by Kiichirō; the tabletop consists of two wide *ate* planks. Electrical cables run in metal pipes which were boldly left exposed.
The Haginos' house is an exception to the Japanese attitude, which usually takes for granted that the battle against winter is fruitless and does not try to insulate houses (usually the Japanese do not even bother to close the front door behind them if they know they will have to leave again). This house is somewhat insulated with double (in the roof) or single (in the perimeter walls) 50-mm-thick phenol foam panels and is heated with a cast-iron wood stove

[→■28]

[→■29]

(average yearly firewood consumption: 19.63 m^3) and a kerosene-burning boiler that heats water, which is circulated in radiators (located underfloor at the foot of large windows; consumption amounts to about 250 litres per year). [→■27] Direct solar gain from the large glazed areas of the southeast and southwest walls can also help in sunny winter days. Sanitary hot water is provided by a propane gas boiler.

The land the Haginos own extends just around the house. Apart from a few berries, nothing can be grown there because it was formerly a forest. The soil is unsuitable both chemically and in terms of grain size. However, Yuki cultivates three fields below the road, which the local elderly farmers no longer use, where she grows the vegetables and legumes the family needs. [→■28,29] Moreover, Yuki bakes bread, harvests wild plants nearby, and makes her own soy sauce and preserves. All food I was offered during my visit comes from the locality, including the wild-boar meat. [→■30]

[→■30] From bottom right, clockwise:
Rice cultivated in natural agricultural methods around Maruyama by Mr. Arai, steamed in an earthenware pot, topping with sesame and salt made at a seaside field using splashing sea water, called "Agehama method"揚浜塩田 in Wajima.
Sakekasujiru 酒粕汁, a soup mixed with *sake* lees from Hakuto Sake Brewery in Wajima and *miso*, with daikon, carrot and *enoki* (hackberry).
Mizuna greens and roasted paprika with salted wild boar meat caught in the village and cooked with a Dutch oven.
"End of winter" sweet: a paste made with white *azuki* bean and *tsukune-imo* (Chinese yam), with the green colour and flavour of *yomogi* (mugwort) inside. This represents Maruyama preparing spring sprouts under the white snow.
Before and after eating, all bowls with different size can be stacked into one piece, a kind of nest of bowls. This set of four bowls is one of the traditional styles of Wajima-nuri lacquerware. This menu is an *ichiju-issai* (一汁一菜) meal with one soup and one side dishes, and rice as a main, which is a typical simple menu in Japan. This time, Yuki added a sweet so she named it *ichiju-issai-ikka* (一汁一菜一菓), which Yuki is considering as a menu for the sweets café she is planning to open on the ground floor of her family house.

Quantitative comparisons and overall discussion

Andrea Bocco Guarneri
(data processing Martina Bocci)

In this final chapter, I will try to propose some quantitative considerations with respect to the cases examined. From a methodological point of view, it is necessary to first state some premises:

- The building materials used are analysed in detail but are presented in the charts aggregated in three macro-categories (vegetal materials; all other natural materials; man-made). For the sake of comparison, these categories are used to describe all the case studies.
- The environmental impacts of buildings are both expressed in absolute values and in values per kilogram, per square metre, and per capita. The surface area is consistently defined as gross internal area (GIA), that is, as the sum total of surface areas measured at the inner face of perimeter walls. This choice was due to the fact that what counts is the amount of space available for living, and also to the fact that in buildings where the envelope is insulated with natural materials such as straw bales, the thickness of perimeter walls can be significant and heavily affects the gross floor area (GFA), that is, the sum total of surface area measured at the outer face of perimeter walls. Similarly, GIV (gross internal volume) was considered, not the whole built volume.
- ICE **[→B121]** and Ökobaudat **[→B376]** databases were chosen to calculate the embodied energy (EE) and 'embodied carbon' (EC) of buildings because they are open access and readily understandable even for inexperienced users, in spite of being based on verifiable sources, and because of their reputation. However, when picking a database, one inevitably needs to embrace the assumptions that come with it. Users are not immediately aware of these assumptions, nor can they modify them to adapt to their own special situations. In the case of this book, this would have been particularly relevant because (similar to what differentiates organic from conventional agriculture) the conventional process—from felling a tree to having a dimensional timber element ready for use at the building site—implies a much greater number of operations (including sawmilling, packaging, and transportation) than what actually happens in an

'alternative' construction, where some of these operations are skipped altogether and others are of very limited extent and sometimes performed without power tools. [→B137] In other words, this means that databases inevitably cannot cover the full range of fine-grain variations in how materials are actually processed and just provide values for conventional manufacturing. This can result in an overestimation of the environmental impact, which is certainly the case here for Villa Strohbunt and Cheia, which were more or less extensively self-built.

- Mainstream databases appear ill-suited for correctly describing the impacts associated with labour-intensive building operations that make use of locally sourced, low-technology, organically grown building materials, which can be found in 'green' buildings, and particularly self-built ones. It should be noted that, even given such limitations, there sometimes exists a disorienting discrepancy between values provided by respected databases. For instance, calculations based on the Ökobaudat database give better results than those based on ICE as long as global warming potential (GWP) is implied, while the reverse is true for primary energy intensity (PEI). These divergences are not only due to obvious differences in the national (UK and German) 'energy mixes' and industrial manufacturing processes, but also because of dissimilar methodology and assumptions in the assessment procedures, particularly (but not only) those concerning the calculation of CO_2 'locked up' in building material of vegetal origin.
- The discrepancy between the data contained in different databases can be so large that sometimes one may question their fundamental reliability. In the case in question, a large part of this divergence is due to the different environmental profiles of timber and timber-based products in the two databases. Specific problems arise regarding the theses underlying this book from the fact that Ökobaudat, while admitting negative values for EC (which favours materials of plant origin), provides very high values for EE of poorly processed plant materials. Since the primary sources are heterogeneous, the comparability of the data is seriously questionable, to the detriment of ecologically aware choices. Particularly disorienting is the case of straw, for which Ökobaudat reports the EE value calculated by FASBA, a body that should promote its use, which is fifty-five times higher than the value found in ICE. In Ökobaudat, the EE value for straw is in turn just slightly less than that for structural steel and more than three times greater than that of fired bricks, whose production must require much more energy. The discrepancy between databases has not yet been adequately investigated, probably because each of them is so far used almost only within the country where it originated and because those who perform LCA assessments usually rely on proprietary software and seldom calculate the environmental impact of a building by adding up the single components manually, as we did. [→B191] The discipline is still very young. A European database covering a full range of building materials and equipped with conversion factors for different countries would be very helpful.
- German or English industrial values were improperly used for all the buildings studied, including vernacular and Japanese buildings, even where the production methods of building materials are probably very different. Nevertheless, given the impossibility of calculating appropriate and contextual values, it was decided to use Ökobaudat and ICE values for all case studies for comparison purposes only.
- Where the products identified were not attributable to the entries in the two databases, EPDs available online were used.
- PEI was accounted in its entirety, regardless of the renewability of the sources, also to try to avoid 'tricks'. It is not particularly important to use renewable energy sources; what matters is to use little energy. [→B74,125,192] Also, because in the specification of building materials, designers, builders, and inhabitants depend on the decisions of others (national energy policies, production methods of manufacturing companies).
- Only phases A1 to A3 ('cradle to gate') have been considered. Phase A4 (transport of mate-

rials from the factory to the construction site) has been omitted owing to the lack of information on where the products used were actually manufactured. This simplification is acceptable because usually, even though road vehicles are used, transport affects EE and EC by a few percentage points. Phase A5 was also excluded because of the impracticability of the accountancy. Even when we were in the ideal position to record the energy used day by day on a construction site, the building team manager refused to do so, as she could not see any usefulness in such a task, in spite of her commitment to green ideals.

- The building services were excluded from the calculations because of their difficult quantification. Often the designers themselves have only approximate information on the matter, as the working project is left to technicians. In general, it can be assumed that the services entail an increase of about one-quarter, [→B162] and this is confirmed by the results we obtained, [→B46] but obviously this depends very much on their complexity. In cases 1, 2, 7, and even 5, we can reasonably expect a much lower incidence of services.
- The environmental impacts considered (i.e., energy use and greenhouse gas emissions) are only calculated for new products, on the basis of the principle, accepted by many, whereby the entire impacts associated with the production of construction products ('embodied impacts') are attributed to the time of production itself. In other words, the impact of everything that constitutes an existing building on which renovation work is carried out, as well as any element that is reused, for example by salvaging from another building, is zero.

The first and crucial step was, as in all environmental assessments, drawing up an inventory. In small, owner-controlled building processes it is common that bills of quantities are incomplete or missing altogether. In fact, this was the situation in most of the case studies. Meticulous inventory work was therefore carried out by Martina Bocci on purposely created 3D 'as built' models.

These models do not necessarily correspond to the project drawings provided by the designers, as changes are often made during the construction phase. The most striking example is Biestøa, whose design weight would have been just under 150 tonnes (its PEI would have been 858 GJ according to ICE, and its GWP-49 tCO_2 according to Ökobaudat), while its weight 'as built' is just under 330 tonnes (resulting in a PEI of 1374 GJ and a GWP of 25 tCO_2 according to the same databases).

The massive buildings are the heaviest. [→■1] Yet, from a construction point of view, it is surprising that a massive masonry building (case 3, Steila Mar) is not the heaviest, but rather load-bearing straw bale buildings 6A and 6B that show low values of 'man-made materials'. Certainly, questions of form affect the result. The volume of these two buildings is large relative to the floor area. Their values of weight/GIA > 2,500 kg/m^2 also explain why their unit EE is high. After these two buildings, the only two exceeding 2,000 kg/m^2 are cases 8 and 10, as the construction technique of Wangelin places limitations on the span and in Biestøa a high weight was implied by foundations and ground insulation.
In addition, the percentage of natural materials is low due to both the AAC masonry and the foam glass against the ground. Cases 1, 4 and 5 are around 1,000 kg/m^2: the data clearly show that framed load-bearing system buildings are more efficient from a structural point of view (less weight for the same surface area). In a similar position is case 2, but on account of its structural material, since it has a massive wooden system (log construction). The Bamboo Ark (7) is out of class because it is a temporary pavilion with no thermal envelope.

The maximum percentage values for natural materials are in cases 1 (which is a traditional building), 5, 6A, 6B, and 7. They are followed by 3 and 2, which is slightly lower despite being a vernacular building because of the concrete piers. All of these can be said to be real 'vegetarian buildings'. The minimum value is in case 12: it weighs a lot because of the concrete basement, but apart from the foundations, it is not made of much. If we look at the vegetal component, it exceeds 50% only in case 2; it is over

		area	weight	EE (ÖBD)			EE (ICE)			GWP (ÖBD)			GWP (ICE)		
		m^2	kg	MJ	MJ/kg	MJ/m^2	MJ	MJ/kg	MJ/m^2	$kgCO_{2eq}$	$kgCO_{2eq}$/kg	$kgCO_{2eq}/m^2$	$kgCO_{2eq}$	$kgCO_{2eq}$/kg	$kgCO_{2eq}/m^2$
1	Hirose House	114	106,880	196,714	1.84	1,726	46,891	0.44	411	-19,535	-0.18	-171.36	2,804	0.03	24.60
1 (r)		114	81,637	196,714	2.41	1,726	46,891	0.57	411	-19,535	-0.24	-171.36	2,804	0.03	24.60
2	Cheia	23	25,738	119,697	4.65	5,168	41,458	1.61	1,790	-12,665	-0.49	-546.86	6,055	0.24	261.45
2 (r)		23	21,744	119,697	5.50	5,168	41,458	1.91	1,790	-12,665	-0.58	-546.86	6,055	0.28	261.45
3	Casa Steila Mar	572	911,500	2,098,102	2.30	3,666	1,017,282	1.12	1,777	-104,428	-0.11	-182.45	71,055	0.08	124.15
3 (r)		572	204,818	2,098,102	10.24	3,666	1,017,282	4.97	1,777	-104,428	-0.51	-182.45	71,055	0.35	124.15
4	Sandberghof	411	469,598	1,522,870	3.24	3,702	1,129,233	2.40	2,745	-34,911	-0.07	-84.86	78,847	0.17	191.65
4 (r)		411	305,981	1,522,870	4.98	3,702	1,129,233	3.69	2,745	-34,911	-0.11	-84.86	78,847	0.26	191.65
5	Villa Strohbunt	103	106,864	152,943	1.43	1,480	43,035	0.40	416	-47,906	-0.45	-463.62	22,360	0.21	216.39
6A	Createrra	65	166,427	802,515	4.82	12,346	870,105	5.23	13,386	-14,701	-0.09	-226.16	43,971	0.26	676.48
6B	Gartist	125	343,872	2,870,826	8.35	22,877	1,462,162	4.25	11,652	-130,775	-0.38	-1,042.11	110,330	0.32	879.19
7	Bamboo Ark	176	29,460	253,430	8.60	1,439	253,430	8.60	1,439	4,845	0.16	27.51	12,223	0.41	69.39
8	Biestøa	153	329,165	1,373,869	4.17	8,989	968,785	2.94	6,339	25,165	0.08	164.65	66,277	0.20	433.63
9	Food Hub	61	67,683	303,307	4.48	4,972	265,489	3.92	4,352	3,604	0.05	59.08	19,844	0.29	325.31
10	Wangeliner Garten	156	340,417	810,835	2.38	5,201	1,645,879	4.83	10,557	8,665	0.03	55.58	103,322	0.30	662.74
11	WISE	2,212	1,966,399	15,159,743	7.71	6,853	9,732,250	4.95	4,400	-178,197	-0.09	-80.56	687,557	0.35	310.83
12	Maruyama-gumi	183	276,623	1,412,038	5.10	7,717	1,205,822	4.36	6,590	9,941	0.04	54.33	96,973	0.35	529.99
	average values				4.55	6,626		3.47	5,066		-0.91	-187.45		0.25	361.99

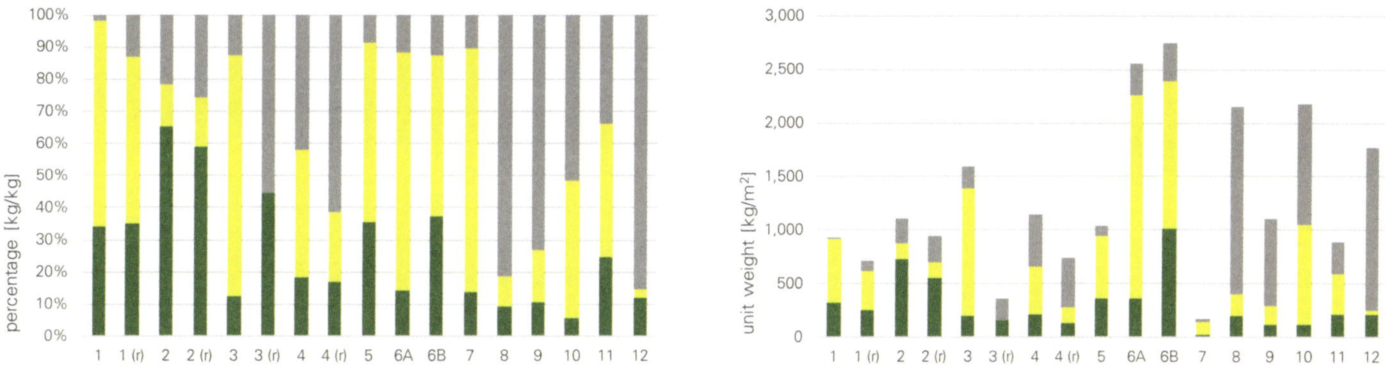

[→■1] left: building weight by material classes
right: unit weight by surface area

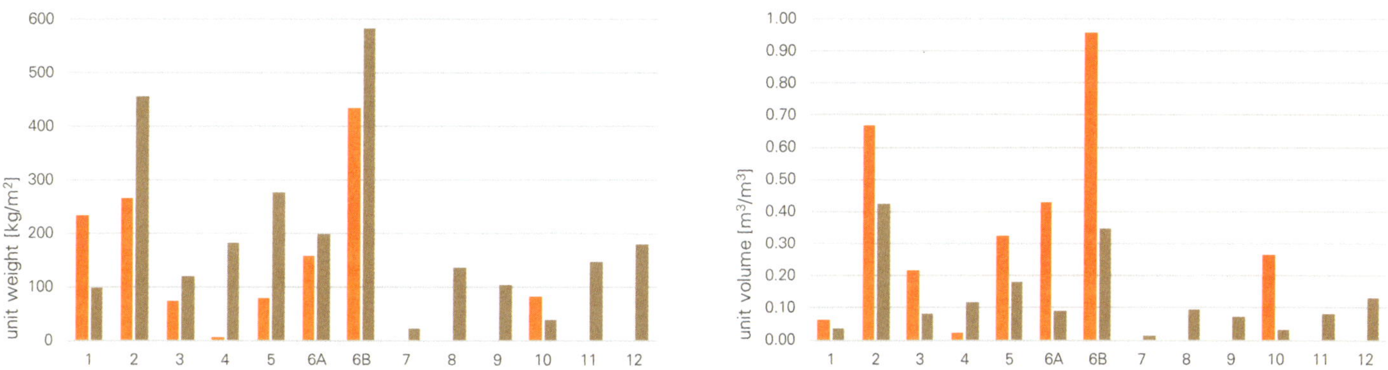

[→■2] left: unit weight of straw and wood by surface area
right: unit volume of straw and wood by total volume

vegetal | other natural | other | straw | wood

one-third in 6B, 5, 3 (retrofit): straw and wood do not weigh much (low density) compared to aggregates.
Cases 1, 2, 4, 5, 7, 8 are load-bearing timber (or bamboo) constructions; 6A, 6B, 10 are load-bearing straw bale constructions, at least partially. [→■2]
Although not load-bearing, timber prevails over straw in 6B (Gartist), which has more timber per unit area than a *Blockbau* house (but not per volume, even if only slightly); it has much more straw, both per surface area and volume, than all the others.
Straw is employed in a range of ways in the eight buildings where it is used; case 1 has a thatched roof, and straw was added to the earth mixture in the walls and in the floor of one of the rooms. In 2 it is similarly used in the roof as such and mixed with other materials in the walls and floors. In 3 it constitutes the thermal insulation of walls and roof. Similarly, in 6A and 10 it takes a load-bearing function. In 4 it is just mixed with earth; in 6B and 5 it fully wraps the building.
In Cheia (2), the straw roof has a high incidence per volume, a little less per surface area; but the value of m^3 straw per m^3 GIV is always higher than that of m^3 wood per m^3 GIV, except in case 4, where in fact straw plays a marginal role (in the mix of soil and straw of the infill panels). This is due to the lower density of straw compared to that of timber. The value of kg timber per m^2 GIA is always higher than that of kg straw per m^2 GIA, except in cases 10 (where timber is used only in certain structural elements, including those of rooms with pitched roofs at the sides) and 1 (where the thatch roof prevails over everything else).
The higher the ratio between the volume of straw or timber and the inhabitable volume, the more inefficient the construction is from a structural point of view as well as in terms of the use of material. (Of course, these are not necessarily the only issues to take into account: thermal mass and embodied energy are just as relevant and point in the opposite direction.) Cases 2 and 6B have a lot of built volume compared to the inhabitable volume; 3 is not significant because these data do not show the masonry mass; 10 has also other important mass (AAC masonry); 5 and 6A are the most efficient in terms of the use of material: envelope and structure are basically all represented in the chart, there is not much else than straw or timber.

To conclude these considerations on the efficiency in the use of building materials, it can be observed that the architectural forms of buildings 6A and 6B do not seem very easy to exploit and do not manage to do without timber. Building 8 is very well devised, but its construction entirely based on timber makes it perhaps only appropriate to Scandinavia and Austria.

The two data sources used are different even at first glance: except in cases 6A and 10 (where the use of cellular glass that ICE overestimates compared to Ökobaudat is high), the values calculated with ICE are lower for all buildings; the average value of PEI is 4.55 MJ/kg (6,626 MJ/m^2) for Ökobaudat, and 3.47 MJ/kg (5,066 MJ/m^2) for ICE, i.e., on average, 31% higher values in the German database than in the English one. [→■3,4,5]
The unit EE values for the new interventions alone, which are indicated with an 'r' in the charts, are (much) larger than those for the same buildings as a whole. This means that the weight of the materials added with the retrofit interventions is (more or less) modest compared to the total weight of the buildings. In case 3, the difference between the unit EE of the building as a whole and the unit EE of the new intervention alone is emphasised by the timber component in the calculations made with Ökobaudat. However, due to the high weight of the building as a whole, the EE/weight value of the entire building is still among the lowest.
According to ICE, the highest energy intensity by weight is found in case 7, which is not surprising given its extreme lightness, which makes it not comparable with other buildings (for the same reason, its EE/m^2 values are among the lowest). For Ökobaudat, however, 8 and 3 (only new intervention) rate higher on account of the disastrous EE values attributed to wood and wood-based products and their relatively low weight.
If we consider EE/m^2, according to Ökobaudat, the worst value is by far that of case 6B, again because of the overestimation of the impact of timber and the relatively small GIA in relation to the extent of the built volume. Among the results obtained with ICE, 6A, 6B, and 10 stand out. The best values are those of case 5 for both databases, followed by 1, where it should be noted, however, that the account refers

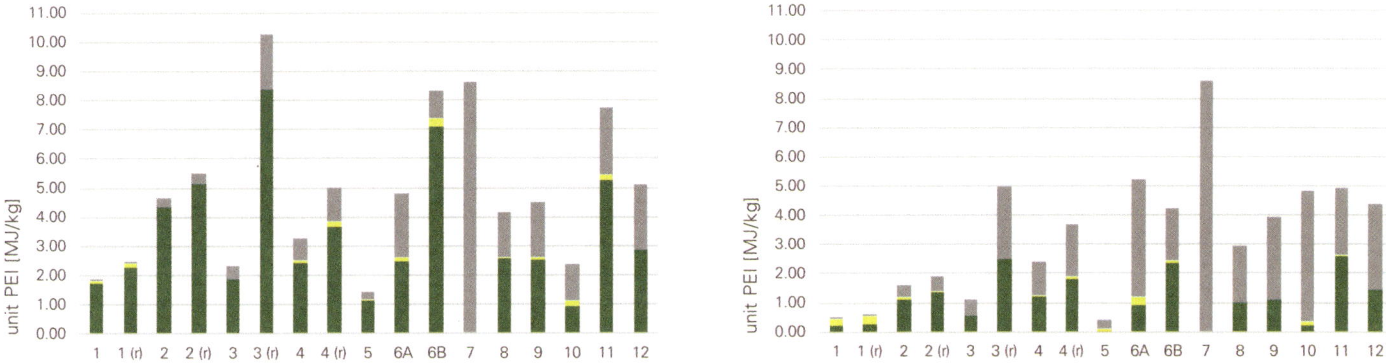

[→■3] unit PEI by weight, left: Ökobaudat; right: ICE

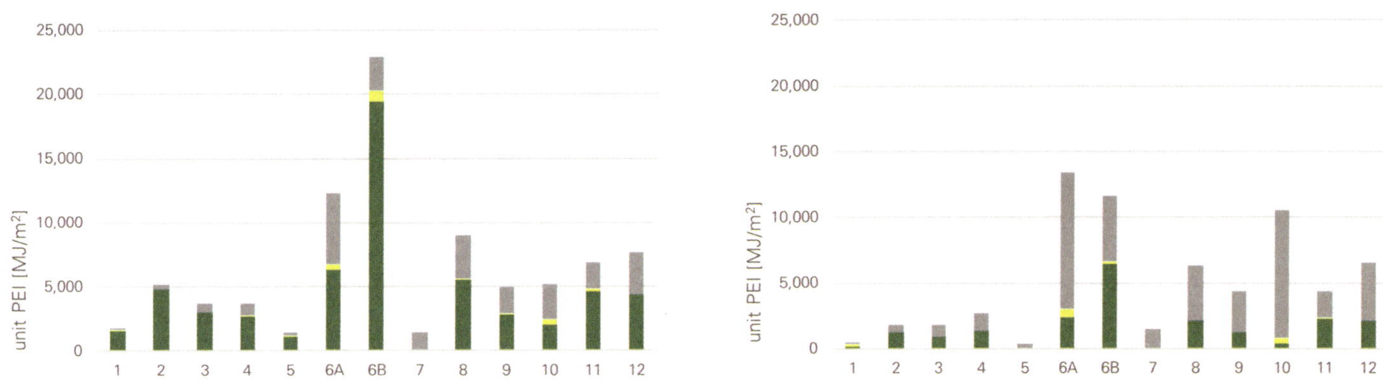

[→■4] unit PEI by surface area, left: Ökobaudat; right: ICE

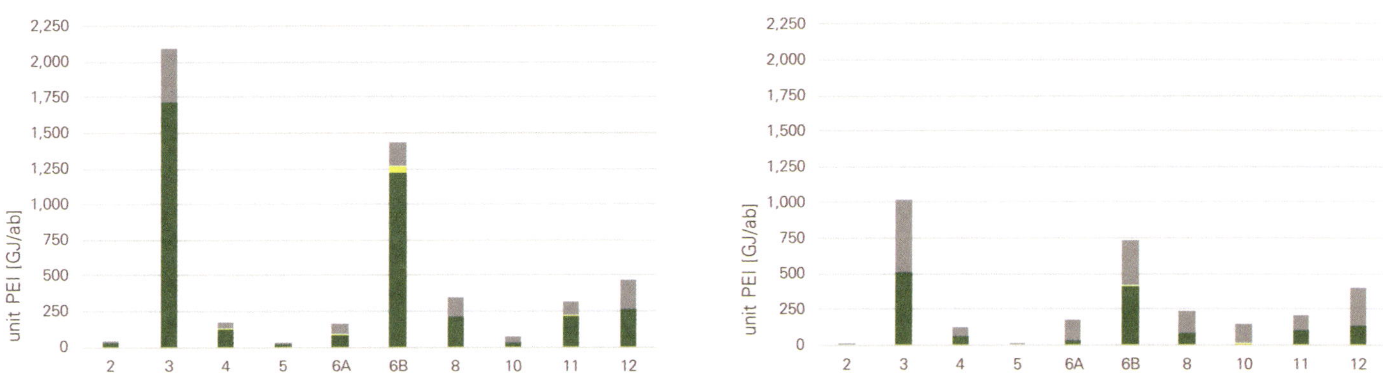

[→■5] unit PEI per inhabitant, left: Ökobaudat; right: ICE

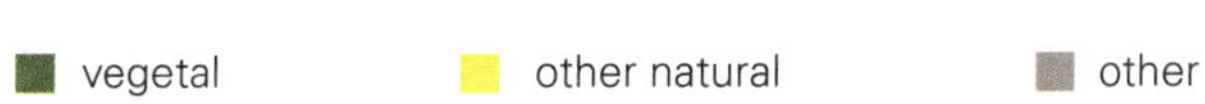

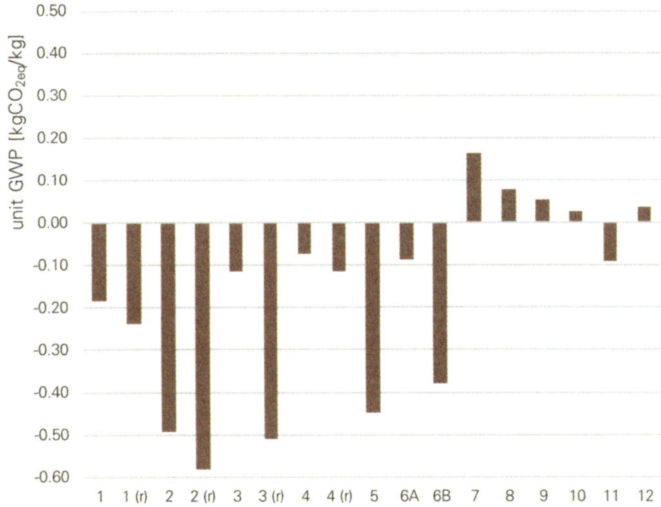

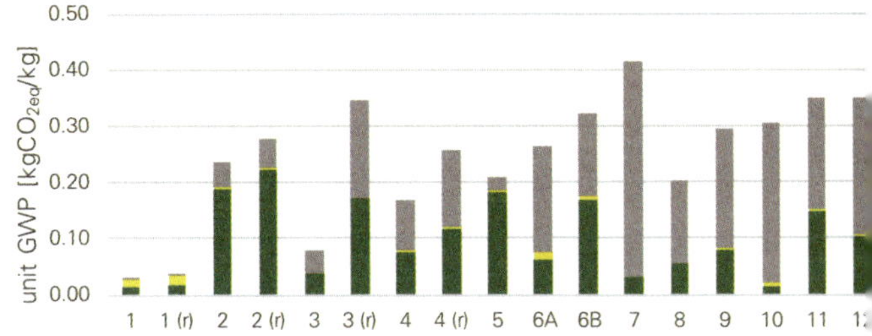

[→■6] unit GWP by weight, left: Ökobaudat; right: ICE

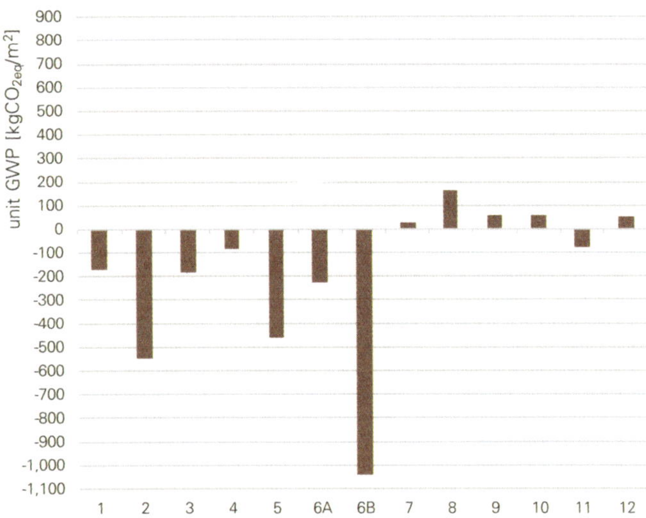

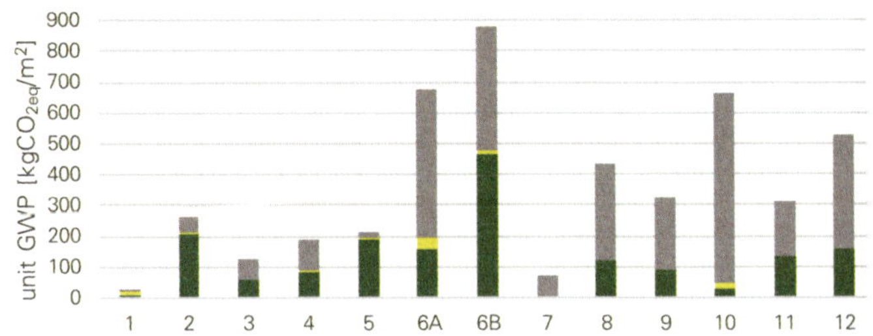

[→■7] unit GWP by surface area, left: Ökobaudat; right: ICE

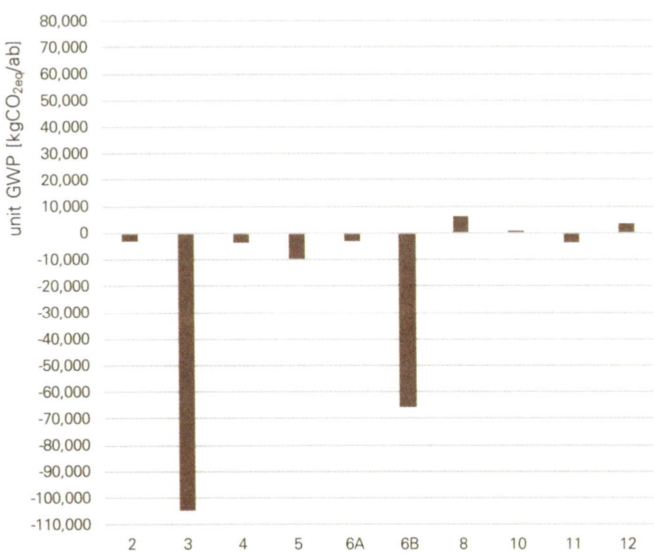

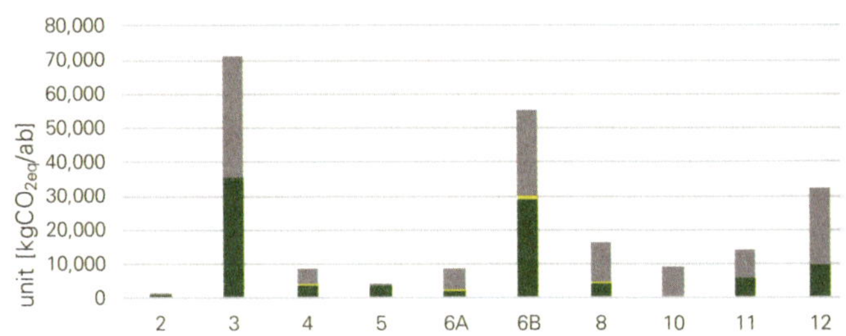

[→■8] unit GWP per inhabitant, left: Ökobaudat; right: ICE

■ all materials together ■ vegetal ■ other natural ■ other

only to the new materials used in the reconstruction at Minkaen and not to those recovered from the original building, and that it offers much lower levels of comfort. It is also fair to say that Villa Strohbunt's EE and EC are a little underestimated because it is necessary to use external spaces to perform domestic functions (the toilet and bathroom are elsewhere).

All buildings have a negative EC (if admitted, as Ökobaudat does), except cases 7 (minimum quantities of bamboo are not enough to compensate for minimum quantities of plastic), 8, 9, and 12 (because of reinforced concrete and/or highly-processed clay materials, and metal elements), and 10 (AAC and especially foam glass). **[→▪6,7,8]** Calculating with ICE, case 7 has the worst EC/kg value, while the results for EC/m^2 are different: case 6B, which for Ökobaudat is the absolute best (that is, it has by far the highest carbon storage intensity), is now among the worst. Ökobaudat also gives good results for cases 2 and 5: an important part of the weight of both buildings is made up of materials that absorb carbon dioxide during their life as plants. Also when comparing the best EC/kg values, the two databases give different results: for Ökobaudat the best is case 2, even better than 5 and 6B, because of the lower weight; while for ICE the best is 1.

Restricting the comparison to the results obtained with ICE, the four buildings with the highest EE/m^2 values also have the highest EC/m^2 values, although in a different order. **[→▪4,7]** Otherwise things remain more or less the same, with the exceptions of cases 2 and 5, which had low EE (very low in the case of 5) and have somewhat remarkably higher EC values. The only building with very low values of both impacts is Hirose.

Accounting for only positive values (as ICE does) allows an easier visualisation of the contributions of the different categories of materials to the total EC. It is interesting to note that non-natural materials contribute more than 50% in cases 4, 6A, and 7 (where their share is almost 94%), 10 (92%), 8 (72%), and 11; instead, in 2 and 5 timber and timber-based materials make an important contribution to EC. Natural non-vegetal materials, on the other hand, have negligible impacts, as was already the case in the calculation of EE.

In the comparison between Villa Strohbunt (5) and Bamboo Ark (7), it should also be considered that at the time of publication of this book, the latter will have already been dismantled, while the former, although with changes in the services and the layout, will still be there and is expected to continue to exist for decades. One more note might be added here. One should not strive for negative carbon accounting, as this might paradoxically result in construction that makes use of any crap, and then adds unnecessary timber-based elements just to lower the EC value.

In the face of so many uncertainties regarding the correctness of the calculations, what the Vales suggested seems to retain validity: "The quickest way to reduce EE is not to worry about calculating it accurately or to try to use materials that have low energy, but quite simply to live in smaller houses." **[→B319:135]** I agree with the plea for fewer square metres per capita, but not with the rest of this statement, as it could be interpreted as a renunciative approach with respect to calculations and an irresponsible one with respect to the importance of choosing materials. Still, they make a valid point. One just needs to consider how much bewilderment can be caused by comparing the EE values shown in Berge's book, in spite of his personal commitment to using natural materials. **[→B25]** The Vales also advocate designing buildings that are long-lasting and easy to repair, recommending tried-and-trusted rather than experimental ways of doing things. **[→B319:189]** Other guidelines that emerge from these analyses are: retrofit and insulate existing buildings; live frugally (i.e. reduce comfort expectations); and opt for multi-family and community buildings over single-family houses. Lastly, if you really have to make new buildings, then maximise passive performance.

The great limit of analyses like these is that they allow more or less detailed comparisons between the cases studied—I have only mentioned the most obvious issues, but many others could—but have no external elements to refer to. In short, are these 'vegetarian' buildings 'better', in terms of environmental impact, than ordinary buildings?

A necessary premise is that many are single-family, or limited-size, buildings and therefore by nature less efficient, from the point of view of the use of materials, than large buildings, as the case studies we investigated confirm.

A first point is that the analysis should of course extend, from an LCA point of view, over the entire life cycle of buildings, while ours is limited to embodied values and does not consider the operational impacts. If these were considered, it would be necessary to introduce into the calculation both the operational energy and the replacements and maintenance (which are usually quite randomly esteemed) over an expected life of the building, the length of which is even more uncertain.

In this book, we have considered only heating OE, which was obtained from statements or measurements made by the inhabitants, and not from calculations (except case 3). [→▪9,10] Some of these OE values (such as that of case 10) are certainly overestimated, because they contain energy consumptions not aimed at space heating, which could not be separated.

The ratio between embodied and operational energy shows very wide variations—from 0.4 to 93.3 according to ICE, from 1.5 to 183.1 according to ÖBD. [→▪11] In itself this is neither 'good' nor 'bad': it merely shows which of the two aspects has been privileged. The goal is the minimisation of both the denominator and the numerator. However, the extreme values of the ratio reveal something significant. At Villa Strohbunt, a very low EE was not enough to obtain very low operational energy (OE/m^2); but this is mainly due to the inefficiency of the heating system, which has now been replaced. Better-performing windows have also been installed. In Gartist and Createrra, energy consumption for heating is very low, but at the same time EE is very high. Further research on building design should focus on how to reduce EE of foundations and below-grade insulation. In fact, it might be challenging to develop solutions to anchor the building on the ground, without the use of artificial materials—such as natural stone foundations, or the ballast used in Bamboo Ark—even in places at risk of earthquakes. In the case of Createrra, it would be useful to detach the building from the ground, but this would be in clashing contradiction with the structural typology.

Perhaps the best balance amongst new buildings is found in Biestøa, in spite of it being burdened, as far as EE is concerned, by unforeseen events (foundations and steel beams added during the works; decrease of the amount of timber employed) and by choices that could have been even more efficient (insulation of the basement). The lowest OE/m^2 would be (assuming the calculated data correspond to reality) Steila Mar, which offers a good case for recovering existing buildings. Moreover, its EE/m^2 values are modest despite the high absolute value (the house is very large). If anything, the patterns of use need to be carefully evaluated: if one considers OE per capita, instead of OE per square metre, one gets a completely different picture. [→▪10] In fact, the lowest values of OE per capita are those of 6A, 6B, 8, and 11: although it must be considered that these buildings have different functions (including residential, educational, workspace) and therefore profoundly different patterns of use. What is certain is that the excellent OE/m^2 performance of 3 and the poor one of 2 are both significantly revisited.

However you look at it, if Maruyama-gumi were in Europe, it would be out of standard in terms of the thermal resistance of the building envelope. In Japan, it can already be considered virtuous, but with three to six times more (possibly natural) insulation, it would be an example to draw inspiration from even in Europe.

I would like to add again that OE is not as important an issue as it is usually considered: we are the living witnesses of the fact that the generations before ours have survived even in houses not or badly heated, and so it is still in Japan. All in all, an energy crisis would be enough to strongly resize OE.

A second point is that there are no systematic reviews of average values of environmental impact (or even just EE and EC) of buildings in the literature. In a previous work, we referred to an article [→B34] where some eighty cases are taken into consideration, and we obtained average values from them; however, these seem so low as to cast doubt on the completeness of the underlying inventories.

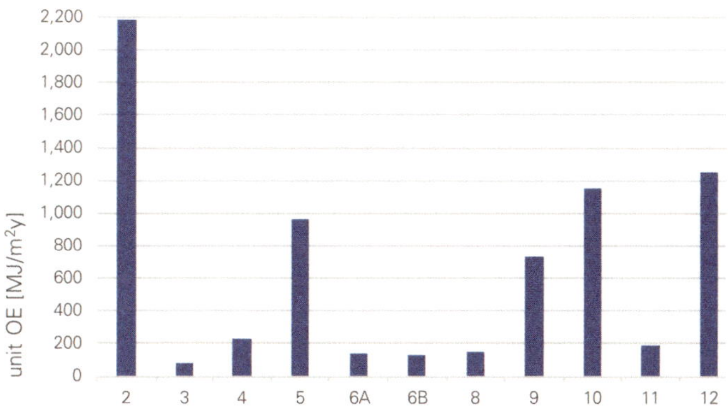

[→■9] unit operational energy by surface area

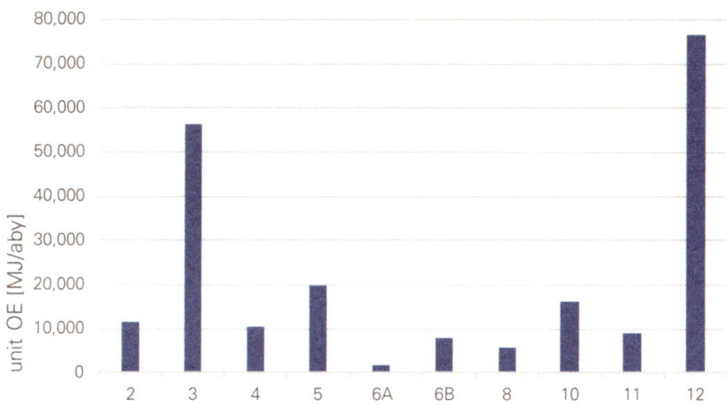

[→■10] unit operational energy per inhabitant

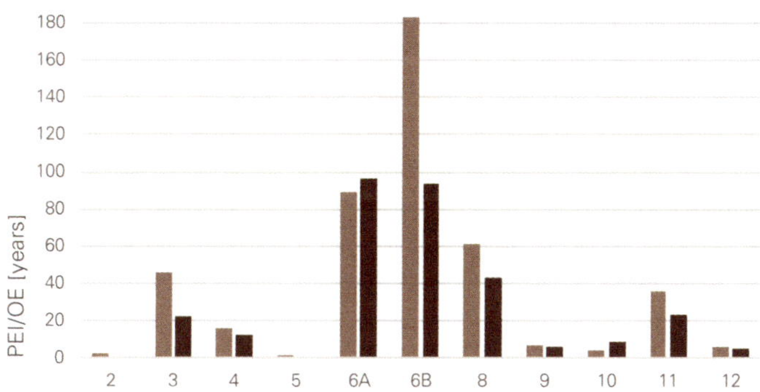

[→■11] ratio PEI/operational energy

■ operational energy ■ Ökobaudat ■ ICE

The authors themselves admit that in some cases projects were analysed, in other buildings 'as built', and that the latter may show environmental impact values twice as large as the former. Moreover, the variations between cases are extremely wide, up to two orders of magnitude. [→B223]

A third point concerns the even more radical question of whether—even in the case in which there were reliable average values of EE and EC to refer to—the fact that a building shows lower values than these average values could be a reason for satisfaction. The reference should rather be the 'absolute environmental sustainability' threshold, [→B35,224], or 'fair share' [→B320], i.e., it should not have relatively less impact than the average but rather impact within the limits of the ecosystem. There is no doubt that this is the direction to take, but there is still a long way to go, much more than with regard to the previous point. The issue is very complex and embraces many more parameters than EE and EC alone, but beyond this there is a delicate problem regarding the allocation of the maximum allowable threshold to each sector of human activity (how much for buildings, for transport, for food, and so forth). The proxy proposed by the authors, far from being indisputable, is in fact to allocate according to the incidence of each of these sectors on the monetary economy.

I suspect that to stay within the limits of sustainability one should possibly live in a way that is not dramatically different from the traditional way in vernacular buildings. In fact, per capita EE values are really low in cases 2 and 5 only. [→■5] Probably, our expectations of comfort (and in some cases, the regulatory requirements) have gone too far to allow us to be sustainable, regardless of the quality of the energy performance of buildings. However, the retrofit of the built heritage would probably be sufficient to stay within the limits of 'sustainability', provided that space is intensely exploited.

Finally, the question of how to evaluate even more complex and multidimensional impacts, which have to do with the social, economic, and cultural vitality of the territories, the quality of life, biodiversity, the ability to transmit knowledge and awareness, is completely open. This is certainly not the place to address issues of this magnitude; cases 9 through 12 are, among many others, possible examples of local commitment in these areas.

In retrospect, it might be argued that 'green architecture' has been practised by two different generations. First came a generation of committed pioneers who accumulated a great deal of practical experience, but lacked the tools for verifying quantitatively the results of their work in terms of energy consumption and conservation. This generation was succeeded by another prepared to use protocols made available in the meantime, that often contents itself with satisfying them without critically verifying their substantial adherence to the principles of sustainability.
This account is certainly caricatured. Yet these two approaches still coexist, and seldom hybridise. On the one hand, there are designers who provide largely aesthetic descriptions; though inspired by environmental ideals and clear about their objectives, they lack experience with using and interpreting data. On the other hand, there are building energy designers and accountants, who instead are good with numbers and can get results that comply with the standards but lack a critical perspective. In a way, I have tried to take the good side of either approach.
Despite the careful choice of case studies and an attempt to meticulously inventory the building materials employed in the works under consideration, the results were not wholly satisfactory, perhaps because of the latter. This research has raised doubts about the completeness of the few comparative studies available and urges for progress in building databases and for improvement in calculation methods.

References

References are given according to ISO 690:1987 and are listed in alphabetical order by author. As in the body of the text, people are named according to local customs: the surname comes after the first name in most European languages; first in Japanese and in some other languages such as Hungarian.

1 *Agri-Culture. The Act of Life*, Kanazawa: Hokuriku Regional Agricultural Administration Office-Ministry of Agriculture, Forestry and Fisheries, 2013

2 Kristina Akermann et al., *Terra Europae. Earthen architecture in the European Union*, Pisa: ETS, 2011

3 Akikawa Yuka, "Philadelphia kara Okunoto e. Jimoto shokunin to yujin to jibuntachi de tsukuritsuzukeru. Noto Mii no ie (Wajima-shi, Ishikawa-ken)", *Confort*, August 2009, p. 103–109 [「フィラデルフィアから奥能登へ。地元職人と友人と自分たちでつくり続ける。能登三井の家 (石川県輪島市) 設計萩野紀一郎」取材、文: 秋川ゆか、撮影: 北田英治、コンフォルト、2009 年8月号]

4 Leon Battista Alberti, *Della architettura, libri dieci*, 1485, as quoted in Aldo Castellano, *La casa rurale in Italia*, Milan: Electa, 1986

5 Christopher Alexander, *A pattern language. Towns, buildings, construction*, New York: Oxford University Press, 1977

6 Christopher Alexander, *The timeless way of building*, New York: Oxford University Press, 1979

7 Christopher Alexander, *The nature of order. An essay on the art of building and the nature of the universe*, London: Taylor & Francis, 2002

8 Paul Allen, *Crazy Idealists? The CAT Story*, Machynlleth: The Centre for Alternative Technology, 1995

9 Miguel A. Altieri, *Agroecology. The scientific basis of alternative agriculture*, Boulder: Westview Press, 1987

10 Günther Anders, *Die Antiquierheit des Menschen*, Munich: Verlag C. H. Beck, 1956

11 Andō Kunihiro, *Kayabuki no Minzokugaku: seikatsu gijutsu to shite no minka*, Tokyo: Haru Shobō, 1983 [安藤邦宏著『茅葺きの民俗学–生活技術としての民家』はる書房1983年)]

12 Massimo Angelini, *Minima ruralia*, Savona: Pentagora, 2013

13 Architecture and Humanity (ed.), *Design Like You Give a Damn. Architectural Responses to Humanitarian crises*, New York: Metropolis Books, 2006

14 "Ark of Bamboo" [sic], *Shinkenchiku*, 12, 2011, p. 107–116, 183 [「竹の会所–復興の方舟」新建築 2011年12月号 107–116頁及び183頁、2011年]

15 Atelier Werner Schmidt, *Aufbau Ausstellungsgebäude, Gartist GmbH* [www.youtube.com/watch?v=Yy-J4tXQ3_0]

16 Nishat Awan; Tatjana Schneider; Jeremy Till, *Spatial Agency. Other Ways of Doing Architecture*, London: Routledge, 2011

17 Alexandru Baboş, *Tracing a sacred building tradition. Wooden churches, carpenters and founders in Maramureş until the turn of the 18th century*, Lund: Lund University, 2004

18 James Baldwin; Stewart Brand (eds.), *Soft-tech*, Harmondsworth: Penguin, 1978

19 "Bamboo Ark", *WA* [*World Architecture*], 8, 2013, p. 108–115

20 Ana Bârcă, *Plastica arhitecturii rurale. Sistem de reprezentări formale şi mentale*, Bucharest: Ad Libri, 2007

21 Rémi Baudouï; Philippe Poitié (eds.), *André Ravéreau. L'atelier du désert*, Marseille: Editions Parenthèses, 2003

22 Tom Bender et al., *Rainbook: Resources for Appropriate Technology*, New York: Schocken Books, 1977

23 Stefano Benvenuti; Vanessa Malandrin; Alberto Pardossi, "Germination ecology of wild living walls for sustainable vertical garden in urban environment", *Scientia Horticolturae*, 203, 2016, p. 185–191

24 Janine M. Benyus, *Biomimicry. Innovation Inspired by Nature*, New York: Morrow, 1997

25 Bjørn Berge, *The Ecology of Building Materials*, London: Architectural Press, 2009[2] [first Norwegian edition 1992]

26 Bjørn Berge, "The engine is not responding. A critique of the automatic energy-saving home", *Arkitektur*, 1, 2011, p. 62–67

27 Bjørn Berge, *Absolute passive energy design. Achieving passive house level by utilizing hygrothermal properties of wood* (Interim report to project HelTREnkelt), Gaia Lista/Asplan Viak/Treteknisk Institutt/Silvinova, December 2014

28 Fikret Berkes, *Sacred Ecology*, New York: Routledge, 2012

29 Franco Berrino, *Il cibo dell'uomo. La via della salute tra conoscenza scientifica e antiche saggezze*, Milan: Franco Angeli, 2016[2]

30 Wendell Berry, *The Gift of Good Land. Further Essays Cultural and Agricultural*, Berkeley: Counterpoint, 1981

31 Wendell Berry, *The Art of the Commonplace. The Agrarian Essays of Wendell Berry*, Berkeley: Counterpoint, 2002

32 *La Biennale di Venezia. 15ª Mostra internazionale di architettura*, Venice: Marsilio, 2016

33 Philippe Bihouix, *L'Age des Low-tech. Vers une civilisation techniquement soutenable*, Paris: Seuil, 2014

34 Harpa Birgisdóttir et al., "IEA EBC annex 57 'evaluation of embodied energy and CO_2eq for building construction'. Case Studies demonstrating Embodied Energy and Embodied Greenhouse Gas Emissions in Building", *Energy and Buildings*, 154, 2017, p. 72–80

35 Anders Bjørn; Michael Zwicky Hauschild, "Introducing carrying capacity-based normalisation in LCA: framework and development of references at midpoint level", *International Journal of Life Cycle Assessment*, 20, 2015

36 William Blacker, *Along the Enchanted Way. A Romanian Story*, London: John Murray, 2009

37 Peter Blundell Jones, "Woodland retreat", *The Architects' Journal*, 27 September 1989, p. 26–31

38 Peter Blundell Jones, "Tra modernità e tradizione", *Spazio e Società*, 55, July–September 1991, p. 12–27

39 Peter Blundell Jones, "Il profumo del legno", *Spazio e Società*, 89, January–March 2000, p. 20–31

40 Peter Blundell Jones; John Sergeant, "New meanings from old buildings", *Architectural Research Quarterly*, 5, 4, 2001, p. 312–331

41 Peter Blundell Jones, *Modern architecture through case studies*, Oxford: Architectural Press, 2002

42 Peter Blundell Jones, "Wales Institute for Sustainable Education by David Lea and Pat Borer", *The Architectural Review*, 21 December 2010

43 Andrea Bocco, "Oltre i confini", *Costruire*, 313, June 2009, p. 88–91

44 Andrea Bocco Guarneri, *Werner Schmidt, Architekt. Ökologie, Handwerk, Erfindung*, Vienna: Ambra Verlag, 2013

45 Andrea Bocco; Gianfranco Cavaglià, *Flessibile come di pietra. Tattiche di sopravvivenza e pratiche di costruzione nei villaggi montani*, Torino: CELID, 2008

46 Andrea Bocco; Martina Gerace; Susanna Pollini, *The environmental impact of Sieben Linden Ecovillage*, Abingdon: Routledge, 2019

47 Varis Bokalders; Maria Block, *The Whole Building Handbook. How to Design Healthy, Efficient and Sustainable Buildings*, London: Earthscan, 2010 [original Swedish edition 2004]

48 Werner Boote, *The Green Lie*, e&a film, 2018

49 Pat Borer, *The CAT 'WISE' Project. Wales Institute for Sustainable Education*

50 Pat Borer, *The evolution of CAT*

51 Pat Borer, personal communication

52 Godfrey Boyle; Peter Harper (eds.), *Radical Technology. Food, Shelter, Tools, Materials, Energy, Communication, Autonomy, Community*, London: Pantheon Books, 1976

53 Stewart Brand, *How Buildings Learn. What happens after they're built*, New York: Viking, 1994

54 Francesca Bretzel et al., "Wildflowers: From conserving biodiversity to urban greening—A review", *Urban Forestry & Urban Greening*, 20, 2016, p. 428–436

55 Azby Brown, *The Genius of Japanese Carpentry*, Tokyo: Kodansha International, 1989

56 Azby Brown, *Just Enough. Lessons in living green from traditional Japan*, Tokyo: Kodansha International, 2009

57 Corneliu Bucur, *Muzeul civilizației populare tradiționale "ASTRA"*, Sibiu: Editura "ASTRA MUSEUM", 2007

58 Corneliu Bucur; Valer Deleanu; Cornelia Gongolea, *Civilizație milenara românească in Muzeul ASTRA*, Sibiu: Editura "ASTRA MUSEUM", 1995

59 Corneliu Bucur; Cornelia Gongolea, *Ghid muzeul tehnicii populare*, Sibiu: Editura "ASTRA MUSEUM", 1986

60 Sarah Bunker et al. (eds.), *Low Impact Living Communities in Britain*, London: Diggers and Dreamers Publications, 2014

61 Enrico Camanni, *La nuova vita delle Alpi*, Torino: Bollati Boringhieri, 2002

62 Colin Campbell, *Whole. Rethinking the Science of Nutrition*, Dallas: BenBella Books, 2013

63 Fritjof Capra, *The Turning Point. Science, Society, and the Rising Culture*, New York: Simon & Schuster, 1982

64 Fritjof Capra, *The Web of Life*, New York: Doubleday, 1996

65 Chiara Catalano et al., "I tetti verdi di tipo estensivo: Biodiversità ad alta quota", *Reticula*, 12, 2016, p. 1–10

66 Centre for Alternative Technology, *An Alternative Energy Strategy for the UK*, Machynlleth: Centre for Alternative Technology Publications, 1977

67 Centre for Alternative Technology, *Zero Carbon Britain. Making It Happen*, Machynlleth: Centre for Alternative Technology Publications, 2017

68 Centre for Alternative Technology, *Raising Ambition. Zero Carbon Scenarios from Across the Globe*, Machynlleth: Centre for Alternative Technology Publications, 2018

69 Giorgio Ceragioli; Nuccia Comoglio Maritano, *Note introduttive alla tecnologia dell'architettura*, Torino: CLUT, 1989

70 Herman Daly, *Steady-State Economics*, San Francisco: Freeman Press, 19902

71 Christopher Day, *Places of the Soul*, Wellingborough: The Aquarian Press, 1990

72 Christopher Day, *Spirit and Place*, Oxford: Architectural Press, 2002

73 Kris De Decker, "Restoring the Old Way of Warming: Heating People, not Places", *Low-Tech Magazine*, 11 February 2015 [https://www.lowtechmagazine.com/2015/02/heating-people-not-spaces.html]

74 Kris De Decker, "Bedazzled by Energy Efficiency", *Low-Tech Magazine*, 9 January 2018 [https://www.lowtechmagazine.com/2018/01/bedazzled-by-energy-efficiency.html]

75 Kris De Decker, "We Can't Do It Ourselves", *Low-Tech Magazine*, 5 July 2018 [http://www.lowtechmagazine.com/2018/07/we-cant-do-it-ourselves.html]

76 Laurence Despins, "Habiter une maison citoyenne", *Maison & Travaux*, 175 (supplément), November–December 2003, p. 56–61

77 Rudolf Ilja Doernach, *Archi Bio. Biosophie + Archaitektur*, Karlsruhe: Verlag C. F. Müller, 1986

78 Leila Dregger, *Tamera. Ein Modell für die Zukunft*, Bad Belzig: Verlag Meiga, 2010

79 Anantha Kumar Duraiappah et al. (eds.), *Satoyama—satoumi ecosystems and human well-being. Socio-ecological production landscapes of Japan*, Tokyo: United Nations University Press, 2012

80 Nurgül Ece, *Baubiologie. Kriterien und architektonische Gestaltung*, Basel: Birkhäuser, 2018

81 *Egao no atsumaru basho—chiiki o mimamoru "Sai no kami"* [笑顔の集まる場所 ー地域を見護る "才の神"]

82 David Eisenberg, *Beyond Green Building & Codes: Seeing a Bigger Picture*, CAZREN & YCCA, Hassayampa Inn, Prescott, Az., 5 December 2009

83 Lynne Elizabeth; Cassandra Adams (eds.), *Alternative Construction. Contemporary Natural Building Methods*, Hoboken N.J.: John Wiley and Sons, 2005

84 Hildegard Elsner, *Wikinger Museum Haithabu. Schaufenster einer frühen Stadt*, Neumünster: Wachholtz, 1989

85 Heino Engel, *Measure and Construction of the Japanese House*, Boston: Tuttle Publishing, 1985

86 FAL e.V., *Wer nicht ins Horn stößt … 20 Jahre verwegene Ideen*, Ganzlin: FAL e.V., 2010

87 Mamoun Fansa, *Düppel, ein lebendiges Dorf aus dem Mittelalter*, Mainz: Nünnerich-Asmus-Verlag, 2014

88 Hassan Fathy, *Architecture for the Poor. An Experiment in Rural Egypt*, Chicago: University of Chicago Press, 1976

89 Luc Floissac, *La construction en paille. Principes fondamentaux, Techniques de mises en œuvre, Exemples de réalisations*, Mens: Terre Vivante, 2012

90 Kenneth Frampton (ed.), *Technology Place and Architecture. The Jerusalem Seminar in Architecture*, New York: Rizzoli, 1998

91 Siri Frech; Babette Seurell; Andreas Willisch (eds.), *Neu Land gewinnen. Die Zukunft in Ostdeutschland gestalten*, Berlin: Ch-Links Verlag, 2017, p. 126–135

92 Marianne Fredriksson; Bengt Warne, *På akacians villkor. Att bygga och bo i samklang med naturen*, Gothenburg: Warne Förlag AB, 1993

93 Andrew Freear; Elena Barthel, *Rural Studio at twenty. Designing and building in Hale County, Alabama*, New York: Princeton Architectural Press, 2014

94 Pierre Frey, *Learning from Vernacular. Pour une nouvelle architecture vernaculaire*, Arles: Actes Sud, 2010

95 Pierre Frey, *Simón Vélez, architecte. La maîtrise du bambou*, Arles: Actes Sud, 2013

96 Yona Friedman, *L'architecture de survie. Oú s'invente aujourd'hui le monde de demain*, Paris: Casterman, 1978

97 Irmela Fromme; Uta Herz, *Lehm- und Kalkputze. Mörtel herstellen, Wände verputzen, Oberflächen gestalten*, Staufen bei Freiburg: Ökobuch, 2012

98 Fukuoka Masanobu, *The One-Straw Revolution. An Introduction to Natural Farming*, Emmaus, Pa.: Rodale Press, 1978 [original Japanese edition 1975]

99 Furue Ryōnin, *Nihon Minka-en Monogatari*, Kawasaki: Tamagawa Shinbun, 1996 [古江亮仁著 『日本民家園物語』 多摩川新聞社1996年]

100 Mahatma K. Gandhi, *The Gospel of Swadeshi*, Bombay: Bharatiya Vidya Bhavan, 1967

101 Siegfried Gaß; Heide Drüsedau; Jürgen Hennicke (eds.), *IL31 Bambus*, Stuttgart: Institut für leichte Flächentragwerke, 1985

102 Giancarlo Gariglio; Fabio Giavedoni; Fabio Pracchia (eds.), *Guida al vino quotidiano*, Bra: Slow Food Editore, 2013

103 Dominique Gauzin-Müller et al., *Habiter écologique: quelles architectures pour une ville durable?*, Arles: Actes Sud, 2009

104 Manfred Gerner, *Fachwerk. Entwicklung, Instandsetzung, Neubau*, Munich: Deutsche Verlags-Anstalt, 2007

105 Khosrow Ghavami et al. (eds.), *Non-Conventional Materials and Technologies for Sustainable Engineering*, Dürnten: Trans Tech Publications, 2014

106 Jean Giono, *Lettre aux paysans sur la pauvreté et la paix*, Paris: B. Grasset, 1938

107 Gino Girolomoni, *Ritorna la vita sulle colline. L'esperienza della cooperativa Alce Nero*, Pesaro: Metauro edizioni, 2004[2]

108 Henry H. Glassie, "Architects, Vernacular Traditions, and Society", *Traditional Dwellings and Settlements Review*, 1, 2, 1990, p. 9–21

109 Edward Goldsmith, *The way. An ecological worldview*, Maidenhead: Veltune Publishing, 2014[3]

110 Green House Living, *Nature Housing*, 11 April 2014 [https://www.youtube.com/watch?v=jL4m1_BbJQc]

111 Gerhard Habartha (ed.), *Das Hundertwasser-Haus*, Vienna: Österreichischer Bundesverlag, 1985

112 Hagino Atelier, *Aenokoto*, Wajima: Maruyama-gumi, February 2012

113 Hagino Yuki, *Maruyama Honzō. Tochi ni nezashita kurashi no koyomi*, 2014 [萩野由紀作『まるやま本草 – 土地に根ざしたくらしの暦』]

114 Hagino Yuki, "Doma to yama ga tsunagaru satoyama no kurashi", *Confort*, August 2016, p. 98–99 [「土間と山がつながる、里山の暮らし」 文: 萩のゆき、コンフォルト、2016年8月号]

115 Hagino Yuki, "Providing Education Self-Sufficiently in *Satoyama*", in: Yiu Evonne; Nagata Akira (eds.), *The Road to Globally Important Agricultural Heritage Systems*, Kanazawa: UNU-IAS OUIK, 2018, p. 50–53

116 Hagino Yuki; Itō Koji, "Through activities of 'Team Maruyama', an organization providing learning experiences rooted in the land", *Journal of Rural Planning*, 6, 2014, p. 49–51 [萩野由紀、伊藤浩二「土地に根ざした学びの場「まるやま組」の活動をとおして」農村計画学会誌2014年6月号、49–51頁]

117 Hagino Yuki; Itō Koji; Hagino Kiichiro, "'Forest of Yoboshi-go': Place-Based Learning in the Satoyama in Noto", *1st Asian Conference on Biocultural Diversity*, Nanao, 27–29 October 2016, p. 55–57 [アジア生物文化多様性国際会議第一回、石川県七尾市、2016年10月27日～29日 萩野由紀、伊藤浩二「「よぼし子の森」: 能登の里山地域における土地に根ざした学びの場」55–57頁]

118 Matthew Hall; Rick Lindsay; Meror Krayenhoff (eds.), *Modern Earth Buildings. Materials, Engineering, Constructions and Applications*, Oxford: Woodhead Publishing, 2012

119 Francis Hallé, *Éloge de la plante. Pour une nouvelle biologie*, Paris: Éditions du Seuil, 1999

120 Francis Hallé, *Plaidoyer pour l'Arbre*, Arles: Actes Sud, 2005

121 Geoff Hammond; Craig Jones, *Inventory of carbon & energy*, University of Bath, 2011 [https://www.carbonsolutions.com/Resources/ICE%20V2.0%20-%20Jan%202011.xls]

122 Hara Miori, personal communication

123 Peter Harper, *The Centre for Alternative Technology: an 'extreme' ngo? Ngos at the crossroads*, The Oxford Research Centre for Humanities, University of Oxford, July 2015

124 Peter Harper, personal communication

125 Kent A. Harries; Bhavna Sharma, *Nonconventional and Vernacular Construction Materials*, Sawston: Woodhead Publishing, 2016

126 Cindy Harris; Pat Borer, *The Whole House Book. Ecological Building Design and Materials*, Machynlleth: Centre for Alternative Technology, 2005

127 Richard Harris et al., "The Wales Institute for Sustainable Education (WISE): Non-conventional materials in mainstream construction", *Proceedings of the 11th International Conference on Non-conventional Materials and Technologies*, Bath, 6–9 September 2009

128 Emilia Hazelip, *Agricoltura sinergica*, Florence, Terra Nuova, 2014

129 Barrett Hazeltine; Lars Wanhammar; Christopher Bull, *Appropriate Technology. Tools, Choices, and Implications*, New York: Academic Press, 1999

130 Dominique Hes; Chrisna du Plessis, *Designing for hope. Pathways to Regenerative Sustainability*, Abingdon: Routledge, 2014

131 Ot Hoffmann, *Handbuch für begrünte und genutzte Dächer*, Leinfelden-Echterdingen: Verlagsanstalt Alexander Koch, 1987

132 David Holmgren, *Permaculture. Principles & Pathways beyond Sustainability*, Hepburn. Vic.: Holmgren Design Services, 2002

133 Sepp Holzer, *Sepp Holzers Permakultur*, Graz: Leopold Stocker Verlag, 2004

134 Sepp Holzer; Leila Dregger, *Wüste oder Paradies*, Graz: Leopold Stocker Verlag, 2011

135 Sepp Holzer; Konrad Liebchen, *Sepp Holzer. Der Agrar-Rebell*, Graz: Leopold Stocker Verlag, 2002

136 Hugo Houben; Hubert Guillaud, *Traité de construction en terre*, Marseille: Editions Parenthèses, 2015[4] [first edition 1989]

137 Theodor Hugues; Ludwig Steiger; Johann Weber, *Timber Construction. Details Products Case Studies*, Basel: Birkhäuser, 2004

138 Ivan Illich, *Tools for Conviviality*, Glasgow: Fontana/Collins, 1973

139 Ivan Illich, *Energy and Equity*, London: Calder & Boyars, 1974

140 Ivan Illich, *Toward a History of Needs*, New York: Pantheon Books, 1978

141 Grigore Ionescu, *Arhitectura populara Românească*, Bucharest: Tehnică, 1957

142 Ishikawa Hajime (ed.), *Visual Guide to Living Landscape in Kamiyama*, Fujisawa: Keio University, 2017 [『神山暮らしの風景図鑑』慶応義塾大学SFC石川初研究室、2017]

143 Hans Jonas, *Das Prinzip Verantwortung. Versuch einer Ethik für die technologische Zivilisation*, Frankfurt am Main: Insel Verlag, 1979

144 Barbara Jones, *Building with Straw Bales. A Practical Guide for the UK and Ireland*, Totnes: Green Books, 2009[2]

145 Lisa Junghans; Uta Herz, *Lehmarchitektur erleben. Bezahlbares Bauen für die Seele*, Ganzlin: FAL e.V., 2017

146 Dirk Junklewitz, "Ein Pionier. Interview mit Ot Hoffmann", *Biotope City*, 11 September 2017 [http://www.biotope-city.net/article/interview-mit-ot-hoffmann-ungek-rzte-fassung]

147 Marcel Kalberer; Micky Remann, *Das Weidenbaubuch. Die Kunst, lebende Bauwerke zu gestalten*, Aarau: AT Verlag, 1999

148 Lloyd Kahn (ed.), *Shelter*, Bolinas: Shelter Publications, 1973

149 Christian Kaiser, *Ökologische Altbausanierung. Gesundes und nachhaltiges Bauen und Sanieren*, Berlin: VDE, 2017[2]

150 Kanda Seiji, *Kamiyama Shinkaron. Jinkō genshō o kanōsei ni kaeru machi-zukuri*, Kyoto: Gakugei shuppan-sha, 2018 [神田誠司著『神山進化論 – 人口減少を可能性に変えるまちづくり』学芸出版社、2018年]

151 Kawaguchi Yoshikazu; Toriyama Toshiko, *Kodomo no mirai to shizen. Shizennō-kosodate-kazoku o kataru* [子どもの未来と自然農 ~川口由一 自然農·子育て·家族を語る~, 川口由一鳥山敏子]

152 Alex Kerr, *Lost Japan*, Hawthorn, Vic.: Lonely Planet Publications, 1996

153 Kikuchi Akira, "Cosmetic agriculturalism: Ishikawa-ken Wajima-shi 'Shiroyone no senmaida' no baai", in: Iwamoto Michiya (ed.), *Furusato shigenka to minzokugaku*, Tokyo: Yoshikawa kōbunkan, 2007, p. 88–106 [岩本通弥編『ふるさと資源化と民俗学』 吉川弘文館、2007年、所収、菊地暁「コスメティック·アグリカルチュラリズム—石川県輪島市「白米の千枚田」の場合」]

154 Kikuchi Akira, "La glocalisation de la protection du patrimoine folklorique: l'exemple des coutumes liées à la riziculture dans le nord de la péninsule de Noto", *Ebisu*, 52, 2015, p. 233–289 [http://ebisu.revues.org/1694]

155 Andrew Kimbrell (ed.), *Fatal Harvest. The Tragedy of Industrial Agriculture*, Washington, D.C.: Island Press, 2002

156 Bruce King, "Structural Properties of Alternative Building Materials", in Lynne Elizabeth; Cassandra Adams (eds.), *Alternative Construction. Contemporary Natural Building Methods*, Hoboken: John Wiley and Sons, 2005, p. 71–83

157 Bruce King, *Design of Straw Bale Buildings. The State of the Art*, San Rafael, CA: Green Building Press, 2006

158 Franklin Hiram King, *Farmers of Forty Centuries; or, permanent agriculture in China, Korea and Japan*, Madison, Wis.: [p.n.i.], 1911

159 Andrea Klein; Michael Grabner, "Analysis of Construction Timber in Rural Austria: Wooden Log Walls", *International Journal of Architectural Heritage*, 9, 5, 2015, p. 553–563

160 Koji S. et al., "Human Capacity Building in the GIAHS 'Noto's Satoyama and Satoumi' in Japan", *1st Asian Conference on Bio-cultural Diversity*, Nanao, 27–29 October 2016, p. 53–54

161 Holger König, *Wege zum gesunden Bauen*, Staufen bei Freiburg: Ökobuch, 1997

162 Holger König et al., *A life cycle approach to buildings. Principles Calculations Design tools*, Munich: Institut für internationale Architektur-Dokumentation, 2010

163 Leonard Koren, *Wabi-Sabi: for Artists, Designers, Poets and Philosophers*, Berkeley, CA: Stone Bridge Press, 1994

164 Silje Kathrin Korsnes, *Fukt- og varmeutveksling i innvendige overflater*, Master's thesis, Trondheim: NTNU [Norges teknisk-naturvitenskapelige universitet], 2012 [https://pdfs.semanticscholar.org/a432/eca7e1035811728f632fc11979e2d1f9d2a8.pdf]

165 Lucien Kroll, *Ecologie urbane*, Milan: Franco Angeli, 2001

166 Lucien Kroll, *Tout est paysage*, Paris: Sens & Tonka, 20122

167 Lucien Kroll, *Techniques contre humanisme*, Paris: Sens & Tonka, 2016

168 Peter Krusche et al., *Ökologisches Bauen*, Wiesbaden: Bauverlag, 1982

169 Kudō Yoshiaki (ed.), *Nihon no Minka 3. Nōka III/Kinki*, Tokyo: Gakken, 1981 [工藤圭章編『日本の民家第3巻農家 3 近畿』学習研究社 1981]

170 Kunkovács László, *Ősépítmények. Népi építészetünk archaikus rétege*, [Budapest]: Kós Károly Alapítvány-Örökség Könyvműhely, 2000

171 Thomas Lange; Geoffrey Pugh, *The Economics of German Unification. An introduction*, Cheltenham: Edward Elgar Pub., 1998

172 Christian Lassure; Dominique Repérant, *Cabanes en pierre sèche de France*, Saint-Remy-de-Provence: Edisud, 2004

173 Jacqueline R. LeBlanc et al., "Building resilience in nonprofit food hubs", *Journal of Agriculture, Food Systems, and Community Development*, 4, 3, 2014, p. 121–135

174 Iola Lenzi, "An interview with architect/artist Eko Prawoto" [https://www.esplanade.com/learn/in-depth/visual-arts/eko-prawoto]

175 Aldo Leopold, *A Sand County Almanac, and Sketches here and there*, New York: Oxford University Press, 1949

176 Andres Lepik (ed.), *Small scale big change. New architecture of social engagement*, New York: The Museum of Modern Art, 2010

177 Lisa Licitra Ponti, *Gio Ponti. L'opera*, Milan: Leonardo Editore, 1990

178 Howard Liddell, *Eco-minimalism. The antidote to eco-bling*, London: Riba Publishing, 2008

179 Karen T. Liftin, *Ecovillages. Lessons for sustainable community*, Cambridge: Polity Press, 2014

180 R. Link, *Symbio Housing. Bengt Warne's designs for living in harmony with nature*, 1984

181 Adolf Loos, *Ins Leere gesprochen 1897–1900*, Paris: Georges Crès, 1921

182 Reinhard Loske (ed.), *Zukunftsfähiges Deutschland. Ein Beitrag zu einer global nachhaltigen Entwicklung*, Basel: Birkhäuser, 1996

183 James Lovelock, *Gaia. A New Look at Life on Earth*, Oxford: Oxford University Press, 1979 [2000[3]]

184 Alberto Magnaghi, *Il progetto locale. Verso la coscienza di luogo*, Torino: Bollati Boringhieri, 2010

185 Friedemann Mahlke, *Schwerelos erdverbunden—vom Leichtbau zum Lehmbau. Das Werk des Architekten Gernot Minke*, Staufen bei Freiburg: Ökobuch, 2007

186 Stefano Mancuso, *Plant Revolution. Le piante hanno già inventato il nostro futuro*, Florence: Giunti, 2017

187 Stefano Mancuso; Alessandra Viola, *Verde brillante. Sensibilità e intelligenza del mondo vegetale*, Florence: Giunti, 2013

188 Wolf Mangelsdorf, "Building with Plant Materials", in: Sandra Piesik (ed.), *Habitat. Vernacular Architecture for a Changing Planet*, London: Thames & Hudson, 2017, p. 526–531

189 Ezio Manzini, *Politiche del quotidiano*, Rome: Edizioni di Comunità, 2018

190 Ezio Manzini; François Jégou, *Quotidiano sostenibile. Scenari di vita urbana*, Milan: Edizioni Ambiente, 2003

191 Alejandro Martínez Rocamora; Jaime Solís-Guzmán; Madelyn Marrero, "LCA databases focused on construction materials: A review", *Renewable and Sustainable Energy Reviews*, 58, 2016, p. 565–573

192 Kelvin Mason, "Icon of green building. Interview with Pat Borer", *Green building*, 21, 1, 2011

193 Claus Mattheck, *Design in der Natur. Der Baum als Lehrmeister*, Freiburg im Breisgau: Rombach, 1992

194 Neil May; Caroline Rye, *Responsible Retrofit of Traditional Buildings. A report on existing research and guidance with recommendations*, London: STBA, 2012

195 Edward Mazria, *The passive solar energy book. A complete guide to passive solar home, greenhouse, and building design*, Emmaus, Pa.: Rodale Press, 1979

196 John McKean, *Learning from Segal. Walter Segal's life, work and influence*, Basel: Birkhäuser, 1989.

197 Jean-Pierre Ménard, "Maison Sidler à Félines-sur-Rimandoule (Drôme)", *Systèmes solaires*, 151, September–October 2002, p. 34–40

198 Elias Messinas; Dan Price (eds.), *The Book #1: Voices for Sustainability*, Ecoweek, 2016

199 Reinhold Messner, *Che tempo che fa*, broadcast interview, Rai 3, 27 December 2009

200 Gernot Minke, *Experimentelles Bauen: ein Werkbericht zum 20-jährigen Bestehen des Forschungslabors für Experimentelles Bauen*, Universität Gesamthochschule Kassel, Freiburg: Ökobuch, 1995

201 Gernot Minke, *Handbuch Lehmbau. Baustoffkunde, Techniken, Lehmarchitektur*, Staufen bei Freiburg: Ökobuch, 20097

202 Gernot Minke, *Dächer begrünen—einfach und wirkungsvoll. Planung, Ausführungshinweise, Praxistipps*, Staufen bei Freiburg: Ökobuch, 2010[4]

203 Gernot Minke, *Cúpulas y Bóvedas para vivir y trabajar, para hacer música y meditar. Obras del Arquitecto Gernot Minke desde los años 1975 hasta 2010*, Cali: Merlín ID, 2011

204 Gernot Minke; Benjamin Krick, *Handbuch Strohballenbau. Grundlagen, Konstruktion, Beispiele*, Staufen bei Freiburg: Ökobuch, 2009

205 Bill Mollison, *Permaculture. A Designer's Manual*, Tyalgum NSW: Tagari, 1988

206 Bill Mollison, *Introduction to Permaculture*, Tyalgum NSW: Tagari, 1991

207 Oliver Moore et al., "Reflexive resilience and community supported agriculture: The case that emerged from a place", *Journal of Agriculture, Food Systems, and Community Development*, 4, 3, 2014, p. 137–150

208 Rowan Moore, "The Wales Institute for Sustainable Education, Machynlleth", *The Guardian*, 18 June 2010

209 Maximilian Moser; Erwin Thoma, *Die sanfte Medizin der Bäume. Gesund leben mit altem und neuem Wissen*, Salzburg: Servus, 2014

210 Lewis Mumford, "Authoritarian and Democratic Technics", *Technics and Civilization*, 5, 1964, p. 1–8

211 Lewis Mumford, *The Myth of the Machine. II. The Pentagon of Power*, New York: Harcourt Brace Jovanovich, 1970

212 Arne Næss, *Ecology, Community, and Lifestyle*, Cambridge: Cambridge University Press, 1989

213 Nagai Takuo; Toki Hirokazu, "Aged Changes of Vibration Characteristics and Mechanical Properties of Actual Bamboo Building", *Elegance in Structures*, proceedings of the IABSE conference, Nara, 2015

214 Nagai Takuo; Toki Hirokazu, "Evaluation of Design Strength of Bamboo and Development of Joint Making Method with Manual Work: Design and construction of emergency temporary building made of bamboo material (Part 2)", *AIJ J. Technol. Des.*, 52, 22 October 2016, pp. 925–928 [永井拓生、陶器浩一「竹の設計強度の算定および人力施工が可能な接合法の開発－竹を構造材料として用いた応急仮設建築物の設計・施工の実例その2－」日本建築学会技術報告集2016年 22 巻 52 号 p. 925–928]

215 Nakamura Kōji; Kada Ryōhei (eds.), *Satoyama fukken. Noto kara no hasshin*, Tokyo: Sōrinsha, 2010 [中村浩二、嘉田良平著『里山復権―能登からの発信』創森社、2010年]

216 Nakano Koji, "Man nakani 'kama' gaaru—Tokushima 'Kamaya' 'Kama & store'", *Ryōritsūshin*, June 2018 [中野晃治 「真ん中に "かま" がある – 徳島「かま屋」「かま&ストア」」、『料理通信』2018年6月号]

217 Nakao Nanae; Futani Tomoo, *Minka wa nan no ki de dekiteiruka*, Kawasaki: Nihon minka-en, 2011 [中尾七重、布谷知夫「民家は何の木で出来ているか」日本民家園叢書 No. 10]

218 Namihei Odaira, "Tôki Hirokazu, le partage avant tout", *Zoom Japon*, 19 April 2012, p. 7

219 Dilip Nandwani (ed.), *Urban Horticulture. Sustainability for the Future*, Cham: Springer, 2018

220 Henrik Kofoed Nielsen, "Eco House Biestøa. Indoor climate performance", *7. Passivhus Norden. Sustainable Cities and Buildings Conference Proceedings*, Copenhagen, 20–21 August 2015

221 *Nihon Minka-en shūzō-hin mokuroku 6: Kyū Hirose-ke jūtaku*, Kawasaki: Nihon Minka-en, 2006 [『日本民家園収蔵品目録6 旧広瀬家住宅』日本民家園2006年]

222 *NOCMAT 2015 [Winnipeg] conference proceedings* [umanitoba.ca/faculties/engineering/departments/ce2p2e/alternative_village/nocmat2015/index.html]

223 Freja Nygaard Rasmussen et al., "Analysing methodological choices in calculations of embodied energy and GHG emissions from buildings", *Energy and Buildings*, 158, 2018, p. 1487–1498

224 Kathrine Nykjær-Brejnrod et al., "The absolute environmental performance of buildings", *Buildings and environment*, 119, 2017, p. 87–98

225 Eugene P. Odum, *Ecology. The link between the natural and the social sciences*, New York: Holt, Rinehart and Winston, 1975[2]

226 Ōkawa Naomi, *Nihon no Minka*, Tokyo: Shakai-Shisōsha, 1962 [大河直躬著『日本の民家その美しさと構造』教養文庫、社会思想社、1962年]

227 Jean-Pierre Oliva; Antoine Bosse-Platière; Claude Aubert, *Maisons écologiques d'aujourd'hui*, Mens: Terre Vivante, 2002

228 Jean-Pierre Oliva; Samuel Courgey, *L'isolation thermique écologique*, Mens: Terre Vivante, 2010

229 Paul Oliver (ed.), *Encyclopaedia of vernacular architecture of the world*, Cambridge: Cambridge University Press, 1997

230 Paul Oliver, *Dwellings. The Vernacular House World Wide*, London: Phaidon, 2003

231 Paul Oliver, *Built to Meet Needs. Cultural Issues in Vernacular Architecture*, Oxford: Architectural Press, 2006

232 Ōno Satoshi, *Minka Mura no Tabi*, Tokoname: INAX, 1993 [大野敏著『民家村の旅』INAX、1993年]

233 Ōno Satoshi; Osaka Hiroshi; Yasuda Tetsuya (eds.), *Nihon Minkaen. Japan Open-Air Folk House Museum*, Kawasaki: Nihon Minkaen, 2014[2]

234 *Osterie d'Italia. Sussidiario del mangiarbere all'italiana*, Bra: Arcigola Slowfood, 1990 [latest ed. 2019]

235 Publius Ovidius Naso, *Metamorphoseon libri XV* [modern English translation: Oxford: Oxford University Press, 2008]

236 Maurizio Pallante, *Le tecnologie di armonia*, Torino: Bollati Boringhieri, 1994

237 Victor Papanek, *The Green Imperative. Ecology and Ethics in Design and Architecture*, London: Thames & Hudson, 1995

238 Raj Patel, *Stuffed and Starved. Markets, power, and the hidden battle for the world food system*, London: Portobello, 2007

239 David Pearson, *Earth to spirit*, San Francisco: Chronicle Books, 1995

240 Olof Persson; Patrik Wennerstål, *Energimodellering av naturhus. En studie av Sundby naturhus*, Helsingborg: LTH Ingenjörshögskolan Lunds universitet, 2015

241 Carlo Petrini, *Terra Madre. Come non farci mangiare dal cibo*, Florence: Giunti/Bra: Slow Food Editore, 2009

242 Carlo Petrini, *Buono, pulito e giusto. Principî di una nuova gastronomia*, Torino: Einaudi, 2011

243 Carlo Petrini; Gigi Padovani, *Slow Food revolution. Da Arcigola a Terra Madre una nuova cultura del cibo e della vita*, Milan: Rizzoli, 2005

244 Achim Pilz, "Soziale Ästhetik. Interview mit Anna Heringer", *Wohnung + Gesundheit*, 157, winter 2015, p. 5–8

245 Maitreyi Dorothee Piontek, *Das Tao der Frau. Energiearbeit, Selbstheilung, Sexualität*, Kreuzlingen: Ariston Verlag, 1995

246 Maitreyi Dorothee Piontek, *Weibliches Manifest. Entdecke deine authentische und lustvolle Spiritualität*, Munich: Ansata, 2009

247 Jan Douwe van der Ploeg, *The New Peasantries. Struggles for Autonomy and Sustainability in an Era of Empire and Globalization*, Earthscan: London, 2008

248 Viktor Herbert Pöttler, *Alte Volksarchitektur*, Graz: Verlag Styria, 1984

249 Viktor Herbert Pöttler, *Gebaute Urväterweisheit. Gründung, Planung und Aufbau*

des Österreichischen Freilichtmuseums zu Stübing bei Graz, Graz: Akademische Druck- u. Verlagsanstalt, 2005

250 Michela Potito; Roberta Borghesi, *Genuino clandestino. Viaggio tra le agri-culture resistenti ai tempi delle grandi opere*, Florence: AAM Terra Nuova, 2015

251 Giannozzo Pucci, *La rivoluzione integrale. Idee e proposte ispirate all'ecologia integrale dell'enciclica Laudato si'*, Florence: Libreria Editrice Fiorentina, 2017

252 Pierre Rabhi; Nicolas Hulot, *Graines de possibles. Regards croisés sur l'écologie*, Paris: Calmann-Lévy, 2005

253 Guillermo Ráfales Sancho, *Werner Schmidt, innovation and ecology*, Master's thesis, Zaragoza: Escuela de Ingeniería y Arquitectura Eina, 2017

254 Ellen Therese Rasmussen et al., *Evaluation of indoor climate in a newly built Økohus with focus on passive measures and natural ventilation*, Bachelor thesis, Grimstad: Universitetet i Agder, 2015

255 Redactia Ziarului Unirea, "Vacanță ca pe vremea strămoșilor, în două case dintr-un sat izolat din județul Alba. Turiștii pot afla cum trăiau țăranii în urmă cu 100 de ani", *Unirea*, 19 July 2017 [ziarulunirea.ro/foto-vacanta-ca-pe-vremea-stramosilor-in-doua-case-dintr-un-sat-izolat-din-judetul-alba-turistii-pot-afla-cum-traiau-taranii-in-urma-cu-100-de-ani-430851/]

256 Sten Rentzhog, *Open air museums. The history and future of a visionary idea*, Östersund: Jamtli/Stockholm: Carlsson, 2007

257 Emily Reynolds, *Japan's Clay Walls. A Glimpse into their Plaster Craft*, [p.n.i.]: Create Space Independent Publishing Platform, 2009

258 Michael Reynolds, *Earthship. How to Build Your Own*, Taos, N.M.: Solar Survival Press, 1990

259 Vicky Richardson, *New Vernacular Architecture*, New York: Watson-Guptill Publications, 2001

260 Michele Riefoli, *Mangiar sano e naturale*, Cesena: Macro Edizioni, 2011

261 Elena Rigano; Lucia Corti, *CasaClima R. Edifici storici ad alta efficienza energetica*, Padua: Overview, 2013

262 Gerhard A. Ritter, *The price of German unity. Reunification and the crisis of the welfare state*, Oxford: Oxford University Press, 2011

263 Matt Ross, *Captain Fantastic*, Electric City Entertainment, 2016

264 Theodore Roszak, *The Making of a Counter Culture: Reflections on the Technocratic Society and its Youthful Opposition*, New York: Anchor Books, 1969

265 Bernardo Rudofsky, "Non ci vuole un nuovo modo di costruire ci vuole un nuovo modo di vivere", *Domus*, 123, 1938, p. 6–15

266 Bernard Rudofsky, *Architecture without Architects. A short introduction to non-pedigreed architecture*, New York: The Museum of Modern Art, 1964

267 Bernard Rudofsky, *The Prodigious Builders. Notes toward a natural history of architecture with special regard to those species that are traditionally neglected or downright ignored*, New York: Harcourt Brace Jovanovich, 1977

268 Bernard Rudofsky, *Now I Lay Me down to Eat. Notes and footnotes on the lost art of living*, Garden City, N. Y.: Anchor Press-Doubleday, 1980

269 Bernard Rudofsky, *Sparta-Sybaris. Keine neue Bauweise, eine neue Lebensweise tut not*, Salzburg: Residenz/VM, 1987

270 Carole Ryan, *Traditional Construction for a Sustainable Future*, Abingdon: Spon Press, 2011

271 Sasaki Masayuki, "Sōzōnōson to wa nanika, naze ima, chūmoku o atsumeru noka", in: Sasaki Masayuki; Kawaida Sachiko; Hagiwara Masaya (eds.), *Sōzōnōson: kaso o kurieitibu ni ikiru senryaku*, Tokyo: Gakugei shuppan-sha, 2014 [佐々木雅幸、川井田祥子、萩原雅也著『創造農村: 過疎をクリエイティブに生きる戦略』学芸出版社所収、佐々木雅幸:「創造農村とは何か、なぜ今、注目を集めるのか」]

272 Ute Schauer; Franz Volhard, *Sandberghof Bestandsaufnahme*, 2005

273 Ute Schauer; Franz Volhard, *Sandberghof—gemeinsam Wohnen im Alter. Umbau und Sanierung in Darmstadt*, 2008

274 Eda Schaur (ed.), *IL41 Intelligent Bauen*, Stuttgart: Institut für leichte Flächentragwerke, 1995

275 Klaus Schillberg, *Altbausanierung mit Naturbaustoffen*, Aarau: AT Verlag, 1996

276 Klaus Schillberg; Heinz Knieriemen, *Bauen und Sanieren mit Lehm. Kork, Hanf und Schilf in modernen Lehmbautechniken*, Vaihingen-Roßwag: Edition Simha, 2013

277 Valentin Șchiopu, "Suliman, magnificii", *Pressone*, 22 April 2018 [https://pressone.ro/suliman-magnificii/]

278 Isabell Schultz, „Starke Bündel. Eine kurze Geschichte des Strohballenbaus", *Oya*, 36, 2016

279 Ernst Friedrich Schumacher, *Small Is Beautiful. Economics as if People Mattered*, New York: Harper & Row, 1975

280 Schweizerisches Freilichtmuseum Ballenberg (ed.), *Jahrbuch 1998. Schweizerisches Freilichtmuseum Ballenberg*, vol. 2, Thun: Ott Verlag + Druck, 1998

281 Schweizerisches Freilichtmuseum Ballenberg (ed.), *Jahrbuch 2000. Schweizerisches Freilichtmuseum Ballenberg*, vol. 3, Thun: Ott Verlag + Druck, 2000

282 Schweizerisches Freilichtmuseum Ballenberg (ed.), *4. Wissenschaftliches Jahrbuch 2003. Schweizerisches Freilichtmuseum Ballenberg*, Baden: HIER + JETZT, 2003

283 Sekiguchi Kinya, *Kyū hirose-ke jūtaku ichiku shūri kōji hōkoku-sho*, Kawasaki: Nihon Minka-en, 1971 [関口欣也旧広瀬家住宅移築修理工事報告書, 川崎: 日本民家園, 昭和四十六年]

284 Luigi Sertorio, *Storia dell'abbondanza*, Torino: Bollati Boringhieri, 2002

285 Luigi Sertorio, *Vivere in nicchia e pensare globale*, Torino: Bollati Boringhieri, 2005

286 Allan Shepherd, *Voices from a disused quarry. An oral history of the Centre for Alternative Technology*, Machynlleth: Centre for Alternative Technology Publications, 2015

287 "Shiga-kenritsu Daigaku Toki Hirokazu kenkyushitsu + Takahashi Kōgyō: Hitobito ga machi no shōrai o katariau fukkō kyoten—chiiki no take o tsukatte gakusei ga tezukuri", *Architekton Plus*, 00, December 2011, p. 6–11 [「滋賀県立大学陶器浩一研究室＋高橋工業: 人々がまちの将来を語り合う復興拠点–地域の竹を使って学生が手づくり」アルキテクトンプラス vol. 00, December 2011、6–11頁]

288 Vandana Shiva, *Staying Alive. Women, Ecology and Survival in India*, New Delhi: Zed Press, 1988

289 Olivier Sidler, *La rénovation à très basse consommation d'énergie des bâtiments existants*, Institut négaWatt/Enertech, 2016

290 Florea Stănculescu, *Case și gospodării la țara*, [Bucharest]: [Maur], 1927

291 Chironya Stanellé; Iris Kunze (eds.), *20 Jahre Ökodorf Sieben Linden*, Poppau: Freundeskreis Ökodorf, 2017

292 William Stanwix; Alex Sparrow, *The Hempcrete Book. Designing and Building with Hemp-Lime*, Cambridge: Green Books, 2014

293 James Steele, *Ecological Architecture. A critical history*, London: Thames & Hudson, 2005

294 Ciprian Anghel Ștefan, *Monumente de arhitectură tradițională din Muzeul ASTRA Sibiu*, Sibiu: Editura "ASTRA Museum", 2010

295 Mariya Stoycheva, personal communication

296 Marianne Suhr; Roger Hunt, *The Old House Eco Handbook. A practical guide to retrofitting for energy efficiency and sustainability*, London: Frances Lincoln, 2013

297 Gabriel Suliman, *Moara din Munții Apuseni* [www.sprijina.ro/cauze/moara-din-muntiiapuseni?fbclid=IwAR0GRLDDuVVB6BgLrchaB7ott1OBageJ96ZrofTpUR_KQcVGfFTqyka1zS0]

298 Suzuki Mitsuru, *Minka*, Tokyo: Shōgakukan, 1975 [鈴木充著『民家』小学館、1975年]

299 John L. Talbott, *Simply build green. A technical guide to the ecological houses at the Findhorn Foundation*, Findhorn: Findhorn Foundation Development Wing, 1993

300 Tanaka [Kei]; Inoue Masafumi et al., "Fundamental Study on Mechanical Property of Bamboo: Part 3 Consideration of Compression Strength and Buckling Behavior", *The Japanese Institute of Architectural Institute of Kyushu Branch Research Report*, 44, March 2005, p. 461–464 [田中圭、井上正文他「丸竹の材料特性に関する基礎的研究 : (その3)圧縮強度及び座屈の挙動に関する考察(建築構造)」日本建築学会研究報告. 九州支部. 1, 構造系 (44) 461–464, Mar 2005]

301 John Thackara, *In the Bubble. Design per un futuro sostenibile*, Torino: Allemandi, 2008

302 Thomas Thiis-Evensen, *Archetypes in Architecture*, Oslo: Norwegian University Press, 1987

303 Thiruvalluvar, *Tirukkuṟaḷ* [most recent English translation by Jyothirllata Girija, Allahabad: Cyberwit, 2015]

304 Erwin Thoma, *Für lange Zeit. Leben und Bauen mit Holz—alte Weisheiten für moderne Technologien*, Vienna: Brandstätter, 2003

305 Erwin Thoma, *Die geheime Sprache der Bäume. Und wie die Wissenschaft sie entschlüsselt*, Salzburg: Ecowin Verlag, 2012

306 Erwin Thoma, *Dich sah ich wachsen. Über das uralte und neue Leben mit Holz, Wald und Mond*, Vienna: Brandstätter, 2013[9]

307 Christopher Tilley et al. (eds.), *Handbook of Material Culture*, London: Sage, 2006

308 Elizabeth Tilley et al., *Compendium des systèmes et technologies d'assainissement*, Dübendorf: Eawag, 2008

309 John Todd; Nancy Jack Todd, *Tomorrow is our permanent address. The search for an ecological science of design as embodied in the bioshelter*, New York: Harper & Row, 1980

310 Robert "Bob" W. Todd, "Notes from the Centre for Alternative Technology", *mimeo*, 18 July 1979

311 Toki Hirokazu; Nagai Takuo, "Design and Construction of Bamboo Spatial Structure Using Bended Bamboo Arch and Handmade Joint", *Elegance in Structures*, proceedings of the IABSE conference, Nara, 2015

312 Toki Hirokazu; Nagai Takuo, "Spatial Structure Using Bamboo as Structural Material: Design and construction of emergency temporary building made of bamboo material (Part 1)", *AIJ J. Technol. Des.*, 49, 21 October 2015, pp. 1007–1012 [陶器浩一、永井拓生「竹を構造材料として用いた空間構造の設計および施工–竹を構造材料として用いた応急仮設建築物の設計・施工の実例 その1–」日本建築学会技術報告集2015年21巻49号1007–1012頁]

313 Toyo Ito Museum of Architecture, *Project Omishima. Transforming into the most beautiful island in Japan*, Imabari: TIMA, 2016 [伊東豊雄建築ミュージアム刊『日本一美しい島・大三島をつくろうプロジェクト』]

314 TU Berlin, *Stroh im Haus, statt Stroh im Kopf*, Berlin: Energieseminar—Institut für Energietechnik, 2006

315 John F.C. Turner, *Housing by people*, London: Marion Boyars Publishers, 1976

316 Liban Usman, *Sikhall naturhus, mätning och simulering av temperatur och luftfuktighet*, Karlstads Universitet, 2016

317 Brenda Vale; Robert Vale, *Green Architecture*, London: Thames & Hudson, 1992

318 Brenda Vale; Robert Vale, *The New Autonomous House*, London: Thames & Hudson, 2000

319 Robert Vale; Brenda Vale, *Time to Eat the Dog? The Real Guide to Sustainable Living*, London: Thames & Hudson, 2009

320 Robert Vale; Brenda Vale (eds.), *Living within a Fair Share Ecological Footprint*, Abingdon: Routledge, 2013

321 Luigi Veronelli, *Terra e libertà. Critical Wine. Sensibilità planetaria, agricoltura contadina e rivoluzione dei consumi*, Rome: DeriveApprodi, 2004

322 Luigi Veronelli, Pablo Echaurren, *Le parole della terra. Manuale per enodissidenti e gastroribelli*, Viterbo: Stampa alternativa, 2003

323 Adam Voelcker, *David Lea. An Architect of Principle*, London: Artifice, 2015

324 Franz Volhard, *Leichtlehmbau. Alter Baustoff—neue Technik*, Karlsruhe: C. F. Müller, 1983

325 Franz Volhard, *Impulse für den Lehmbau—Zeitgemäßes Bauen mit Holz und Lehm*, Ganzlin: FAL e.V., 2015, p. 7–9

326 Franz Volhard, *Bauen mit Leichtlehm. Handbuch für das Bauen mit Holz und Lehm*, Basel: Birkhäuser, 2016 [English edition: *Light earth building. A handbook for building with wood and earth*]

327 Franz Volhard; Ulrich Röhlen, *Lehmbau-Regeln, Begriffe Baustoffe Bauteile*, Wiesbaden: Springer Vieweg, 1998

328 Peter Walker et al. (eds.), *11th International Conference on Non-conventional Materials and Technologies. NOCMAT 2009. Conference proceedings*, Bath: University of Bath, 2009

329 Bengt Warne, *Report from a cultural exchange Sweden-USA*, Stockholm, 1982

330 Bengt Warne, *Symbio Housing Symposiums. List of common questions and answers at the symposiums*, Stockholm, 1982

331 Bengt Warne; K. Warne, *Man and Nature: the house of the future?*, Stockholm: Natur och kultur, 1980

332 Tony Watkins, *The human house. Sustainable Design*, Wellington: Karaka Bay Press, 2009

333 Adam Weismann; Katy Bryce, *Building with cob. A step-by-step guide*, Totnes: Green Books, 2006

334 Ernst Ulrich von Weiszäcker; Amory B. Lovins; L. Hunter Lovins, *Factor Four. Doubling Wealth, Halving Resource Use*, London: Earthscan, 1998

335 Malcolm Wells, *The Earth-sheltered house. An architect's sketchbook*, White River Junction, Vt.: Chelsea Green Pub., 1998

336 Elke Wiegand; Martin Stengel; Dirk Scharmer, *Ecovillage Sieben Linden with straw bale construction*, World Habitat Awards 2006 Building and Social Housing Foundation, Sieben Linden, 2006

337 Christopher G. Williams, *Craftsmen of necessity*, New York: Vintage Books, 1974

338 Tom Woolley, *Natural building. A guide to materials and techniques*, Ramsbury: The Crowood Press, 2006

339 Tom Woolley, *Low Impact Building. Housing using renewable materials*, Chichester: Wiley-Blackwell, 2013

340 Virginia Worthington, "Nutritional Quality of Organic Versus Conventional Fruits, Vegetables, and Grains", *The Journal of Alternative and Complementary Medicine*, 7, 2, 2001, p. 161–173

341 David Wright, *Natural solar architecture. A passive primer*, New York: Van Nostrand Reinhold, 1978

342 Michael Würfel, *Dorf ohne Kirche. Die ganz große Führung durch das Ökodorf Sieben Linden*, Beetzendorf: Eurotopia-Buchversand, 2012

343 Yoshimoto Mitsuhiro, "Kamiyama's Success in Creative Depopulation", *Field. A journal of socially-engaged art criticism*, 8, fall 2017

344 Yuki Masami, "Designing the Communication of Traditional Ecological Knowledge: A Noto Case Study", in: Scott Slovic; Swarnalatha Rangarajan; Vidya Sarveswaran (eds.), *Routledge Handbook of Ecocriticism and Environmental Communication*, Abingdon: Routledge, 2019, p. 279–290

345 Mirko Zardini; Giovanna Borasi, *Actions. What you can do with the city*, Montréal: Canadian Centre for Architecture, 2009

346 Ernst Zürcher, "Lunar Rhythms in Forestry Traditions. Lunar-Correlated Phenomena in Tree Biology and Wood Properties", *Earth, Moon and Planets*, 85–86, 2001, p. 463–478

347 Ernst Zürcher et al., "Looking for differences in wood properties as a function of the felling date: lunar phase-correlated variations in the drying behavior of Norway Spruce (*Picea abies* Karst.) and Sweet Chestnut (*Castanea sativa* Mill.)", *Trees*, 24, 2010, p. 31–41

348 Ernst Zürcher; Christian Rogenmoser, "Considering reversible Variations in Wood Properties: possible Applications in the Choice of the Tree-Felling Date?", *Proceedings of the International Convention of Society of Wood Science and Technology and United Nations Economic Commission for Europe—Timber Committee*, Genève, 11–14 October 2010

349 Klaus Zwerger, *Wood and Wood Joints. Building Traditions of Europe, Japan and China*, Basel: Birkhäuser, 2012[2]

350 www.atelierwernerschmidt.ch

351 www.bosch-stiftung.de

352 www.caneloproject.com

353 www.canyaviva.com

354 www.cat.org.uk

355 www.dachverband-lehm.de

356 www.facebook.com/SatulCheia

357 fal-ev.de

358 foodhub.co.jp

359 www.gaiaarkitekter.no

360 gartist.ch

361 gernotminke.gernotminke.de

362 www.in-kamiyama.jp

363 www.ipogea.org

364 www.jpc-net.jp

365 www.kanazawa-u.ac.jp

366 kitokuras.jp

367 www.lehmmuseum.de

368 lernpunktlehm.de

369 www.lowtechmagazine.com

370 www.mannmaru.jp

371 maruyamagumi.blog102.fc2.com

372 minke-strawbaledome.blogspot.com

373 www.mlit.go.jp

374 newdaughters.org

375 www.nihonminkaen.jp

376 www.nutritionstudies.org

377 www.oekobaudat.de

378 okohuset.blogspot.com

379 www.patborer.co.uk

380 peterharper.org

381 www.ruralstudio.org

382 sandberghof.org

383 www.schauer-volhard.de

384 siebenlinden.org

385 www.venussplash.com

386 www.wangeliner-garten.de

387 www.wangeliner-workcamp.de

Picture credits

ABG = Andrea Bocco Guarneri

Vegetarian architecture: a theoretical proposal

1 Ochiai, Higashi-Iya, Tokushima prefecture, Japan. ABG, 2016.
2 Segger House, Blaen Camel, Cilceninn, Dyfed, Wales. Virginia Bertolotti, 2017.
3 Farahuset, Jølle, Farsund, Vest-Agder, Norway. ABG, 2018.
4 Kitokuras, Ayauta-gun, Marugame city, Kagawa prefecture, Japan. Kitokuras, 2009.
5 Low-temperature (left) and high-temperature (right) dried timber at Kitokuras, Japan. Kitokuras, 2009.
6 Slow-growth (left) and fast-growth (right) timber at Kitokuras, Japan. ABG, 2016.
7 Peniarth Uchaf, Llanegryn, Gwynedd, Wales. Virginia Bertolotti, 2017.
8 Bamboo House II, Bodaiji-gun, Konan city, Shiga prefecture, Japan. ABG, 2019.
9 Rauchstubenhaus Großschrotter at the Österr. Freilichtmuseum Stübing bei Graz, Austria. ABG, 2011.
10 *Pătul* of a farm from Târgu Cărbuneşti at the Muzeul Civilizaţiei Populare Tradiţionale ASTRA, Sibiu, Romania. ABG, 2018.
11 Bamboo House II, Bodaiji-gun, Konan city, Shiga prefecture, Japan. ABG, 2019.
12 Kodama desk. Kodama project, 2014.
13 Ipanema table. Andrea Zanini, 2018.
14 Lake One, Tamera, Monte do Cerro, Odemira, Portugal. ABG, 2011.
15 Ōmishima, Imabari city, Ehime prefecture, Japan. ABG, 2016.
16 Kyrkhult farmhouse at Skansen, Stockholm, Sweden. ABG, 2007.
17 Sikhall Naturhus, Brålanda, Vänersborg, Sweden. Andrea Antolloni, 2017.
18 Wikinger-Museum Haithabu, Busdorf, Schleswig, Germany. ABG, 2012.
19 Wikinger-Museum Haithabu, Busdorf, Schleswig, Germany. ABG, 2012.
20 Ōmishima Minna no ie, Ōmishima, Imabaricity, Ehimeprefecture, Japan. ABG, 2016.
21 Bamboo Ark, Oyakaigan, Motoyoshi-cho, Kesennuma City, Miyagi prefecture, Japan. Toki lab, 2012.
22 Industrially grown strawberries. Cristiana Peano, 2019.
23 Chiiori House, Higashi-Iya, Tokushima prefecture, Japan. Taki Yosuke, 2016.
24 *Cămară de alimente* of a farm from Goieşti-Vidra at the Muzeul Civilizaţiei Populare Tradiţionale ASTRA, Sibiu, Romania. ABG, 2018.
25 Valbjørsetra mountain farm at the Maihaugen open-air museum, Lillehammer, Norway. ABG, 2012.
26 Aula, Tamera, Monte do Cerro, Odemira, Portugal. ABG, 2018.
27 Chiiori House, Higashi-Iya, Tokushima prefecture, Japan. ABG, 2016.
28 Vasalishof, EVA Lanxmeer, Culemborg, Gelderland province, the Netherlands. ABG, 2009.
29 Kitokuras, Ayauta-gun, Marugame city, Kagawa prefecture, Japan. ABG, 2016.
30 Maison Sidler, Félines-sur-Rimandoule, Drôme, France. Olivier Sidler, 2011.
31 Museumsdorf Düppel, Berlin-Zehlendorf, Germany. ABG, 2019.
32 Peniarth Uchaf, Llanegryn, Gwynedd, Wales. Virginia Bertolotti, 2017.
33 Rural Studio Farm greenhouse, Newbern, Alabama, USA. Timothy Hursley, 2016.
34 Gonjiro, Tateyama, Chiba prefecture, Japan. ABG, 2016.
35 Schafbrühl, Tübingen, Germany. ABG, 2009.
36 Sikhall Naturhus, Brålanda, Vänersborg, Sweden. Andrea Antolloni, 2017.
37 Sikhall Naturhus, Brålanda, Vänersborg, Sweden. Andrea Antolloni, 2017.
38 Segger House, Blaen Camel, Cilceninn, Dyfed, Wales. Virginia Bertolotti, 2017.
39 Farahuset, Jølle, Farsund, Vest-Agder, Norway. ABG, 2018.

1. Captive vernacular: Hirose House at Nihon Minka-en

1 Perspective section of Hirose house from **B233**.
2 Hirose house, Kamihagiwara, Enzan-gun, Kōshū city, Yamanashi prefecture. Nihon Minkaen archive 20_57 R123–14, 1969.
3 Survey plan of Hirose house from **B283**. [広瀬家報告書]
4 Hirose house, Kamihagiwara, Enzan-gun, Kōshū city, Yamanashi prefecture. Nihon Minkaen archive 21_81 C8–1, 1969.
5 Hirose house at Nihon Minkaen, Kawasaki city, Kanagawa prefecture, Japan. ABG, 2016.
6 Hirose house at Nihon Minkaen. ABG, 2016.
7 Hirose house at Nihon Minkaen. Nihon Minkaen archive 22_81, 1969.
8 Hirose house at Nihon Minkaen. Nihon Minkaen archive 22_34 R147–5, 1969.
9 Hirose house at Nihon Minkaen. Nihon Minkaen archive 22_5 R140–15, 1969.
10 Hirose house at Nihon Minkaen. Nihon Minkaen archive 21_89 C8–9, 1969.
11 Hirose house at Nihon Minkaen. Nihon Minkaen archive 22_24 R141–19, 1969.
12 Hirose house at Nihon Minkaen. Taki Yosuke, 2016.
13 Hirose house at Nihon Minkaen. Nihon Minkaen archive 22_38 R143–12 + 22_42 R146–4 + 22_44 R146–2 + 22_49 R143–26 + 22_53 R143–28 + 22_56 R148–4, 1969.
14 Hirose house at Nihon Minkaen. Nihon Minkaen archive 22_60 R147–6, 1969.
15 Hirose house at Nihon Minkaen. Nihon Minkaen archive 22_62R148–27, 1969.
16 Inoue house, Iga city, Mie prefecture, Japan. Martina Imeroni, 2017.
17 Hirose house at Nihon Minkaen. Taki Yosuke, 2016.
18 Hirose house at Nihon Minkaen. ABG, 2016.
19 Section and plan of Hirose House. Martina Bocci, 2019.
20 Hirose house at Nihon Minkaen. ABG, 2016.
21 Detail of *irori*, *iroko*, and *doma* from **B233**.
22 Survey plan of Hirose house from **B283**. [広瀬家報告書]

2. Wild vernacular: Cheia

1 Rameţ, Alba county, Romania. Daniliuc Sorin, 2018.
2 Laura Praja house, Cheia, Rameţ commune, Alba county, Romania. ABG, 2018.
3 Plan of *gospodăria* Ilieş Ioana, Valea Stejarului, Vadu Izei, Maramureş. Arhiva de relevee a Departamentului de Istoria & Teoria Arhitecturii şi Conservarea Patrimoniului "Sanda Voiculescu" Rv.235.03, 1968.
4 Suliman House, Cheia, Rameţ commune, Alba county, Romania. Satul Cheia, 2017.
5 Suliman House, Cheia. ABG, 2018.
6 Suliman House, Cheia. Daniliuc Sorin, 2018.
7 Suliman House, Cheia. ABG, 2018.
8 Casa Gavrilă (Suliman House), Cheia. Satul Cheia, 2018.
9 Suliman House, Cheia. Satul Cheia, 2018.
10 Casa Gavrilă (Suliman House), Cheia. From **B277**.
11 Casa Gavrilă (Suliman House), Cheia. ABG, 2018.
12 Casa Gavrilă (Suliman House), Cheia. Satul Cheia, 2016.
13 Casa Gavrilă (Suliman House), Cheia. ABG, 2018.
14 Casa Gavrilă (Suliman House), Cheia. Satul Cheia, 2016.
15 Casa Gavrilă (Suliman House), Cheia. Satul Cheia, 2016.
16 Casa Paraschiva (Suliman House), Cheia. ABG, 2018.
17 Section and plan of Casa Paraschiva. Martina Bocci, 2019.
18 Casa Paraschiva (Suliman House), Cheia. Satul Cheia, 2016.
19 Construction sequence of Casa Paraschiva. Martina Bocci, 2019.
20 Casa Paraschiva (Suliman House), Cheia. ABG, 2018.
21 Casa Paraschiva (Suliman House), Cheia. Satul Cheia, 2016.
22 Casa Paraschiva (Suliman House), Cheia. ABG, 2018.

3. Straw-based retrofit: Casa Steila Mar

1 Casa Steila Mar, Susch, Zernez, Graubünden, Switzerland. Lucia Degonda, 2017.
2 Casa Steila Mar, Susch. Lucia Degonda, 2017.
3 Casa Steila Mar, Susch. Atelier Werner Schmidt, 2013.
4 Casa Steila Mar, Susch. ABG, 2018.
5 Casa Steila Mar, Susch. Atelier Werner Schmidt, 2013.
6 Plans of Casa Steila Mar. Martina Bocci, 2019.
7 Casa Steila Mar, Susch. Lucia Degonda, 2017.
8 Renovation sequence of Casa Steila Mar. Martina Bocci, 2019.

9 Casa Steila Mar, Susch. Lucia Degonda, 2017.
10 Casa Steila Mar, Susch. Atelier Werner Schmidt, 2013.
11 Casa Steila Mar, Susch. Atelier Werner Schmidt, 2013.
12 Casa Steila Mar, Susch. Atelier Werner Schmidt, 2013.
13 Section of Casa Steila Mar. Martina Bocci, 2019.
14 Casa Steila Mar, Susch. ABG, 2018.
15 Casa Steila Mar, Susch. ABG, 2018.
16 Casa Steila Mar, Susch. ABG, 2018.
17 Casa Steila Mar, Susch. ABG, 2018.

4. Earth-based retrofit: Sandberghof

1 Haus J, Darmstadt-Bessungen, Germany. Martina Bocci, 2017.
2 Haus Eilberg, Mörfelden, Mörfelden-Walldorf, Germany. Martina Bocci, 2017.
3 Sandberghof, Darmstadt-Bessungen, Germany. Sandberghof gemeinsam wohnen in Bessungen GbR, 2016.
4 Sandberghof, Bessungen. ABG, 2019.
5 Sandberghof, Bessungen. Sandberghof gemeinsam wohnen in Bessungen GbR, 2017.
6 Sandberghof, Bessungen. ABG, 2019.
7 Plan of Sandberghof. Schauer+Volhard modified by Martina Bocci, 2019.
8 Sandberghof, Bessungen. Schauer+Volhard, 2008.
9 Sandberghof, Bessungen. Schauer+Volhard, 2007.
10 Sandberghof, Bessungen. Schauer+Volhard, 2007.
11 Section of Sandberghof's main building. Schauer+Volhard modified by Martina Bocci, 2019.
12 Sandberghof, Bessungen. Thomas Ott, 2005.
13 Axonometric projection of Sandberghof's main building. Damian Kuna, 2019.
14 Sandberghof, Bessungen. Schauer+Volhard, 2005.
15 Plans of Sandberghof's main building (original state). Schauer+Volhard, 2005, from **B272**.
16 Sandberghof, Bessungen. Schauer+Volhard, 2005.
17 Sandberghof, Bessungen. Martina Bocci, 2017.
18 Sandberghof, Bessungen. ABG, 2019.
19 Sandberghof, Bessungen. Schauer+Volhard, 2006.
20 Sandberghof, Bessungen. Schauer+Volhard, 2006.
21 Sandberghof, Bessungen. Schauer+Volhard, 2005.
22 Haus Eilberg, Mörfelden, Mörfelden-Walldorf, Germany. Schauer+Volhard, 1998.
23 Sandberghof, Bessungen. Schauer+Volhard, 2005.
24 Sandberghof, Bessungen. Thomas Ott, 2006.
25 Sandberghof, Bessungen. Martina Bocci, 2017.

5. Radical vegetarianism: Villa Strohbunt at Sieben Linden

1 Sieben Linden Ecovillage, Beetzendorf, Germany. ABG, 2013.
2 General plan of Sieben Linden Ecovillage, Beetzendorf. Martina Gerace, 2018.
3 Regiohaus and Sonneneck, Sieben Linden Ecovillage. ABG, 2013.
4 Nordriegel and Regiohaus, Sieben Linden Ecovillage. ABG, 2013.
5 Sieben Linden Ecovillage, Beetzendorf. ABG, 2013.
6 Sieben Linden Ecovillage, Beetzendorf. ABG, 2013.
7 Sieben Linden Ecovillage, Beetzendorf. ABG, 2013.
8 Sieben Linden Ecovillage, Beetzendorf. ABG, 2015.
9 Strohpolis, Sieben Linden Ecovillage. ABG, 2015.
10 Nordschonung, Sieben Linden Ecovillage. Susanna Pollini, 2017.
11 Villa Strohbunt, Sieben Linden Ecovillage. ABG, 2013.
12 Villa Strohbunt, Sieben Linden Ecovillage. Bill Steen, 2009.
13 Villa Strohbunt, Sieben Linden Ecovillage. ABG, 2010.
14 Villa Strohbunt, Sieben Linden Ecovillage. ABG, 2010.
15 Axonometric projection of Villa Strohbunt. Martina Bocci, 2019.
16 Villa Strohbunt, Sieben Linden Ecovillage. Bill Steen, 2009.
17 Villa Strohbunt, Sieben Linden Ecovillage. ABG, 2013.
18 Villa Strohbunt, Sieben Linden Ecovillage. Alberto Valentino, 2013.
19 Section and plans of Villa Strohbunt. Martina Bocci, 2019.
20 Libelle, Sieben Linden Ecovillage. ABG, 2015.
21 Strohballenkuppeln, Sieben Linden Ecovillage. ABG, 2010.
22 Villa Communia, Sieben Linden Ecovillage. ABG, 2010.
23 Villa Strohbunt, Sieben Linden Ecovillage. Bill Steen, 2009.
24 Villa Strohbunt, Sieben Linden Ecovillage. Bill Steen, 2009.

6. Massive structures: Createrra and Gartist

1 Kindergarden in Sorsum, Hildesheim, Germany. Martina Bocci, 2017.
2 Haus am Wasserturm 17, Kassel, Germany. Martina Bocci, 2017.
3 Createrra office, Hrubý Šúr, Bratislava, Slovakia. Bjørn Kierulf/Createrra, 2012.
4 Section and plan of Createrra office. Martina Bocci, 2019.
5 Createrra office, Hrubý Šúr. Bjørn Kierulf/Createrra, 2012.
6 Createrra office, Hrubý Šúr. Bjørn Kierulf/Createrra, 2010.
7 Createrra office, Hrubý Šúr. Bjørn Kierulf/Createrra, 2010.
8 Createrra office, Hrubý Šúr. Bjørn Kierulf/Createrra, 2010.
9 Createrra office, Hrubý Šúr. Bjørn Kierulf/Createrra, 2010.
10 Createrra office, Hrubý Šúr. ABG, 2011.
11 Createrra office, Hrubý Šúr. ABG, 2011.
12 Createrra office, Hrubý Šúr. ABG, 2011.
13 Createrra office, Hrubý Šúr. Bjørn Kierulf/Createrra, 2010.
14 Section of Gartist office. Werner Schmidt, 2016.
15 Bubikon/ZH, Switzerland. Atelier Werner Schmidt, 2017.
16 Plan of Gartist office. Werner Schmidt, 2016.
17 Gartist office, Bubikon/ZH, Switzerland. Atelier Werner Schmidt, 2017.
18 Plans of Gartist office. Martina Bocci, 2019.
19 Gartist office, Bubikon. Joel Kunz, 2018.
20 Gartist office, Bubikon. Joel Kunz, 2018.
21 Gartist office, Bubikon. Joel Kunz, 2018.
22 Gartist office, Bubikon. Atelier Werner Schmidt, 2017.
23 Gartist office, Bubikon. Atelier Werner Schmidt, 2016.
24 Gartist office, Bubikon. Atelier Werner Schmidt, 2017.
25 Section of Gartist office. Martina Bocci, 2019.
26 Gartist office, Bubikon. Atelier Werner Schmidt, 2017.
27 Gartist office, Bubikon. Atelier Werner Schmidt, 2017.
28 Gartist office, Bubikon. Atelier Werner Schmidt, 2017.
29 Gartist office, Bubikon. Gartist GmbH, 2018.
30 Gartist office, Bubikon. Gartist GmbH, 2016.

7. Framed structure: Bamboo Ark

1 Bamboo ark, Oyakaigan, Motoyoshi-cho, Kesennuma City, Miyagi prefecture, Japan. Toki lab, 2012.
2 Instructions for tying joints. Toki lab, 2011.
3 Load-deformation chart from **B214**.
4 Bending shape analysis from **B312**.
5 Section and plan of Bamboo ark. Toki lab, 2011.
6 Shiga Prefecture University Campus, Hikone, Shiga Prefecture, Japan. Toki lab, 2011.
7 Bamboo ark, Kesennuma city. Toki lab, 2011.
8 Assembly diagrams of twoof the main types of frames. Toki lab, 2011.
9 Bamboo ark, Kesennuma city. Toki lab, 2011.
10 Bamboo ark, Kesennuma city. Toki lab, 2011.
11 Model of Bamboo ark roof, Shiga Prefecture University Campus, Hikone. ABG, 2019.
12 Bamboo ark, Kesennuma city. Toki lab, 2011.
13 Bamboo ark, Kesennuma city. Toki lab, 2012.
14 Bamboo ark, Kesennuma city. Toki lab, 2012.
15 Bamboo ark, Kesennuma city. Toki lab, 2012.
16 Bamboo ark, Kesennuma city. Toki lab, 2012.
17 Bamboo ark, Kesennuma city. Toki lab, 2011.
18 Bamboo House II, Bodaiji, Konan City, Shiga prefecture. ABG, 2019.
19 Bamboo House II, Bodaiji, Konan City, Shiga prefecture. ABG, 2019.

8. Passive performance: Biestøa

1 House in Nordhassel, Farsund, Norway. ABG, 2018.
2 Trekkfuglbu på Lista fyr, Farsund, Norway. ABG, 2018.
3 Farahuset, Jølle, Farsund, Norway. ABG, 2018.
4 Biestøa house, Grimstad, Norway. ABG, 2018.
5 Biestøa house, Grimstad, Norway. ABG, 2018.
6 Biestøa house, Grimstad, Norway. ABG, 2018.
7 Biestøa house, Grimstad, Norway. ABG, 2018.

8 Biestøa house, Grimstad, Norway. ABG, 2018.
9 Biestøa house, Grimstad, Norway. ABG, 2018.
10 Biestøa house, Grimstad, Norway. ABG, 2018.
11 Biestøa house, Grimstad, Norway. Giuseppe Salomone, 2018.
12 Biestøa house, Grimstad, Norway. ABG, 2018.
13 Plans of Biestøa house. Martina Bocci, 2019.
14 Biestøa house, Grimstad, Norway. ABG, 2018.
15 Biestøa house, Grimstad, Norway. ABG, 2018.
16 Biestøa house, Grimstad, Norway. ABG, 2018.
17 Exploded axonometric of Biestøa house. Martina Bocci, 2019.
18 Section of Biestøa house. Martina Bocci, 2019.
19 Biestøa house, Grimstad, Norway. ABG, 2018.
20 Biestøa house, Grimstad, Norway. ABG, 2018.

9. Food economy system: Kamiyama Food Hub

1 *Daisuki Kamiyama walking map.* Inlet in top left corner: sketch of Kamiyama food hub premises. Tase Michio 田瀬理夫, 2016.
2 Nishiokubo, Kamiyama town, Tokushima prefecture, Japan. ABG, 2019.
3 Yorii, Kamiyama town, Tokushima prefecture, Japan. ABG, 2019.
4 Yorii, Kamiyama town, Tokushima prefecture, Japan. ABG, 2019.
5 Engawa office, Yorii, Kamiyama town, Tokushima prefecture, Japan. ABG, 2019.
6 Kamiyama food hub farm, Yorii, Kamiyama town, Tokushima prefecture, Japan. ABG, 2019.
7 Yorii, Kamiyama town, Tokushima prefecture, Japan. ABG, 2019.
8 Kama pan & store, Yorii, Kamiyama town, Tokushima prefecture, Japan. Food hub project, 2017.
9 Kama pan & store, Kamiyama. ABG, 2019.
10 Section and plan of Kama pan & store. Shimazu Architectural Design Office, 2016.
11 Kama pan & store, Kamiyama. Food hub project, 2017.
12 Kamiyama town, Tokushima prefecture, Japan. Food hub project, 2017.
13 Kamaya, Yorii, Kamiyama town, Tokushima prefecture, Japan. Food hub project, 2017.
14 Kamaya, Kamiyama. Food hub project, 2017.
15 Kamaya, Kamiyama. ABG, 2019.
16 Kamaya, Kamiyama. ABG, 2019.
17 Kamiyama food hub, Kamiyama. Food hub project, 2017–2018.
18 Kamiyama food hub, Kamiyama. Food hub project, 2016.
19 Kamiyama food hub, Kamiyama. Food hub project, 2016.
20 Kamaya, Kamiyama. Food hub project, 2017.
21 Kamiyama food hub, Kamiyama. Food hub project, 2016.

10. Soil and earth: Wangeliner Garten

1 Lehmmuseum, Gnevsdorf, Buchberg, Germany. ABG, 2018.
2 Lehmmuseum, Gnevsdorf, Buchberg, Germany. ABG, 2018.
3 Wangeliner garten satellite view. Reworked from Google earth, 2019.
4 Wangeliner garten, Wangelin, Buchberg, Germany. ABG, 2018.
5 Europäische Bildungsstatte für Lehmbau, Wangelin, Buchberg, Germany. ABG, 2018.
6 Lehmkloster, Europäische Bildungsstatte für Lehmbau, Wangelin, Buchberg, Germany. ABG, 2018.
7 Wangeliner garten, Wangelin. Sabine, 2011.
8 Kritzower See, Kritzow, Germany. ABG, 2018.
9 Garden café, Wangeliner garten, Wangelin. ABG, 2018.
10 Garden café, Wangeliner garten. ABG, 2018.
11 Lehmhaus, Wangeliner garten. ABG, 2018.
12 Garden café, Wangeliner garten. ABG, 2018.
13 Garden café, Wangeliner garten. ABG, 2018.
14 Gästehaus, Wangelinger garten, ABG, 2018.
15 Lodgings, Tamera, Monte do Cerro, Odemira, Portugal. ABG, 2018.
16 Plan and sections of the Gästehaus. Martina Bocci and Federica Rossetto, 2019.
17 Gästehaus, Wangeliner garten. ABG, 2018.
18 Gästehaus, Wangeliner garten. ABG, 2018.
19 Gästehaus, Wangeliner garten. Ajeschka/Marcin Kolakowski, 2011.
20 Gästehaus, Wangeliner garten. Ajeschka/Marcin Kolakowski, 2011.
21 Gästehaus, Wangeliner garten. Sabine/Stephanus/Hiroshi, 2011.
22 Gästehaus, Wangeliner garten. Hiroshi, 2011.
23 Working drawing of Gästehaus vault. Hiroshi, 2011.
24 Wangelin, Buchberg, Germany. ABG, 2018.

11. Education and inspiration: WISE at CAT

1 General plan of CAT premises. CAT modified by Redina Mazelli, 2019.
2 Segal-method house, CAT, Machynlleth, Powys, Wales. ABG, 2010.
3 Eco Cabins, CAT, Machynlleth, Powys, Wales. ABG, 2010.
4 Straw-bale theatre, CAT, Machynlleth, Powys, Wales. ABG, 2010.
5 AtEIC building, CAT, Machynlleth, Powys, Wales. Martina Bocci, 2017.
6 The Whole Home garden, CAT, Machynlleth, Powys, Wales. Centre for Alternative Technology, 2018.
7 David Lea and Pat Borer at WISE opening ceremony, CAT, Machynlleth, Powys, Wales. ABG, 2010.
8 Early scheme for bedrooms on separate site, WISE, CAT. David Lea, from **B323**.
9 Plans of WISE. Pat Borer, 2010.
10 Section of WISE. Pat Borer, 2007.
11 WISE, CAT. ABG, 2010.
12 WISE, CAT. ABG, 2010.
13 Dining space/lobby, WISE, CAT. Martina Bocci, 2017.
14 Entrance porch, WISE, CAT. ABG, 2010.
15 Morgan-Grenville courtyard, WISE, CAT. Martina Bocci, 2017.
16 Sheppard lecture theatre, WISE, CAT. ABG, 2010.
17 East wing staircase, WISE, CAT. ABG, 2010.
18 Open gallery on the north side of north wing, WISE, CAT. ABG, 2010.
19 Upper courtyard, WISE, CAT. ABG, 2010.
20 Building sequence of WISE. Pat Borer, 2007.
21 Foundations of east wing, WISE, CAT. ABG, 2010.
22 Sheppard lecture theatre, WISE, CAT. Martina Bocci, 2017.
23 Lecture theatre ambulatory, WISE, CAT. ABG, 2010.
24 Section of rammed earth wall and ambulatory, WISE. Pat Borer modified by Martina Bocci, 2019.
25 Hemp-crete wall, WISE, CAT. Pat Borer, 2007.
26 Section of south façade of north wing, WISE. Pat Borer modified by Martina Bocci, 2019.
27 Rammed earth wall, WISE, CAT. Martina Bocci, 2017.
28 Rammed earth wall, WISE, CAT. Pat Borer, 2007.

12. Reconciliation: Maruyama-gumi

1 Ichinosaka, Wajima city, Ishikawa prefecture. Hagino Kiichirō, 2008.
2 Map of the township of Mii-machi, Wajima city, Ishikawa prefecture. Adapted from Geospatial Information Authority of Japan, 2019.
3 Ichinosaka, Wajima city, Ishikawa prefecture. Hagino Yuki, 2013.
4 Maruyama, Mii-machi, Wajima city, Ishikawa prefecture. Hagino Kiichirō, 2013–2014–2011.
5 Maruyama-gumi. Hagino Kiichirō, 2011.
6 Maruyama-gumi at Hagino house. Hagino Kiichirō, 2012.
7 Hagino house, Mii-machi. Hagino Kiichirō, 2011.
8 Maruyama-gumi. Hagino Kiichirō, 2012.
9 *Tochi ni nezashita kurashi no koyomi Maruyama honzō* [土地に根ざしたくらしの暦 まるやま本草]. Hagino Yuki, 2014.
10 Maruyama. Hagino Kiichirō, 2010.
11 Hagino house, Mii-machi. ABG, 2019.
12 Wajima city, Ishikawa prefecture. Hagino Kiichirō, 2009.
13 Hagino house, Mii-machi. Hagino Kiichirō, 2010.
14 Axonometric projection of Hagino house. Martina Bocci, 2019.
15 Hagino house, Mii-machi. ABG, 2019.
16 Hagino house, Mii-machi. Hagino Kiichirō, 2008.
17 Hagino house, Mii-machi. Hagino Kiichirō, 2008.
18 Hagino house, Mii-machi. ABG, 2019.
19 Plans of Hagino house. Hagino Kiichirō, 2006.
20 Hagino house, Mii-machi. Hagino Kiichirō, 2010.
21 Hagino house, Mii-machi. Hagino Kiichirō, 2008.
22 Hagino house, Mii-machi. Hagino Kiichirō, 2009.
23 Hagino house, Mii-machi. Hagino Kiichirō, 2009.
24 Hagino house, Mii-machi. Hagino Kiichirō, 2009.
25 Hagino house, Mii-machi. ABG, 2019.
26 Hagino house, Mii-machi. Hagino Kiichirō, 2008.
27 Section of Hagino house. Hagino Kiichirō, 2006.
28 Surroundings of Hagino house. Maruyama-gumi, 2011.
29 Mii, Wajima city, Ishikawa prefecture. ABG, 2019.
30 Hagino house, Mii-machi. ABG, 2019.

Acknowledgements

The introductory essay is a completely reworked and expanded version of an article I wrote on the invitation of Emiliano Michelena, "Tecnología y comportamiento humano", *Revista de arquitectura*, 250, August 2013, p. 46–53.

Some parts of **§5** and **§13** are derived from *The Environmental Impact of Sieben Linden Ecovillage* **[→B46]**. Some short excerpts in **§§0,3,6** are derived from *Werner Schmidt. Ecology Craft Invention* **[→B44]**. Some parts of **§§6,9** are also reworked from articles that previously appeared in 2010/11 in *Il giornale dell'architettura*.

Basic research on some case studies was developed by students in the framework of their master or bachelor thesis: Daniliuc Sorin **[§2]**, Martina Bocci **[§4]**, Martina Gerace **[§5]**, Guillermo Ráfales Sancho and Mathieu Rossi **[§6]**, Giuseppe Salomone **[§8]**, Federica Rossetto **[§10]**. Some contextual information was also collected by Andrea Antolloni **[§0:▪36]**, Virginia Bertolotti **[§ 11]**, Cai Luyang **[§7]**, Jessica Leão França **[§ 7]**, Salvatore Satta **[§0:▪13]**, Alberto Valentino **[§11]**.

Quantitative data regarding the environmental impact of the buildings (standardised technical drawings, 3D models, data mining from them to build the inventories, data processing) were systematised and processed by Martina Bocci, also with the help of Susanna Pollini, also based on preparatory work performed by graduate students of the "Appropriate technology and low-tech architecture" course (2018).

Owners and designers of buildings visited kindly allowed access to their properties, shared information and opinions, and often offered meals—Bjørn Berge **[§8]**, Pat Borer **[§11]**, Anne Evans, Marit Grinaker Smith **[§8]**, Hagino Kibo and Yuki **[§12]**, Lothar Helm **[§4]**, Uta Herz **[§10]**, Klaus Hirrich **[§0]**, Peter and Cynthia Jones, Bjørn Kierulf **[§6]**, Joel Kunz **[§6]**, David Lea **[§11]**, Gernot Minke **[§6]**, Beate Neumerkel **[§10]**, Roar Ousland **[§8]**, Dorothee Piontek **[§3]**, Burkard Rüger **[§10]**, Werner Schmidt **[§3,6]**, Peter Segger, Shiramomo Kaoru **[§9]**, Olivier Sidler, Anders Solvarm, Gabriel and Cristina Suliman **[§2]**, Tanemoto Hiroko **[§9]**, Toki Hirokazu **[§7]**, Franz Volhard **[§4]**.

Arai Hiroshi, Elena Barthel of Rural Studio **[§0:▪33]**, Francesca Bretzel, David Eisenberg, Hara Miori **[§1]**, Gabriella Morini, Peter Harper **[§11]**, Janni Hentrich of Tamera, Itō Koji **[§12]**, Ito Toyo, Alex Kerr, Kumagai Kuniji and Yuuki, Federica Larcher, Moriyama Madoka **[§9]**, Giovanni Munari, Murasawa Kazuteru, Glenn Murcutt, Okabe Akiko, Eko Prawoto, Sanada Junko, Sasagawa Daisuke **[§9]**, Bill Steen **[§5]**, Mariya Stoycheva **[§1]**, Christoph Strünke of Sieben Linden **[§5]**, Annika Tengsrand of the Arkitekturmuseet Stockholm, Teruhisa Mizuno, Andrea Zanini shared documents and information.

Taki Yosuke translated research texts from Japanese and, what's more important, played a continuous role as a builder of wisely selected cultural bridges between Japan and Europe. Shirotani Kosei helped establish connections with Maruyama-gumi **[§12]**. Luisa Montobbio edited our photographs, drawings, and charts.

Research has been funded by an individual research grant of the Politecnico di Torino and a Japan Society for the Promotion of Science (JSPS) fellowship I was awarded in 2015 thanks to the help of Ozasa Takao and Komatsu Hisashi.